Designing
Knitted Textiles

Designing Knitted Textiles

Machine Knitting for Fashion

Florence Spurling

Laurence King Publishing

LAURENCE KING

First published in Great Britain in 2021 by

Laurence King Student & Professional
An imprint of Quercus Editions Ltd
Carmelite House
50 Victoria Embankment
London EC4Y 0DZ

An Hachette UK company

A CIP catalogue record for this book is available
from the British Library

ISBN 978-1-78627-653-7

10 9 8 7 6 5 4 3 2 1

Design by Lizzie Ballantyne

Printed and bound in China by C&C Offset Printing Co Ltd

Papers used by Quercus are from well-managed forests and other
responsible sources.

Front cover: Design by Matilda Norberg. Photography by Ceen Wahren
Back cover: Photography by Marcie Revens

Page 2: Blocks of heavier weight yarn are laid into a fine knit
background using the knit-weave method, providing both pattern
and structure to this delicate silhouette. By label Alice Lee.

Page 6: Numerous folds in the knitted fabric give way to an incredibly
sculptural and experimental form. By Melbourne-based menswear
designer Chris Ran Lin.

See page 193 for information on videos

Contents

Introduction

The process of knitting allows the designer to take total control of the type of fabric they wish to make. Fibre, yarn, colour, pattern, stitch and structure are all fundamental components of the resulting cloth, which provide endless opportunities of inspiration and variation. While knitting by machine is undoubtedly more efficient than by hand, it still shares the same tactile qualities that makes this textile method so appealing. Automation brings regularity and consistency to the stitches within the fabric and allows for extra experimentation due to the speed in which ideas can be executed.

Machine knitting is not a new skill, but its resurgence no doubt stems from an increasing desire to connect with our hands and appreciate the joy in 'making'. The meditative notions of knitting are clear: focusing on the task at hand and the rhythm in which it is completed helps to centre your thoughts and lends an attainable sense of achievement. In regard to sustainability, a custom-knitted garment yields little waste, allowing a considered approach to fashion design. Pieces are shaped to exact measurements, eliminating the need to discard excess materials.

Most designers are introduced to this mode of knitting by a machine that falls within the single-bed domestic category. This is simple to learn on, and its compact size, availability and price point contribute to its popularity within universities, small design studios and home crafters. For these reasons, and the breadth of creative outputs that are possible, the single-bed domestic machine is this book's focus. Because you may find subtle variations (for example, the positioning and names of buttons or settings) between machine models, having a copy of the machine manual as reference is of advantage, allowing you to double-check these components while you work through the text.

Creativity and technical expertise work hand in hand throughout knitwear design. Innovation is born when you push beyond the traditional, yet to achieve this calls for skill. With this in mind, the book aims to provide the reader with an understanding of key techniques and their resulting knitted fabric structures. The more you work through the methods and examples given, the easier it is to understand how the machine settings, the use of tools and manual manipulation can affect the outcome. While these practical elements are not often intuitive, they soon become muscle memory with repetition. Creativity flourishes when you experiment, combine, subvert and remain curious to all of these possibilities.

The book is divided into three parts: Preparation, Materiality, and Construction.

The first section guides the reader through the machine itself, including its various parts, tools and settings. The formation of loops that contribute to knitted fabric is illustrated through key stitch structures, and acquiring the ability to recognize and 'read' this loop layout is advantageous for new knitters. The initial stages of knitting such as casting on and off, using tools and working with yarn are introduced, providing the opportunity to develop basic skills and confidence. Creativity is at the core of this machine knitting guide, and the reader is encouraged to apply their own design sensibility to the provided methods and techniques. To help with this, fibres and yarns, inspiration, research, colour and the iterative artistic process are explored within the context of machine knitting for fashion.

The second section outlines numerous stitch types and techniques that broadly focus on colour and pattern, texture and structure, and openwork and embellishment. Instructions detail the mechanics of each method with customization for both manual and punchcard machines. Design guidelines including sources of inspiration, stitch and pattern placement, and colour and yarn use, provide a starting point to inspire customization of these structures to generate unique fabrications for various fashion contexts.

The final section teaches the reader how to knit beyond a square or rectangle. Constructing a fabric to a certain size calls for it to be shaped, which can be accomplished in various ways according to the design outcome. Finishing processes such as trims, seaming and blocking contribute to professional-looking textiles and garments. Finally, information describing common mistakes are included at the end, to help the knitter to troubleshoot, fix and, most importantly, understand the cause of errors that may occur.

Most of the knitted fabric swatches included in this book were created on a standard-gauge knitting machine. The images display only a small sampling of creative design outcomes that are possible, with the intent to inspire further ideas. Informative illustrations are interspersed throughout the text, which work to demonstrate important technical steps and highlight a range of knitted structures. With the help of this book, you are encouraged to start your own machine knitting journey and discover just how versatile this skill can be.

Florence Spurling

Part 1

Preparation

This tactile loop knitting technique creates a voluminous fabric that highlights the harmonious yarn palette. Designed by Sophie Steller Studio.

Chapter 1

The Knitting Machine

There are many different types of knitting machine, each with its own purpose and technical abilities. Ranging from simple hobby models to advanced computerized systems capable of creating seamless garments in one piece, they address the exceptional breadth of the knitwear industry.

The flat-bed or single-bed domestic knitting machine is the focus of discussion in this book. This is the most popular kind of machine to learn on, and is ideal for students, home crafters, limited production and small design studios alike. With a little practice, it is quick to master and a fantastic tool for developing knitted fabrics and simple garments.

As the name suggests, a single-bed machine has one needle bed only. Its simplest output is single jersey (also called stocking stitch and plain knitting), a two-sided fabric formed of knit stitches on the face and purl stitches on the reverse. A single-bed machine can be transformed into a double-bed machine by the addition of a ribber, allowing a greater range of outcomes, including ribbed and racked fabrics, tubular structures and knit-and-purl combinations to name a few.

Types of Knitting Machine

Machines used in the industry are broadly categorized as fabric machines or garment-length machines. Fabric machines are mostly circular in configuration and knit continuous lengths of fabric to a set width in tube formation. Once off the machine, the tube is usually sliced open, creating a flat fabric from which garment pieces can be cut. Fabric machines can produce knitted yardage very quickly and efficiently, making them ideal for jersey cut-and-sew garments such as T-shirts. Garments created from these machines are assembled and sewn after they have been cut into pieces of the correct size.

Garment-length machines can be flat-bed or circular and are used to produce outcomes that are knitted to a certain size and shape. Items knitted on circular machines such as hosiery may be used in their tubular formation, whereas flat-bed machines are used to knit individual garment panels.

Some industrial machines are capable of making seamless 'whole garments', items such as gloves, legwear and sweaters that are assembled completely on the machine as part of the knitting process, and need minimal finishing. Whereas knitted garment panels consist of separate pieces that must be seamed to create a three-dimensional form, whole garments are knitted entirely without joins, eliminating waste and additional work.

Clockwise from top left: Circular fabric machine, circular sock machine, single-bed domestic machine in designer Emily Watt's studio, Shima Seiki whole-garment machine, and electronic single-bed domestic machine knitting a design by Catherine Tough.

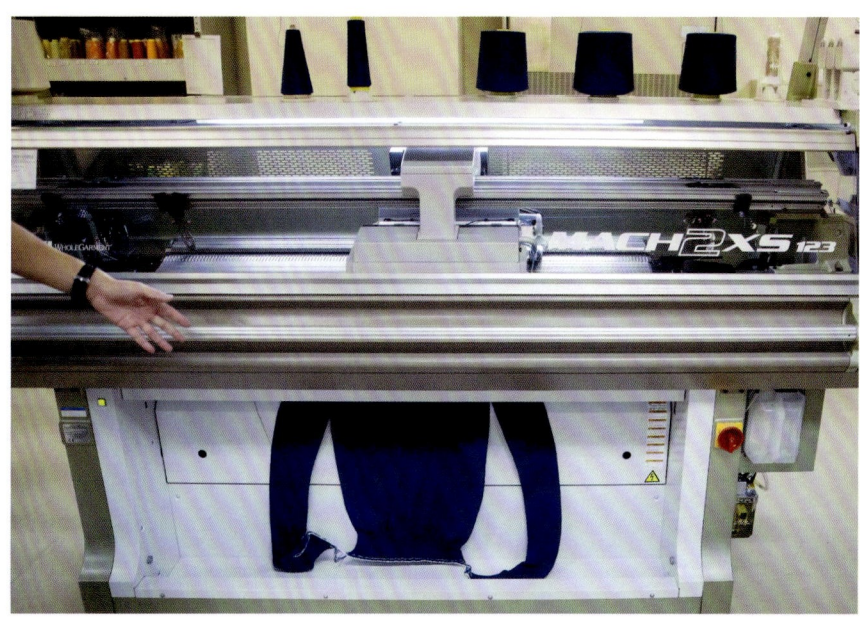

New developments in machines by companies such as Kniterate are designed to bridge the gap between industrial and domestic models. These electronic machines act as a hybrid between the two, with advanced technical capacity, presented in a more affordable, compact and user-friendly output.

Single-bed machine types

Single-bed machines can be split into three groups: manual, punchcard and electronic. Manual machines are the most affordable, and their simplicity means they are quick to learn on. They have no built-in patterning device, meaning that different stitch types are all performed by hand.

Punchcard machines have a built-in patterning system, allowing the user to knit different stitch types or colours more efficiently within the same row. These machines often come with pre-designed punchcards, but blank cards are also available for you to use to design your own patterns. Punchcard machines are widely available and simple to learn on, and can produce an extensive range of professional-looking outcomes.

Electronic models offer an expanded range of knitted stitches, through built-in or computer-controlled pattern selection. They are typically the most expensive and require more skill from the user.

Knitting machine gauge

The gauge refers to the distance between needles on the bed. This divides machines into four categories of gauges: fine, standard, mid and bulky/chunky. The distance dictates the thickness of yarn that can be successfully used. The chart details the various distances (although the gauge may vary slightly between brands).

Purchasing a machine

When you are considering the purchase of a machine, there are many factors to keep in mind. To determine the machine gauge, think about the types of fabric and garment you want to make and the yarn weights you will most frequently be using. See pages 35–36 for help with this decision and to establish the yarn weights suited to each gauge.

The machine's technical and patterning capabilities should also be taken into account, since its affordability will depend on its complexity. View the purchase of a machine as an investment; as long as it is used with care and maintained regularly, it should have a long life.

Second-hand machines are available 'as is' or refurbished, and can be an excellent alternative to buying new. If buying second-hand, enquire about the machine's history, current working order and the availability of new parts. If possible, view it in person, and try it out. Acquiring a machine that has been out of use and requires maintenance (besides just cleaning) can be frustrating for a novice knitter.

Knitting machine gauge

Machine gauge	Needle spacing	Fabric weight
Fine	3.6mm apart	**Lightweight** Versatile for all seasons – summer knits and autumn/winter garments for layering
Standard	4.5 or 5mm apart	**Light to medium weight** Good for transitional-season garments
Mid	6 or 7mm apart	**Medium to thick weight** Sweaters for autumn/winter
Bulky/Chunky	8 or 9mm apart	**Very thick weight** Chunky, hand-knit appearance for winter and outerwear

How the Machine Works

The mechanics of the machine

Regardless of the single-bed machine type, brand or model, they all create knitted fabric in the same way. The appearance and position of the controls may differ, and some machines may lack functions that others have (such as a punchcard facility). The two elements that remain constant, however, are a bed containing needles and a carriage that slides across to create stitches.

The following information is applicable to any flat-bed machine. Should your machine differ visually from the examples given, refer to its user manual.

The carriage

The carriage contains two parts: the main body and the sinker plate. If you remove the carriage from the machine and examine the underside, you will find a mix of cams, magnets, brushes and wheels. The cams are aligned to form three different pathways (lower, middle and upper), through which the needles move. The cams can move and modify the middle pathway alignment, creating an altered route, depending on whether the carriage is set to knit, tuck or miss stitches.

As the carriage passes, magnets are used to open needle latches so that new stitches can be produced. Brushes and wheels further help with the formation of stitches and ensure the fabric is kept close to the bed, in its correct position.

Carriage functions

The levers, buttons and dial of a carriage may differ slightly between brands in appearance, location and name, but the functions remain the same. Shown here are two carriages found on popular models: a Silver Reed machine and a Brother machine. (Please note that Brother machines are also sold under the name KnitKing, and Silver Reed under the names Singer, Studio, Empisal and KnitMaster.)

TIP: *Familiarize yourself with these functions by identifying them on your own machine, checking the user manual for any differences in name and location.*

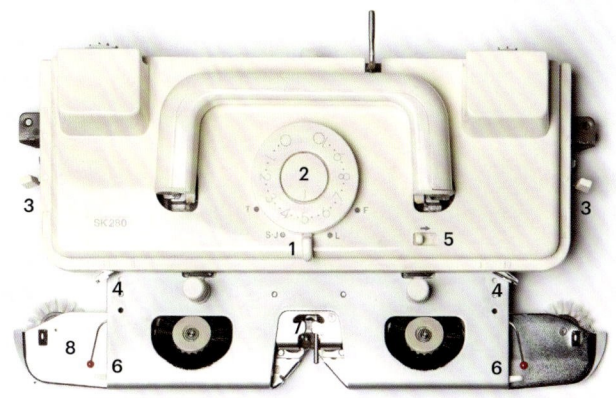

Silver Reed knitting machine carriage.

The underside of a typical single-bed knitting machine carriage.

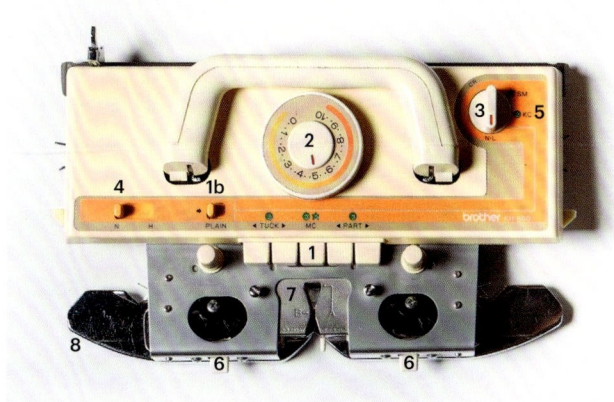

Brother knitting machine carriage.

1. Cam lever/cam buttons

1b. Cam release lever Cams are used to select stitch types, including knit, miss, tuck and Fair Isle. Silver Reed carriages have a lever that can be switched to the selected stitch category, whereas Brother machines have buttons. To deselect a button, use the Cam Button Release Lever.

2. Stitch/tension dial This dial controls the stitch size. The higher the number, the larger the stitch, resulting in a more open fabric. The lower the number, the smaller the stitch, resulting in a denser fabric.

3. Side levers/change knob These have a plain setting for non-punchcard knitting, and a pattern setting for punchcard knitting.

4. Russel levers/holding cam lever When these levers are engaged they set the carriage to the 'holding position' function. In this setting, needles in holding position do not knit.

5. Release lever/carriage release This releases the carriage from a jam. A lever is used for Silver Reed machines, whereas the setting for Brother models is often found on the Change Knob (setting 'CR').

6. Weaving knobs/weaving pattern lever These are used to position the weaving brushes for the woven cast-on method and to create hand- or punchcard-woven patterns. The brushes should be in the dropped position for these techniques and the raised position for plain knitting.

7. Yarn feeder The working yarn coming from the tension unit is positioned securely in the feeder before knitting with it.

8. Sinker plate The sinker plate houses the brushes and wheels within the carriage. It can be unscrewed from the main body of the carriage if there is a jam or when disassembling and storing the machine. When reattaching the sinker plate, ensure that it is aligned correctly with the carriage.

The needle bed

Most knitting machines have four needle positions, represented by letters displayed at the end of the needle bed. Going from the back of the bed to the front, these positions are: Nonworking, Working, Upper Working and Holding. Again, you will notice a slight disparity between machine brands as to how the positions are lettered. Following the same order as above, these are displayed as A, B, C and D on Silver Reed and A, B, D and E on Brother machines. Despite this difference, the needle position function remains the same.

A Position = Nonworking Position (NWP) – Needles are positioned as far back as possible in the needle bed. Needles do not knit.

B Position = Working Position (WP) – Needles are positioned so that the hooks line up with the edge of the needle bed. Needles knit.

C Position (Silver Reed) or D Position (Brother) = Upper Working Position (UWP) – Needles are positioned slightly forwards so that their open latches line up with the edge of the needle bed. Needles knit.

D Position (Silver Reed) or E Position (Brother) = Holding Position (HP) – Needles are positioned as far forward as possible in the needle bed. Needles do not knit when the carriage is set to hold. If hold is not selected, needles knit back to B position.

Although not every machine has them, sinker posts or gate pegs are metal prongs at the edge of the needle bed. Every needle has a sinker post either side of it, and while they should always be clear of stitches and yarn during knitting, they can be used to tension the fabric when casting off.

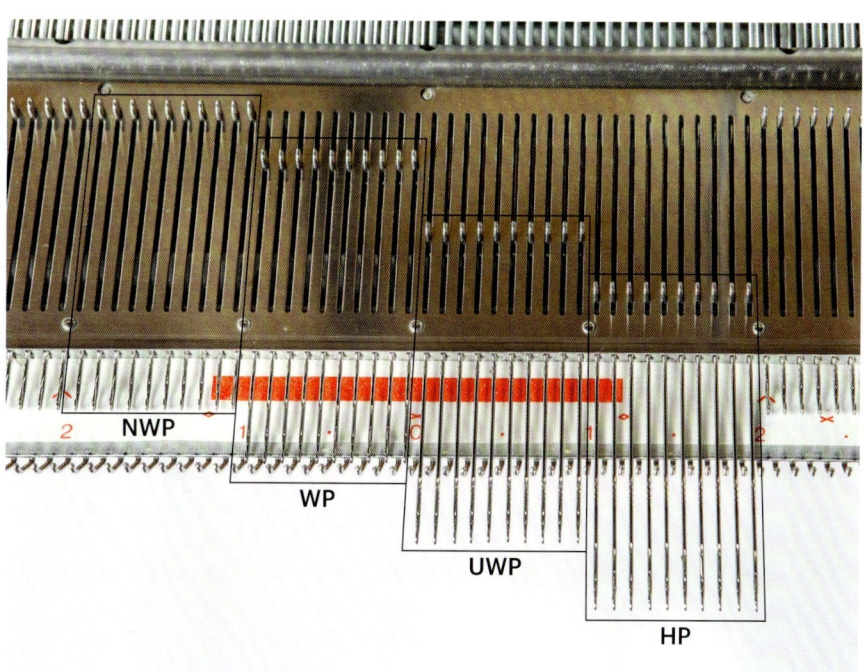

Groups of needles situated in their four different positions in the needle bed.

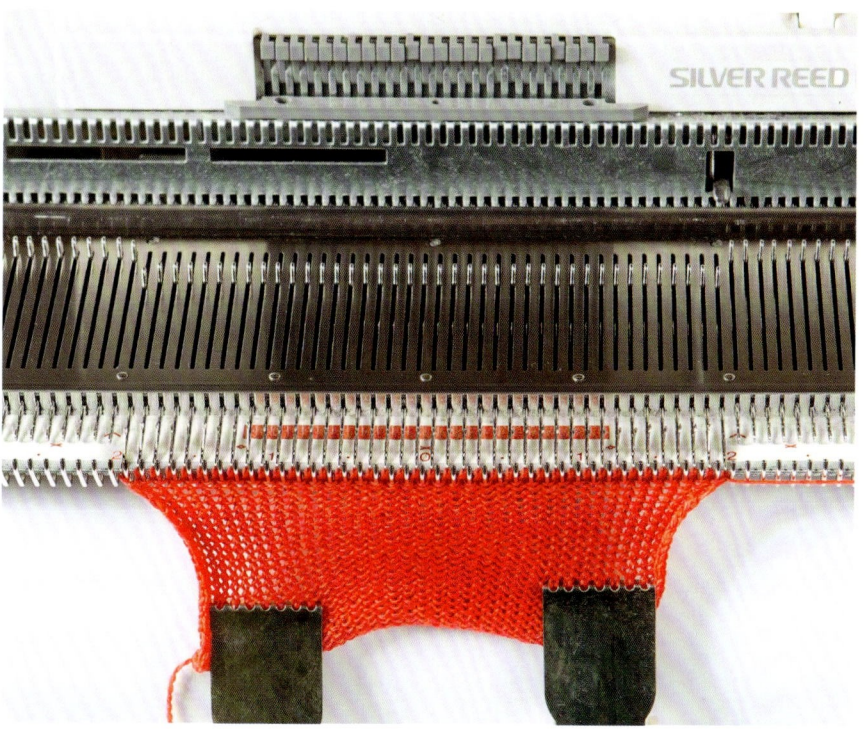

This swatch is knit using 40 needles: 20 needles both sides of the central '0' mark.

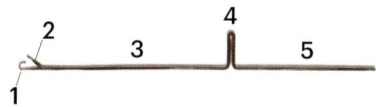

Latch needle.

Latch needles

The needles in the machine bed are called latch needles. Each needle is set in its own groove within the needle bed. The needle butt protrudes through the groove, allowing you to move the needle back and forth. Latch needles consist of five main parts:

1. **Hook** Catches yarn to form new stitches.
2. **Latch** Hinged, meaning that it opens lying against the stem and closes onto the hook. The latch is essential to the formation of stitches.
3. **Stem** Holds the course of stitches just formed.
4. **Butt** Enables the needle to move. As the carriage passes, the needle butt connects with the pathway underneath.
5. **Shank** Supports the needle.

Numbered needle strip

A strip numbers the needles on the bed, from the centre outwards to left and right. This allows you to select the desired number of needles easily, and helps to keep shaping and pattern repeats consistent. Generally, it is recommended to work in the middle of the bed, so that you use roughly the same number of needles on either side of the central '0' mark.

Machine Tools and Accessories

How stitches are formed

The carriage is in control of moving the needles back and forth and feeding yarn into the hooks, to create new stitches. This is how knit stitches are formed:

1. The needle is in working position, with the current stitch held in the needle hook.
2. As the carriage passes the needle, it pushes it forward. This causes the stitch in the hook to slide past the latch and back onto the stem.
3. While the needle is in this forward position, the open hook catches the yarn coming from the carriage feeder.
4. The needle travels back, causing the stitch to slide forward and slip over the now closed latch and the strand of yarn.
5. The needle ends back in working position, with a new stitch sitting in the hook.

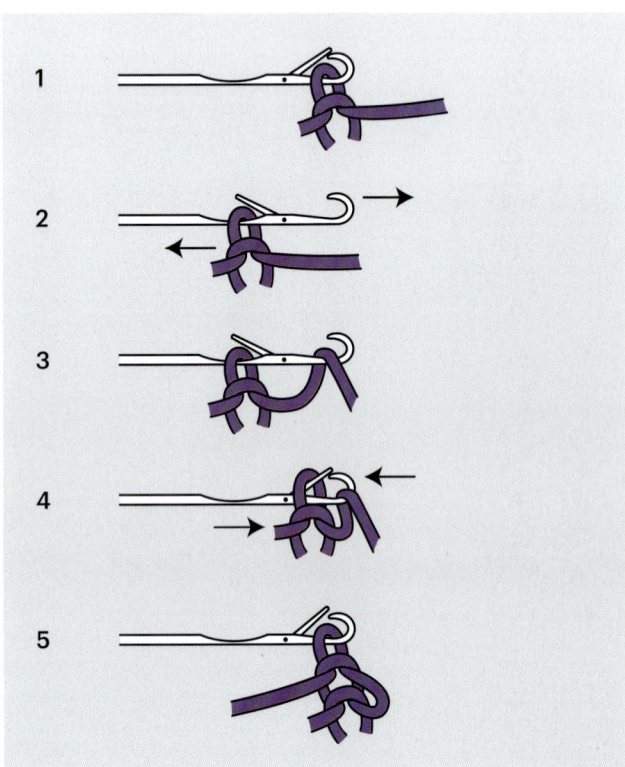

Formation of a knit stitch.

Tools are required for a number of tasks, such as selecting needles, moving stitches, keeping the fabric weighted and finishing your work. All machines, regardless of the type or model, come with basic tools that can often be used among different flat-beds, although items such as transfer tools are gauge-specific. Additional tools may be needed when creating specific stitches or knitting large fabrics, and they can be purchased separately.

Basic tools

1. **Cast-on comb** Adds tension to the fabric from the first row. Useful when working with larger numbers of needles.

2. **Table clamps** Secure the machine bed to the work surface. They fit into slots at both ends of the machine and are tightened to the correct thickness for the table.

3. **Needle pushers** Needle selection tools that allow you to push a number of needles at once, making the process quicker and easier. These come in a variety of configurations, which result in different needle arrangements.

4. **Transfer tools** Used to move stitches, and most commonly have one, two or three prongs. One-prong tools are used for single stitches, and multi-prong tools move groups of stitches.

5. **Claw weights** Come in different shapes and sizes, and are hung on the fabric while knitting. As the fabric grows, they are moved up to ensure the consistent tension needed to form stitches. Depending on the yarn used and the knitting technique, more or fewer weights may be needed to ensure smooth knitting.

6. **Latch tool** Also known as a 'tappet tool'. Essentially a knitting-machine latch needle on a holder. It allows you to reconstruct stitches to create knit stitches on the purl side and vice versa. It is also used to repair accidently dropped stitches.

7. **Cleaning brush** Used for maintenance, to keep the machine free of dust and fluff.

8. **Ravel cord** A smooth synthetic cord used for casting on and to knit one row between the waste and main knitting.

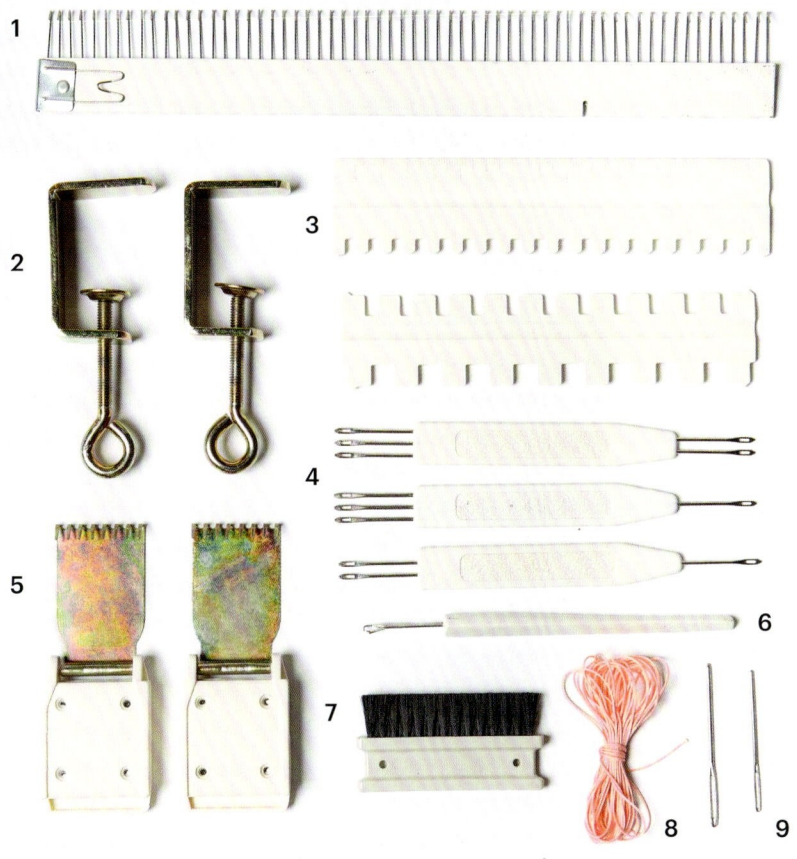

A nylon or slippery yarn that can easily be pulled out from the fabric can also be used for this purpose.

9. Tapestry needle Blunt-ended needle used to sew in loose ends created by casting on, casting off and changing yarns.

Punchcard tools
Blank cards (1) are used to create your own patterns. Pre-designed cards (2) are included with punchcard machines and feature a standard set of patterns. Snaps (3) secure the ends of the card together and a tool (4) is used to punch your design into a blank card.

Left, top: Basic tools.

Left, bottom: Punchcard tools.

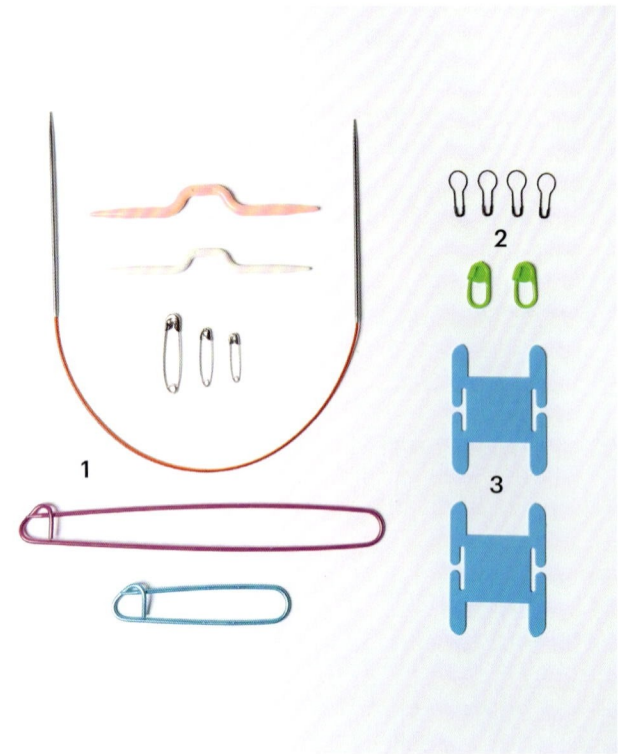

Hand-knitting tools.

A skein of yarn held on a swift while being wound into a centre-pull ball.

Hand-knitting tools

These tools are sold for two-needle hand-knitting, but they can also be helpful with certain techniques of machine-knitting.

1. **Stitch holders** Cable needles, safety pins, small circular needles and clasped stitch holders can all be used to remove, hold and carefully replace stitches.

2. **Stitch markers** Removable stitch markers that slip easily on and off can be used to highlight certain stitches in the fabric. This is particularly useful when working with textured, dark or fine yarn, where the fabric is harder to read.

3. **Bobbins** Techniques such as hand-weaving and intarsia often require several balls or cones of yarn that are worked together. Bobbins are handy for keeping groups of yarns tidy.

Additional equipment

Yarn swift or skein holder Used to prepare yarn for machine-knitting. Yarn that is sold in a skein or hank must be wound into a centre-pull ball before knitting. A yarn swift holds the skein open tautly so that the loose strands can be wound without getting tangled.

Ball winder Winds yarn into balls that pull from the centre, ensuring that it stays stable while feeding through the machine.

Process tools Scissors, ruler, tape measure, notebook and pencil should be on hand throughout the design and knitting process.

Finishing equipment As well as the blunt-ended tapestry needle mentioned before, equipment for blocking and seaming is required if you are to create professional-looking swatches and garments. See Chapter 9 for the tools you will need.

Setting the Machine Up

Threading the machine

In two-needle hand-knitting, the working yarn is held, tensioned and controlled through the movement of the fingers. The tension unit is essentially the equivalent of this for machine-knitting. To prepare for knitting, yarn is threaded through the tension unit, which feeds it to the carriage.

Before you begin, make sure the yarn is positioned securely, either on the floor or on the knitting table. The area around it should be clear of other objects, and the yarn should be able to feed upright to the tension unit without having to stretch diagonally. Each time you start working with a different yarn, make sure it is unwinding freely and evenly from the ball or cone. These measures will prevent tangles, uneven feeding and problems with tension.

The following steps detail how to thread your yarns correctly. Note that some machines do not have the second yarn guide described in Step 5.

Thread the selected yarn:

1. through the tension guide eyelet,
2. between two tension discs and under the guide pin (the tension discs contain a dial that can be further adjusted according to the yarn),
3. through the yarn guide eyelet,
4. through the tension spring eyelet,
5. through the yarn guide eyelet. Finally, place the yarn end into the yarn clip or the carriage yarn feeder.

TIP: *Keep checking the tension unit during knitting. This helps to stay ahead of mistakes occurring if the yarn accidently unthreads from an area in the unit or becomes entangled with another cone.*

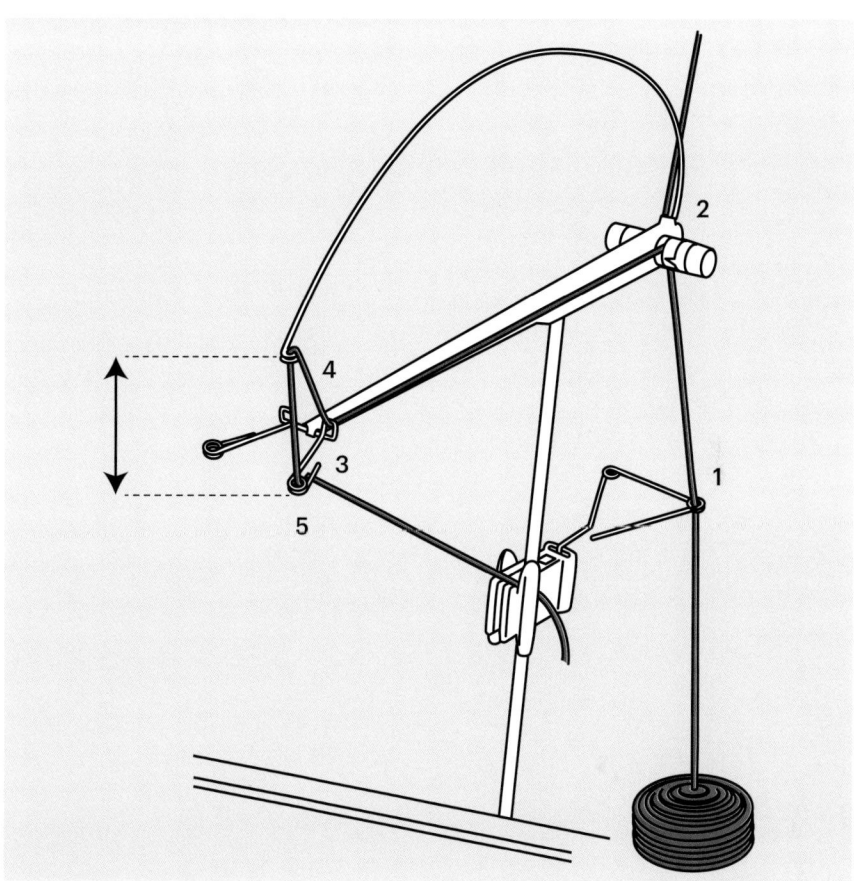

A ball of yarn threaded through one side of the tension unit and held in the yarn clip until it is ready to be used.

Tension dial

The tension dial (attached to the tension discs) can be adjusted to suit the weight of yarn. To determine how:

1. Secure the yarn in the yarn clip or the carriage yarn feeder and look at the distance between the tension spring (Step 4) and yarn guide (Step 5 or Step 3 if the machine does not have the second yarn guide).
2. This distance should be between 10 and 20cm (4–8in). If it is smaller than 10cm (4in), decrease the tension. If it is greater than 20cm (8in), increase the tension.

Stitch size

The stitch size is controlled by the stitch dial on the carriage. When the dial is set to a larger number, the needles take more yarn into each loop, creating a bigger stitch. When a lower number is selected, less yarn is taken into each loop, resulting in a smaller stitch.

The machine gauge determines the yarn weight that will knit successfully on the machine. Using a yarn in the thicker range for that gauge requires a higher stitch size, and using a yarn in the thinner range for that gauge needs a lower stitch size. Using a yarn whose weight calls

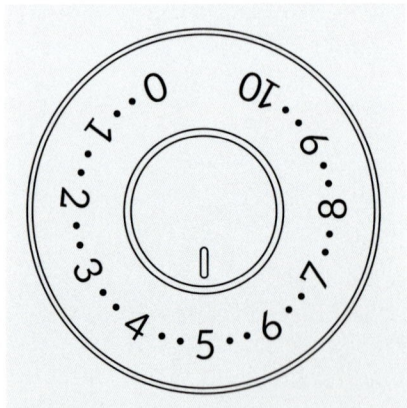

Stitch size dial.

for a stitch size in the middle range of the dial is the ideal for that gauge and will always knit the most effectively, since the machine is calibrated to perform best in this setting.

Most machines have dials that range from 0 to 10 with fractional sizes in between. The stitch size you choose will depend on a few factors, just as two-needle hand-knitters choose smaller or larger needles for certain functional or aesthetic reasons. The most important consideration is that the stitch size be large enough to knit the yarn with ease. If the stitch size is too small for the yarn, stitches won't form properly.

Some techniques, such as tuck and cables, call for a larger stitch than you would use for plain knitting. A higher stitch size will also produce a fabric with better drape, and so is recommended for knitting a shawl, for example. On the other hand, a beanie will generally require a more compact fabric and would consequently benefit from a tighter stitch size. Fluffy or textured yarns can be deceptive in that, although the core may appear fine, the outer hairs or surface interest causes them to knit as if they were much thicker. Imagine that the fuzz

Beginning at stitch size 3 and gradually increasing to stitch size 10, bands of different stitch size are displayed in this swatch, all of which are knit with the same number of stitches and rows. As the stitch size increases, the fabric also becomes larger and has more drape.

or thickest part of the yarn equates to the total diameter, and adjust the stitch size to accommodate it.

It is possible to knit thicker yarns using the every-other-needle method (see page 51). This entails casting on alternate needles, which leaves more space for the stitches. The method has its limitations, though, and the machine may struggle with anything more advanced than single jersey. Yarns that are too fine for the machine can be combined and fed through to knit as one.

If you are working with two or more yarns of varying thickness, there may be a disparity between the appropriate stitch sizes. In this case, choose a number that is a compromise. If this isn't possible – if, for example, the range is too great – you may need to adjust the size from one yarn to another. Bear in mind that extreme differences may distort the sides of the knitting.

Machine manuals contain a guide to help new knitters decide which stitch size corresponds best with their

Stitch size:
6.2

Stitch size:
7

Stitch size:
5.2

Stitch size:
10

Stitch size:
8

Stitch size:
3.1

Small plain knit fabrics display how different yarn types knit on the same machine gauge can call for a varied range of stitch sizes.

intended yarn. However, this choice will become instinctive with practice.

TIP: *As a useful reference, keep a journal with yarn cuttings, the machine gauge and the stitch size. When working with a new yarn, you will be able to compare it with those in your journal and know roughly which number to set the stitch dial to.*

The stitch size of a yarn can also be explored for visual effects. Bands of tighter and looser areas are created by altering the stitch size in the same yarn on the left, and using two very different yarn weights, knit at the same stitch size throughout on the right.

Fabric Structure

A knitted loop.

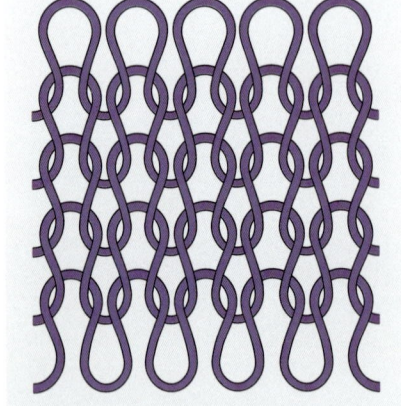

Weft knitting structure.

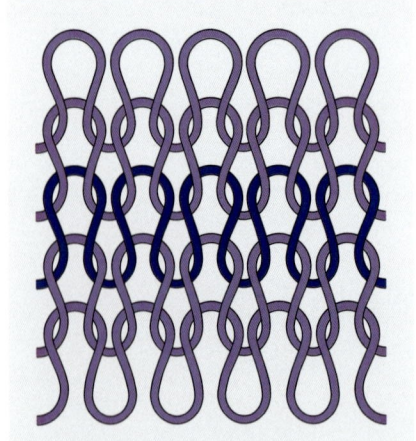

A course of stitches is highlighted.

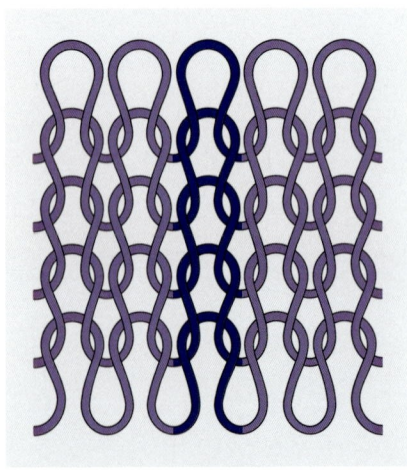

A wale of stitches is highlighted.

The knitted loop

When you are learning to knit, it is a huge advantage to understand the structure of the fabric you are creating. This structure, in its simplest form, is a loop. When the loop is repeated, a knitted fabric is generated. The knitted loop structure may not always be easily noticeable – if, for instance, it is made from an extremely fine or textured yarn. Furthermore, some stitch patterns and occasionally finishing processes can distort the fabric, making it harder to read.

Weft and warp knitting

The knitting industry is divided into two sectors: weft and warp knitting. Although both methods of knitting form a loop structure, the sequence in which the yarn is carried from loop to loop differs, as do the resulting fabrics.

Weft structures are created from a continuous length of yarn that is carried horizontally across the rows to form a series of loops. This is the way fabric is made through two-needle hand-knitting, as well as through the majority of machine-knitting, and it is the method most frequently used to knit textiles and garments.

Warp-knitted fabrics are formed by a yarn that zigzags and creates loops vertically. Each vertical column is created with a separate length of yarn. Because of this, warp structures are more stable than weft structures, which can be unravelled fairly easily. The resulting fabrics tend to be speciality types such as nets and tulle, which are used for lingerie, athletic wear, and curtains and trimmings, as well as alternative outputs such as the automotive industry. Warp knitting is always created on dedicated machines operated by specialists.

Courses and wales

In knitted structures, the horizontal rows of stitches are called 'courses' and the vertical columns of stitches 'wales'.

Technical face and reverse

The terms 'technical face' and 'technical reverse' are generally used when describing the 'right side' and the 'wrong side' of the fabric respectively. The knit side of the fabric is mostly regarded as the technical face, but for some stitches, such as tuck and knit-weave, the purl side is used. This is because the detail in tucked and knit-woven surfaces is more prominent on the reverse, and so should be seen by the viewer.

Ultimately this is a design decision, and the knitter is free to change it according to personal preference and design requirements. The same thinking can apply to the direction of knitting; although fabrics are knitted with the courses running horizontally and the wales running vertically, the resulting fabric may be rotated when it is used.

Stitch types

There are three principal stitch structures in machine-knitting: knit, tuck and miss. They are extremely versatile and allow endless possibilities when they are combined, modified and creatively transformed.

Knit stitch

A knit stitch has a smooth technical face appearing as a V shape.

Technical face, or knit side of a single jersey fabric.

Technical reverse, or purl side of a single jersey fabric.

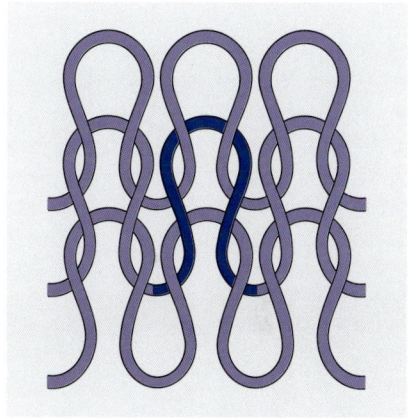

The face of a knit stitch is highlighted.

The purl side of this fabric is chosen as the face because it displays more detail than the knit side.

This fabric is equally interesting on both sides and so either one can be chosen as the face.

V-shaped knit stitches.

Its reverse is a purl stitch, recognizable by its arched appearance. Knit stitch fabrics are known as single jersey, plain knit or stocking stitch. When knitting single jersey on the single-bed machine, the purl side always faces the knitter.

Tuck stitch

A tuck stitch is one that is held on the needle without being knitted. With every pass of the carriage, new yarn is collected on the tucking needle and continues to accumulate, until the needle is instructed to knit again. If too many tucking courses are knitted, it becomes difficult to form the new stitch through which the held stitch and built-up yarn must be drawn.

The held stitch appears elongated, and it creates a raised effect that is more prominent on the purl side of the fabric. In addition to tactile outcomes, multicolour effects can also be created through tucking. Compared to a single-jersey fabric knitted with the same number of stitches and courses, a tucked structure will cause the fabric to appear shorter vertically and wider horizontally.

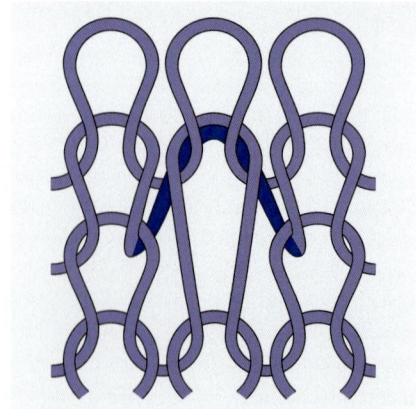

The face of a tuck stitch is highlighted.

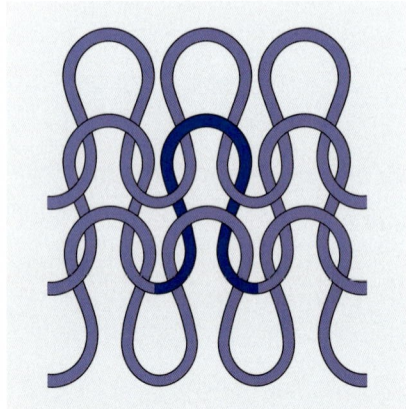

The reverse of a knit stitch (purl stitch) is highlighted.

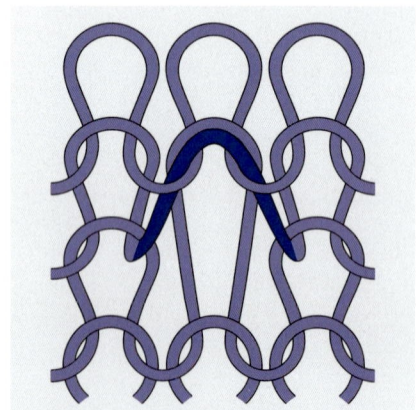

The reverse of a tuck stitch is highlighted.

Arch-shaped purl stitches.

Tuck-stitch pattern fabric displayed on the purl side.

Miss stitch

A miss or slip stitch is formed by the carriage passing and deliberately skipping the selected needle. The miss-stitch needle does not create a new stitch, and a float is produced on the purl side of the fabric. A new float occurs with every consecutively missed course. When the needle is selected to knit again, the miss stitch appears elongated. Slip-stitch patterns produce textural and dimensional fabrics, as well as multicolour stitch patterns.

Compared to a single-jersey fabric knitted with the same number of stitches and courses, a miss-stitch structure will cause the fabric to appear longer vertically and narrower horizontally.

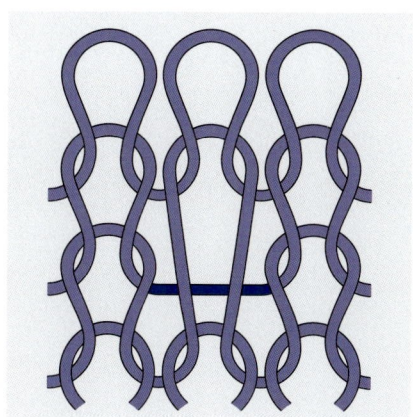
The face of a miss stitch is highlighted.

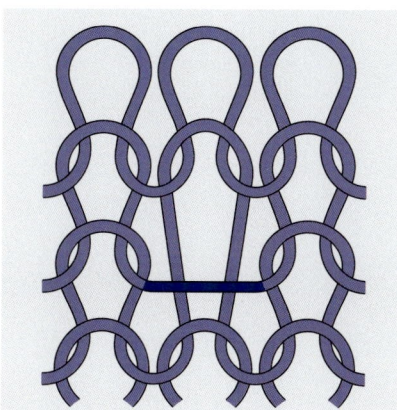
The reverse of a miss stitch is highlighted.

Miss-stitch pattern fabric displayed on the purl side.

Chapter 2

Research and Design

Part of the allure of knitting is being able to create exactly the fabric you desire. Knitters can establish their chosen characteristics within a design and implement them in the fabrication of the textile itself. Because of this, it is important to familiarize yourself with the various fibre types and the properties of their resulting yarns. Exploring and settling on a mix of materials can be akin to an artist choosing the right medium for a painting. It may take a few iterations to find the outcome you want, but the process can be fun and rewarding.

Finding inspiration is an individual process, and it is this notion that explains the extent of unique creative vision that fills the world. The more practised you become as a designer, the more you will notice things around you that excite you visually, or leave you curious and intrigued. Many ideas are well-trodden in the design world, but the way you approach and construct your research can guarantee that you interpret them in a distinctive and personal way.

Sampling ideas on the machine is an important part of the design development process and key to gaining confidence and experimenting with colour, yarn and stitches. Once you have a small collection of initial fabrication outcomes, you can consider how each might work for its end use.

Fibres and Yarns

Fibre and yarn choice is crucial to the functionality of the textile and how suitable it is for its intended design. Elements such as the handle and drape of the fabric, whether it will keep its form through wash and wear, and whether it will provide insulation or ventilation for the wearer determine its suitability. In terms of aesthetics, the fibre and yarn contribute to the colour, texture, structure and mood of the knit.

Fibres

A fibre is an individual, hair-like structure and the raw material used to produce yarn. There are two types: staple and filament, referring to the fibre length. They vary from less than 2.5cm (1in) to miles in length. Shorter fibres that can be measured in centimetres or inches are defined as staple fibres. All natural fibres, except silk, are staple fibres, and must be spun or twisted together to create a long, continuous strand of yarn. Longer, continuous fibres that can be measured in metres or yards are called filament fibres. All manufactured fibres are initially formed as filament fibres, although they are often cut into staple fibres for blending. Silk is the only natural filament fibre.

Each fibre has its own characteristics, which may be seen as advantages or disadvantages depending on the requirements of the design. Such qualities include:

Drape Drape may be desired for a garment such as a waterfall-opening cardigan, but not for a tailored piece such as a tweed-style knit blazer.

Handle Soft, fluffy fibres suit cold-weather clothing for children, whereas smooth, cool fibres could

An organic colour palette created with naturally dyed wool fibre.

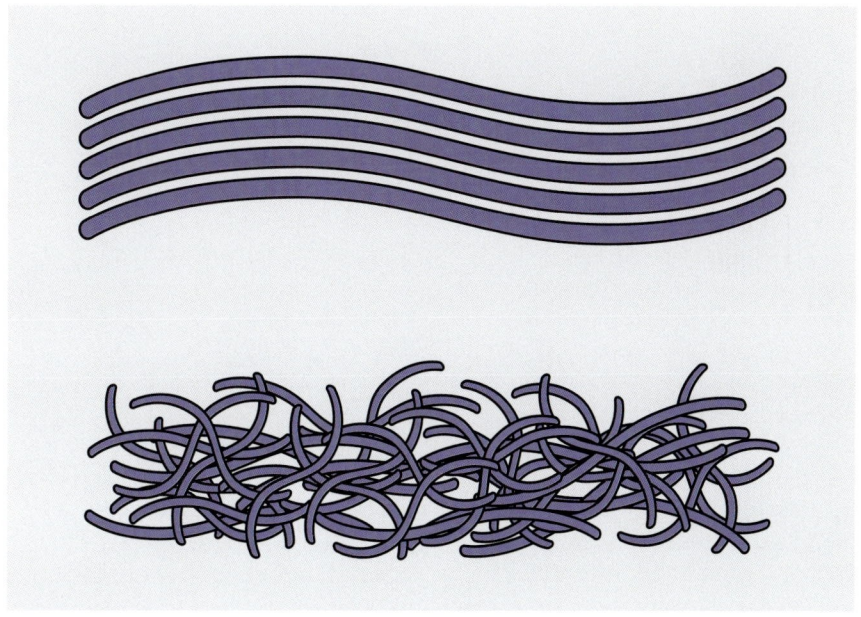
Longer filament (top) and shorter staple (bottom) fibres.

be appropriate for lace-knit beach cover-ups.

Dyeability Fibres that respond well to dye would be suitable for an electric colour palette in neon tones, while those that are harder to penetrate with colour or that display naturally beautiful tones may be better suited to a vintage-style palette.

Elasticity and resilience While the loop structure of knitting is inherently stretchy, some designs require more flexibility than others. Stitch patterns such as cables may call for fibres with elasticity, because of their many lateral transfers, and heavy or oversized silhouettes need resilient fibres so that they don't droop or stretch out of shape.

Durability Strong, hard-wearing fibres may be best for outcomes such as socks, whereas more fragile fibres will add to the delicate appearance of a gauzy piece.

Laundering and care Fibres that are prone to felting or should be hand-washed only could be problematic for baby garments that require frequent cleaning, but are suitable for accessories that need only periodic care.

Price Using predominantly luxury fibres may result in the design becoming overpriced for the intended market, but incorporating a small percentage of these fibres may increase the perceived value of the product.

Sustainability and society A project that collaborates with an indigenous culture and their craft may need to work exclusively with fibres that are derived locally, whereas a collection

Yarns created from natural fibres.

aimed at customers with sensitive skin may use solely hypoallergenic and antibacterial fibres.

Natural fibres

Materials that grow in nature from sources such as animals and plants are known as natural fibres. Those derived from animals are further defined as protein fibres, and they include wool, cashmere, angora, alpaca and silk. Plant-based fibres, such as cotton and linen, are described as cellulose fibres.

Protein fibres
Silk
The silkworm produces silk by pushing fine streams of thick liquid out of small openings in its head; the liquid hardens into filaments when it comes into contact with air. The ensuing fibre is extremely strong, smooth and fine, and is prized for its excellent drape and luxurious hand feel. It is hypoallergenic and

breathable, and responds particularly well to dye, resulting in dazzling, intensely coloured, glossy yarns.

Silk is prone to stretching and, because of the time and work involved in its production, is expensive. The lack of elasticity and the slippery nature of silk yarns can call for extra concentration during knitting, and its inherent delicacy means it must be laundered with care. Traditional silk production raises ethical questions over the farming of silkworms, which are often treated cruelly in order to produce the best fibre. More humane options include ahimsa or 'peace' silk.

Wool
Wool fibre varies in fineness and length according to the breed of sheep, and the climate in which it lives. The softest and highest-quality fibres are generally used for goods that are worn close to the skin, and coarser fibres are better suited to the

Knit in a vibrant shade of silk yarn, this pullover by Julie Hoover for Purl Soho displays the fibre's characteristic drape.

Well-loved wool sweaters are celebrated and combined with new wool knits through needle punching by menswear brand CMMN SWDN.

Alpaca Fair Isle pullover by Kordal Studio, a NYC-based brand driven by sustainable sourcing and manufacture.

interiors market. It is a warm, strong, elastic fibre that drapes and dyes well, making it one of the most popular choices for knitting. The crimped texture of the fibre causes it to trap air and form an insulating barrier, keeping the wearer warm in cold climates and cool in warm climates.

Wool is extremely resilient, with an intrinsic 'memory' that makes it resistant to wrinkles and allows garments to preserve their shape. Its springiness makes it easy to knit with, resulting in even-looking stitches.

Care must be taken when laundering wool products, however, as the fibres can felt if exposed to heat and moisture, or are agitated. Wool is also vulnerable to damage by moths, and the surface of the fabric can pill with wear. Wool may not be suitable for people with sensitive skin, as the lanolin in the fibre can cause prickling or itching.

Speciality hair fibres
Camelids: Alpaca, camel hair, llama and vicuña

The alpaca produces lustrous fibre that is warm and soft, with a silky hand feel. It is durable and creates lightweight, breathable fabrics with excellent drape. The fibre is available in a wide range of beautiful natural tones and also responds well to dyeing. Alpaca can be a good alternative to wool, as it contains no lanolin, making it hypoallergenic and safe for sensitive skin.

Some alpaca yarns are prone to shedding, resulting in excess fluff and fibre when knitting or wearing. The fibre must be laundered with care to avoid felting, and fabrics may also pill from abrasion. Alpaca garments can be susceptible to stretching, because the fibre is less elastic and resilient than wool, and it may sometimes feel more slippery to work with. Because it

is regarded as a speciality fibre, it can command a high price.

It is considered one of the most sustainable fibres, since there is a smaller environmental impact than with other grazing animals, the production process requires no harsh chemicals and the alpacas are treated ethically.

Camel hair is a strong, warm, yet lightweight fibre with thermostatic properties. The softest fibres, such as those found on the undercoat of the animal or taken from baby camel, are reserved for use in clothing. They have an extremely luxurious handle and can be likened to a more affordable cashmere. The natural fibre is typically golden tan and can be dyed to a broad range of colours. Because it does not felt as easily as other animal-fur fibres, laundering is simpler. Camel fibre is less elastic and resilient than wool.

Llama is a lofty, extremely warm, lightweight fibre with excellent

Exclusive vicuña knitwear by Loro Piana.

The looser-gauge of this luxurious ostrich feather adorned scarf by Miss Knitwear displays the delicate and airy qualities of mohair.

Knitted turban and sweater exhibiting cashmere's soft, downy surface texture.

insulating properties. It creates a strong and durable fabric that is also hypoallergenic. The fibre is available in an array of natural shades and also takes dye well. It can be likened to alpaca, but it is not as widely used and remains a specialist choice.

Vicuña is a rare golden fibre that is extremely fine and soft. It is also very warm, with good insulating properties. Owing to the slow growth of the fibre until it can be shorn from the animal, vicuña is incredibly expensive. Its delicacy dictates that it should not be dyed beyond its natural state, a fact that, alongside the price, reserves it for the luxury market.

Goats: Mohair, cashmere and cashgora

Mohair, produced from the Angora goat, is soft, warm, lightweight and very hard-wearing. It is prized for its silky, lustrous sheen and can be dyed easily. Mohair fleece displays a natural curl and is recognizable for its tightly crimped waves or ringlets of fibre. This fluffy structure gives it its characteristic 'ethereal' effect, which can be enhanced when knitted into open-gauge fabrics, or if the textile is brushed. Kid mohair is obtained from the fleece of Angora kids and is even softer.

Mohair creates yarn with less elasticity and resilience than wool. Because it is so fluffy, complicated stitch patterns can be obscured and the knitted fabric can be harder to read. It can also be difficult to unravel stitches, because the hairs of the fibres tend to cling together.

Cashmere comes from the inner coat hair of Cashmere goats, and is a particularly smooth and silky fibre. Although it is very warm, it is also very light, which gives it excellent drape. Recognizable by its luxurious handle,

cashmere is one of the softest fibres, and results in lofty yarns that 'bloom' when knitted. It is elastic and resilient and can also be easily dyed, making it highly sought-after and associated with desirable, timeless, high-quality goods.

Cashmere can be prone to felting if it is not laundered correctly, and it is susceptible to damage by moths. Its inherent softness also means that it is predisposed to pilling and shedding. Cashmere's superior properties and limited production result in a very high price, so it is usually reserved for the luxury market. Its high demand has, however, damaged the Cashmere goat's local environment – through over-population and over-grazing – which has led to ecological imbalances further afield.

Cashgora fibre is the result of breeding Angora and Cashmere goats, and it has similar characteristics to both those fibres. It shares the softness of cashmere, although, since the fibres are slightly longer, it tends to be more durable and less prone to pilling. The resulting yarns are reminiscent of mohair through their lustre, and the fabric has a silky sheen. Cashgora is suitably priced in the middle of pure cashmere and mohair yarns.

Rabbit: Angora

Angora rabbits are bred specifically for their fibre, which is yielded by plucking or shearing their long fur. The fibre is known for its unique halo effect when knitted into fabric, and is very soft and fluffy. Because angora fibre is hollow, it has superior insulating properties, while remaining very lightweight. It is also extremely sleek and lustrous, creating easily recognizable fabrics with a lofty handle.

Angora lacks strength, elasticity and resiliency, and so is often blended with other fibres during the production of yarn. Its fluffiness causes it to shed, and its delicacy means it must be washed carefully. When knitting, it can feel slippery and may not show intricate stitch patterns clearly. Because the manufacturing process of angora fibre is slow and time-consuming, it can be an expensive material to work with. Do your research when buying angora; the treatment of some rabbits can be unethical.

Yak

The fibre found on the undercoat of a yak is similar to cashmere, but less expensive.

Cellulose fibres
Cotton

This fibre is found in the fruit, known as 'bolls', of the cotton plant. Inside the boll casing is a fluffy, white fibre

When knitted, angora's fluffy fibres create garments with a recognizable halo effect. By Ulyana Sergeenko, Autumn/Winter 2018.

that grows around the seeds.

Cotton is a matt fibre with reasonable drape and a soft handle. It is non-allergenic and produces fabrics that are easy to wear, and wash and care for. A very popular choice for warm weather and athletic wear, cotton absorbs moisture and dries quickly. Its comfort, affordability and versatility contribute to its wide use. Cotton can, however, be prone to stretching, and because it lacks elasticity, knitting with it can sometimes be difficult. Cotton farming requires a lot of pesticides and water, causing concern for the surrounding ecosystems and the health of the workers.

'Mercerized' describes cotton that has had its surface fibres burned off, revealing a silkier, smoother yarn that looks extremely lustrous. Fabrics knitted with mercerized cotton possess excellent stitch definition.

The comfort and crisp appearance of cotton makes it a popular choice for summer knits, including this lacey T-shirt by We Are Knitters.

Bast fibres
Linen

Linen is derived from the stem of the flax plant and is naturally tan, off-white or grey. It is a smooth, lustrous fibre with a crisp handle, and is synonymous with warm-weather designs because it absorbs moisture and dries quickly. As well as being very durable, it is lint-free and resists pilling, resulting in practical garments. It also has excellent drape and responds well to dye, with good colourfastness. Some linen yarns may seem to have a coarser hand feel, but they become softer and suppler every time they are laundered.

Linen lacks elasticity, so it is less forgiving during knitting than springier fibres. The lack of stretch and the organic-looking nature of linen yarn can sometimes cause stitches to appear less uniform. Arguably, this adds to the natural beauty of the fibre,

Crisp linen fabrics by Finnish brand Kudokko.

Hemp fibre lends a rustic feel to this patchwork-effect sweater by JW Anderson.

Manufactured fibres

This category of fibre is made from chemical solutions. They generally begin life as pellets, flakes or chips, before being made into a viscous (thick or sticky) liquid for processing. The liquid is forced through a spinneret (a device with lots of holes), in a similar action to water passing through a shower head. The liquid solution then hardens into continuous strands, also known as filament fibres. Manufactured fibres can be split into two categories: synthetic and artificial.

Synthetic fibres are made from petrochemicals and are non-biodegrable. They should be treated with caution during the fabric finishing stage, as they may melt if they come into contact with too much heat.

Artificial, or regenerated fibres, are derived from nature but need either chemical or biochemical intervention to be converted into fibre. Wood and cotton linters (the short fibres left stuck on the cottonseed) are the major sources.

and it can usually be rectified through finishing. Flax is environmentally friendly, requiring little irrigation, chemicals or energy to grow.

Bamboo, hemp and ramie

Bamboo comes from the stem of the bamboo plant, which requires no pesticides or chemicals and little water to grow. The plant can be processed in two ways, resulting in different types of fibre. When it is processed naturally, the resulting fibre is known as 'bamboo linen'; when processed chemically it is called 'bamboo viscose' or 'bamboo rayon' and may be categorized further as an artificial or regenerated fibre.

Bamboo linen is strong, durable and fairly stiff, with a rough handle. It is much less frequently used than bamboo rayon, which has a softer, silkier feel with good drape and a lustrous appearance, and which dyes easily into vibrant shades. Bamboo

viscose remains a popular choice for undergarments and sportswear because of its breathability, comfort and wicking properties. Furthermore, it can block UV rays and is naturally antibacterial and antimicrobial.

Hemp fibre is produced from the hemp plant, which grows easily and quickly in many environments. It is a very strong fibre, similar to linen, but with a rougher hand feel. Hemp dyes easily, and is breathable, anti-microbial and UV resistant.

Ramie is a sleek white fibre that is lustrous and looks like silk. It is extremely absorbent and breathable, making it another ideal warm-weather choice. Although incredibly strong, it lacks elasticity and resilience, and so is often blended with other fibres.

Synthetic fibres
Polyester

Polyester is strong, durable, easy to launder and resistant to wrinkling, stretching and shrinking. It does,

Polyester chips ready to be processed into fibres.

however, lack good elasticity, and can feel scratchy against the skin. It is frequently blended with natural fibres to add strength, and creates fabrics that are simple to care for. Pure polyester yarns often fall into the novelty or fancy category, and are generally very inexpensive. Monofilament is a clear 100 per cent polyester yarn that gives the appearance of transparency when knitted.

Nylon

Nylon is an extremely strong fibre that is also lightweight, with good elasticity and abrasion resistance. It is easy to care for, and can be dyed a wide range of colours. Like polyester, it is frequently blended with other fibres to impart its strength to less durable materials. Unmixed nylon yarns are often classified as novelty types, and are usually very affordable.

Acrylic

Acrylic was developed as a cheaper and easier-to-launder alternative to wool. While it imitates wool fibres well, it does not have the same insulating properties. It is also less breathable, and can have a scratchier handle. Pure acrylic yarns are a popular choice for beginner knitters, as they are easy to work with. The fibre can be dyed to bright colours, blends well with natural fibres, and is versatile and affordable.

Elastane

Also known as Spandex and Lycra, this is an incredibly stretchy fibre that will bounce back to its original shape. This adds to the comfort and fit of close-fitting garments, preventing them from bagging. The fibre is very strong and durable, but remains lightweight, soft and smooth. Only

Yarns created from manufactured fibres.

Monofilament and thicker yarns are juxtaposed together in this fabrication by Molly Henderson, giving the illusion of floating areas.

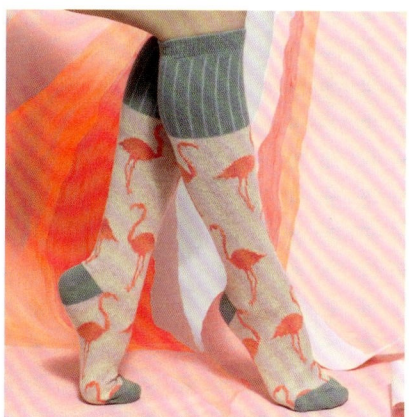

Catherine Tough's flamingo socks are composed from a mix of lambswool and nylon. Nylon adds to the durability, comfort and fit.

a small amount of elastine is needed to add its stretchy properties when blended with other fibres.

Artificial fibres

Viscose

Originally developed as an alternative to silk, this is also known as rayon and is composed of regenerated cellulose usually obtained from wood or cotton

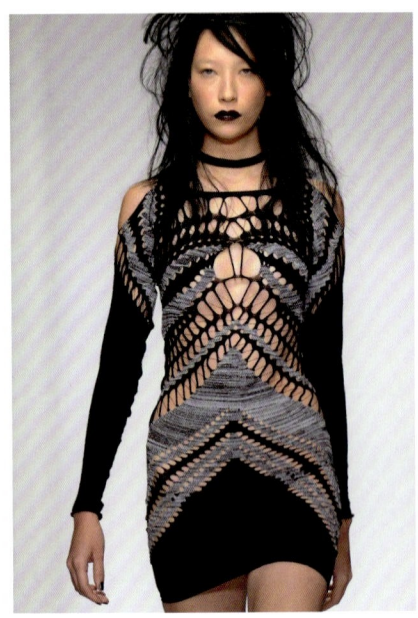

Mark Fast's signature cobweb dresses are knit from stretch yarns to obtain their bodycon silhouette.

linters. Viscose is very lustrous, dyes extremely successfully into vibrant colours and drapes well. It is smooth, soft and comfortable, but it has little elasticity or resilience.

Lyocell

Lyocell is made of regenerated cellulose from wood pulp, and requires less chemical processing than viscose, working with a 'closed-loop system' that secures and reuses most of the chemicals used in its production rather than releasing them into the environment. Lyocell is incredibly strong and comfortable, creating fabrics with great drape and a soft, sleek finish. It is simple to care for, since it does not easily shrink, but it may pill with wear and can be difficult to dye. Tencel is a brand name of Lyocell, manufactured by Lenzing.

Fibre blends

Fibres can be blended to take advantage of their various best characteristics. This is often done to reduce the cost of the yarn and the resulting product. For example, a pure cashmere would result in an extremely expensive garment, but if combined with a cheaper sheep's wool the price would be significantly less without losing the cashmere's softness. Blending can also enhance performance by increasing resilience, making the fabric easier to care for, and improving the way it dyes.

Yarns and yarn types

Yarns are fibres that have been spun or twisted together to create a continuous strand. The amount of twist in a yarn is described as the turns per inch, or TPI. Differing TPI will affect how the yarn looks, and how it performs during knitting and as a fabric. Crepe yarn, for example, is produced by applying as much twist as possible until it reaches a certain point. Crepe yarns have a bumpy, kinked texture that gives rise to a grainy fabrication.

The direction of twist can also differ. A right-hand turn is known as a 'Z' twist, and a left-hand turn as an 'S' twist. When fibre is twisted to create one yarn, it is known as a single yarn. If two or more single yarns are twisted together, a ply yarn is formed. Plied yarns are stronger than single yarns. Two-ply yarn has two yarns twisted together, three-ply has three yarns twisted together, and so on. It is important to note that a yarn with more plies is not necessarily thicker. For example, a four-ply yarn may be thinner than a two-ply yarn if it is created from four fine ends. Yarn can be plied to merge different fibre types, introduce textured or novelty yarns, and add colour interest.

TIP: *You can examine the type of yarn you are using by untwisting a small piece and counting the plies.*

Yarns are constructed to give the knitter an endless array of choice and variety of appearance and function. The design concept is usually the starting point to determine the choice of yarn, but there are other important considerations. These include the intended season, since some yarns may work across the board, but

Left-hand turn or 'S' twist and right-hand turn or 'Z' twist.

Single, two-ply and four-ply yarns.

The range of yarns available to knitters can be very inspiring.

others may be more appropriate for autumn/winter or spring/summer. The outcome of the fabrication must be considered: whether it is a garment, an accessory or a textile that can be used for various products. You should also think about the stitches to be used; some yarns lend themselves to crisp stitch definition, but others may blur and camouflage complex patterns. Drape and structure should also be reflected on, particularly in reference to the garment's silhouette. Finally, factor in the target market, and the intended customers' preferences.

Novelty yarns

This category of yarn can be either single or plied from any fibre or mix of fibres. Effects are introduced into the yarn, resulting in variations in colour, pattern and texture. Innovation is abundant, providing the knitter with ceaseless inspiration. Examples of common novelty yarns are: spiral/

corkscrew, crepe, loop, snarl, chenille, knopp and tape.

Non-traditional yarns can also be used, either by directly feeding them into the machine, or by weaving them into the surface while knitting. Fabric strips, elastic, fine wire, leather cord and more can produce unusual effects, as long as care is not taken to push the machine beyond its limits.

Yarn weight and yarn count

Yarns marketed for two-needle hand-knitting and those sold on cones can be used for machine-knitting. While hand-knitting yarns may serve well for smaller projects and sampling, it is much more economical to use yarn purchased on cones for larger yardage and garments.

When shopping for yarn to use on your machine, you will find that hand-knitting yarns sold in skeins or balls employ a different system to detail their weight from yarns wound on cones. For yarn on cones, the yarn count number specifies the fineness to which the yarn has been spun, and is detailed as a length-to-weight ratio. The count affects the price, weight, opacity, handle and drapeability of the knitted fabric. Several numbering systems are used, depending on the type of yarn. Some are direct numbering systems – meaning the lower the number, the finer the yarn. Others are indirect numbering systems – meaning the lower the number, the thicker the yarn.

Use the table as a guide to help select yarns weights for the relevant machine gauge. Due to its frequency of use,

Machine gauge (gg)	Hand-knitting weights	Machine-knitting weight*
Fine 10–12gg	0–1 (Lace–Super Fine) UK – 1–2 ply US – Lace, Light Fingering	8–18
Standard 7gg	1–2 (Super Fine–Fine) UK – 3–4 ply US – Fingering, Sock, Light Sport	4.5–7
Mid 5gg	3–4 (Light–Medium) UK – DK US – Sport, DK, Light Worsted	3–4.5
Bulky/Chunky 3gg	4–5 (Medium–Bulky) UK – Aran, Chunky US – Worsted, Bulky	1–2

*(Nm metric yarn count number reduced)

the metric (Nm) system is detailed here for coned yarn. This is an indirect numbering system that communicates the ply of the yarn followed by the strand size. To find out if it can be used on your machine, find the lowest common denominator of the count number and fit into the chart. For example, if the yarn count number of a cone of cashmere is 2/30, the count equals 1/15 when reduced. The strand size of 15 therefore, fits in the range given for the fine-gauge machine.

Some yarns may fit into different boxes to how they are listed because the fibre and construction can cause variations in weight. Note that in UK hand-knitting terms 'ply' refers to weight and not the number of strands.

Preparing yarn for the machine

When preparing to knit, it is important to take time to set your yarn up properly. Yarn from cones winds freely and evenly, usually with little hassle. The exception is when shiny or slippery yarns are used. With these yarns, once an end starts knitting, it often pulls several others off the cone with it, causing them to tangle. This can be avoided with a yarn sock, made by cutting the foot off an old stocking, tying it securely over the cone and cutting a small hole in the top to feed the yarn end through.

All yarn that is not purchased on cones must be rewound into balls suitable for machine-knitting. Hand-knitting yarn is bought in skeins or balls, neither of which will feed freely through the machine without getting tangled or flying around. A skein is placed on an umbrella swift, which holds it taut. A ball winder is then used to rewind it into a ball that will stay upright and stable while it feeds through the yarn tension unit.

TIP: *Hand-knitting yarn balls can be prepared simply with a ball winder, but it is advisable to keep them in a container during this process to stop them running around the floor and getting caught. A box with a hole in the lid for the yarn to pull through works well, and a paper bag should suffice if you are in a pinch.*

Keeping yarn notes

Exploring different yarns is such a significant part of the design process that it is worth getting into the habit of keeping a yarn record in a notebook or sketchbook. When pursuing a new design or project, or simply an idea, a good approach is to gather a mix of yarns and knit small single-jersey swatches. This exercise enables you to familiarize yourself with the yarn, assess the stitch size and decide if the aesthetic and functionality corresponds with the design concept. Note down as many of these key points as possible:

- Yarn manufacturer
- Yarn name
- Fibre content
- Shade dye lot number
- Yarn weight
- Stitch size

A skein (1), cone (2), hand-knitting ball (3), and centre-pull ball (4) of yarn.

Jagger Spun
'Maine Line'

100% Wool (WO)

Colour: Sand
Dye lot #19409

2/8

Stitch size: 7

Zegna Baruffa

70% Virgin Wool (VW)
20% Silk (SE)
10% Cashmere (WS)

Colour: Raw white

Stitch size: 8

Swift Yarns
'Swift High Street'

70% Merino Wool (WO)
30% Silk (SE)

Colour: Sugar Plum Fairy

Fingering Weight

Stitch size: 6

Recording the details of different yarns can be a useful exercise during the design development process.

The Design Process

Design approach

When embarking on a machine-knitting design journey, there are a few directions to take. This may be specific to your individual working style, or to the project. Since knitters create the fabric themselves, the textile often serves as the starting point. You may be trying to create a certain mood, and that will lend itself to an end product that shares the same feel.

You could also start with a particular technique, such as creating optical illusions with stripes, or giving the fabric definition through the use of cables. Alternatively, the end project may provide the basis for the design. Approaching the fabrication knowing it is intended for a decorative bag, for example, allows you to work backwards and craft the knitted textile accordingly.

Design brief

Regardless of which design approach you take, the springboard will be initial inspiration, a design concept or a brief. These will vary according to whether you are designing for yourself or working on a student project or in the industry.

If designing for yourself, your initial concept may be open and flexible, so that it can change and develop freely as you experiment on the knitting machine. A student project may start with a set brief that establishes the initial direction, but also allows freedom and creativity in how you interpret it. Professional work, however, whether it be freelance or within a larger commercial company, will almost certainly demand that you work on a much more focused path and within tighter design parameters. You might liken the design brief to a creative contract between yourself

The direction of Penny Charlotte Gibb's knitwear collection was inspired by skiwear and the aesthetic of après ski. She focused heavily on creating striped fabrics in differing colour combinations and design layouts.

Mindful materials are the focus of this project by Megan Stone, in which she celebrates earth-friendly fibres and the beautiful colours that can be achieved through natural dyeing.

and your client. Naturally, the design journey may fork in different directions as you work, but frequently rereading and familiarizing yourself with the design brief and set requirements along the way will ensure that your creativity stays focused.

When embarking on the design process, there are a number of important factors to consider:

- **Season** If the intended outcome is specific to a season, it will directly affect your choice of yarn, gauge and stitches. Cold-weather garments typically dictate heavier yarns that are spun from warm fibres. The resulting fabrics tend to be compact or textured, to keep the wearer insulated. When designing for warm temperatures, finer yarns are knit into airy, lightweight fabrics and medium- or heavier-weight yarns tend to be knitted loosely or into open, lacy structures.

- **Customer** Do your research to ensure you are informed about your customer profile or target market. The demographic, socio-economic background and psychographic behaviour of your customer can be investigated through interviews and market research, and by analyzing trend-forecasting data.

- **Price range** This will have a direct impact on the materials and the complexity of the design. Starting at the high end of the spectrum, the market categories can be defined as:

1. Bespoke: One-of-a-kind pieces made to measure for an individual client to their preferences and size.

Chia Lee's 'Kopitiam' project explores the cultural significance of the traditional Malaysian coffee shop. Her materials and techniques were inspired by the unique amalgamation of objects, textures and patterns experienced through first-hand visits, photographs and memories.

2. Couture: Precision-made garments crafted entirely by hand.
3. Ready-to-wear: Luxury brands that usually show a collection at least twice a year.
4. Diffusion brands (US Bridge): More affordable lines that have been developed by the luxury market.
5. High-end high street (US Better): Includes brands that often cater for a particular customer or category and have a defined style and aesthetic.
6. Middle- and mass-market high street (US Moderate): Garments manufactured in high volumes and designed to appeal to a wider audience.
7. Value market (US Budget): Garments made from lower-quality materials and available at an easily attainable price point.

- **Occasion** Determine whether the finished piece will be daywear, eveningwear, casualwear, sportswear or other. For example, designing for athletic wear requires fabrics that are technical and performance-driven using high-stretch yarns and stitches that create durable and resilient textiles that allow fluid movement.

- **Materials** As the building blocks of knitted textiles, fibres and yarns should be considered and evaluated at every step.

- **Sustainability and ethics** This might dictate the source and type of material used, as well as factoring the life cycle of the garment or product into the design process. A requirement, for example, may be to use only yarns created from domestically grown, naturally dyed fibres.

Inspiration and research

Inspiration can come in countless forms and can be taken from many aspects of life. Research is a crucial part of developing your inspiration into a considered, exciting design concept.

There are two categories of research: primary, or first-hand; and secondary, or second-hand. Primary research includes material that you have observed, in person, in the real world, such as drawing during a museum visit, taking photographs during an excursion, collecting shells and pebbles from the beach or interviewing someone. Secondary research is done using books, the internet,

'A Bigger Splash' collection by Ilana Avital draws upon the colours and shapes within David Hockney's paintings to direct her own fabrications.

Catherine Sinclair uses photographs of her natural surroundings in the north-west of Scotland to inform her design development of knitted textiles for interiors.

cinema, magazines and music – for instance, exploring a book of 1970s fashion, studying Swedish textiles online, or taking in the colours of Wes Anderson films. As this material is original to its creator, it is important you interpret it in your own way when drawing ideas from it. Both types of research inform a well-rounded design concept, but it is primary research that gives the designer strength and the ability to be innovative.

Sources of inspiration

There is no right or wrong approach to finding inspiration, as long as it fuels the direction of your design work. You could look into various categories:

1. **Processes** Delving into creative processes, whether textile or not, allows you to think differently when it comes to your own craft. Tactile woven tapestries, elaborate brickwork patterns or the structure of coiled baskets may cause you to question how you might approach knitted fabric with the eyes of a weaver, a mason or a basket maker.

2. **Natural world** The patterns, colours, forms and movements of flora and fauna have always provided abundant inspiration for textile designers. You could interpret them through different viewpoints (macro and zoomed out, for example), according to the transition of time and season, or through the impact of humans and technology.

3. **Urban landscape** Human contribution to our landscape and environment and the continuous development of our urban surroundings can be examined in myriad ways.

4. **Motion** Movement can influence a series of creative discoveries to do with energetic patterns, shifting lines and the transcending of volume and shape.

5. **Emotion and experience** A personal approach that draws on the collection of emotions we display and our experiences in the world. Topics with a strong social context or cultural importance may be the focus here.

6. **Artists and designers** Whether they are prominent or less well-known, the work of other artists and designers may initiate your creative journey. Researching their life and experiences, their inspiration, their working process and the results can trigger a vision in your own mind.

Sketchbooks by Beth Simmons show her sources of inspiration are a launch pad for her design work.

Different approaches to sketchbooks. Clockwise from top left:
by Rachel Coppard, Amy Bant, Jasmine Lynch, and Catherine Sinclair.

Moodboard by Songbird Studio, based in NYC, for their collection inspired by nostalgia for traditions of the past. It features key images, yarns and swatches using locally sourced natural fibres.

Although it is beneficial to understand what others are doing or have done, be careful not to replicate or imitate their style. Instead, use it as a launch pad to prompt your own interpretation.

Sketchbook

Once you have established your initial concept, a sketchbook or process book is essential for collecting research and design development work. Everyone approaches this in their own way, but regardless of whether you prefer to use a traditional book, loose sheets or a mix of physical and digital pages, having the information collated will help tremendously.

There is no formula; your sketchbook is a personal reflection of you as a designer. Some people may find sketching and drawing essential, while others may prefer to play directly with materials to get their ideas flowing. The key notion is that the sketchbook helps you to gather and collect information, record your findings and analyze your

process. Once you have a good body of ideas represented through image and text, you can use them to explore colour, texture, yarn and stitch concepts. Sketchbooks are valuable tools that allow others to see how your mind works as a designer. This is an advantage when presenting in an interview – for college or career – or pitching to a client.

Mood boards

While a sketchbook usually serves as an ongoing space to collect, develop and reflect, a mood or story board displays the most important elements in an edited way that communicates your vision clearly. Mood boards usually summarize the design concept by displaying key ideas using imagery, text, colour swatches, yarn and other materials. Take time when selecting and juxtaposing these elements to ensure the result is carefully considered. When you move on to design development, a mood board acts as a quick reference, and it is useful for conveying concepts to a client or during a presentation.

Colour and yarn

The colour of a textile or garment is often the main feature a consumer notices, and it can attract them to a product. Because of this, it is crucial as a designer to be knowledgeable, experienced and confident about colour. Colour is subjective, and views and tastes differ among groups of varying age, gender and culture.

The colour wheel can be a tool to understand the basics of colour theory and guide your choices into groups that are seen as universally harmonious. Red, yellow and blue are the primary colours, which are mixed in pairs to create the secondary colours orange, green and purple. Tertiary colours are composed when a primary colour is mixed with a secondary colour. Colours that sit directly opposite each other on the wheel – for example blue and orange – are known as complementary.

Designers are often directed in their colour choices by forecasting agencies, which predict trends and provide information on the use of colour palettes for different seasons and products. These reports cover an international market, and are

available for different age groups and geographical locations. Although trend-forecasting packages are useful for obtaining key information quickly, they can be costly and are not available to everyone. It is good practice, therefore, to learn how to make your own colour decisions from your inspiration, research and design work.

Your design concept is likely to suggest a colour story, and drawing, mark-making and collaging are excellent ways to explore ideas in a personal style. Whether your choice is inspired by an object seen at first hand, a photograph or a research image, try to examine and analyze the palette. Determine how many colours there are, how they work with one

Top: Interesting colour groupings found through collaging by Becky Mars.

Above: Naturally dyed palette by Joanna Fowles.

The colour wheel.

another, and how they sit together proportionally. Focus on the other elements of the object or photograph, and analyze the impact those make on your area of focus. Light and texture will contribute to different tones, densities and effects. Painting this palette out, either by hand or digitally, will help you to consider all these elements carefully. When using paint, always mix your own colours to truly reflect what you see.

Once you have explored this stage, you can translate your findings into an initial yarn selection. As you source yarns, match them to your colour palette, keeping in mind the proportion and tone. The type of yarn will cause colours to display differently, and can be employed to create interesting effects. Using the same colour or tone in a mix of fibre and yarn types can produce exciting results. For example, the components of a wool-and-silk yarn dyed blue will display the silk as a much more vibrant tone than the wool. Wrapping small pieces of yarn around white card is a popular way to explore the harmony of initial yarn ideas, and to analyze how yarns work with one another. Several of these wrappings can be created within a single colour story to help you visualize different combinations and approaches.

Ultimately, the way you approach colour and yarn is very personal. Some people work intuitively with colour, while others may need clearer direction and be more focused on seasonal trends. Keep in mind that although basic colour theory is helpful, there are no rules when it comes to the choices you make. The more you experiment with unexpected combinations, the more likely you are to come up with new and different colour groupings.

P 663 C

P 664 C

P 7527 C

P 5305 C

P 535 C

P 7546 C

P 532 C

Striped Jersey
35% Wool, 35% Linen,
30% Baby Alpaca
75% Cotton, 25% Linen

Striped Jersey
100% Cotton
100% Linen

Jersey Knit
66% Linen, 28%
Viscose, 6% Cotton

Machine Knit Jersey
100% Cotton

English Lace
100% Cotton

'Grapevine' Lace
60% Baby Alpaca, 40%
Pima Cotton

Jersey Knit
100% Linen

Lightweight Canvas
55% Hemp, 45%
Organic Cotton

Top: Work in progress by Kit Couture, identifying key colours within inspiration images and matching them through yarn selection.

Above: Colour and material story by Allie McMurphy.

Amber Hards' sampling process.

Sampling

A great way to explore ideas freely on the machine is to collect yarns that are relevant to your design concept and knit swatches that develop in complexity or refinement.

Once you have a group of samples, use them to analyze your choice of colour and yarn, and your stitch development. Sketch, photograph or collage from them to form your next set of iterations. As you progress to more concrete ideas, increase the size of the swatches to help you visualize how each would behave as a working fabrication.

Sustainability

It is imperative that, as a designer, you have an understanding of sustainability in the fashion and textile industry. Be mindful of the ecological impact of your work, from material sourcing to manufacture. The life cycle of a product should also be measured, by taking into account the long-term implications of the design.

Materials

The choice of fibre and yarn plays a critical role in the sustainability of a textile or garment. Natural fibres are typically seen as greener than their manufactured counterparts, owing to the renewability and biodegradability of their raw materials. Chemicals are habitually associated with manufactured fibres, as are the notions of factories and pollution. While these ideas about manufactured fibres are not wrong, those made from natural sources can also have a negative ecological effect. When assessing the impact of a material, consider resources such as energy, water, chemicals and land, as well as the waste and emissions that are produced during its fabrication.

There are ongoing innovations in fibre manufacturing that focus on bringing cleaner alternatives to the knitwear market. For example, Brooklyn-based AlgiKnit Inc. is developing yarns from kelp (seaweed), a renewable source that grows abundantly in the ocean without the use of pesticides or fertilizers. The fibre is durable yet rapidly degradable, and is suited for garments, accessories, footwear and interiors.

With the rise of technology, fresh perspectives and a flourishing interest in bringing sustainable options to the knitwear market, the arrival of new fibres will surely face ongoing expansion.

Visible mending by Collingwood-Norris adds new life to a previously-loved garment.

Life cycle

Fast fashion and low-cost 'throwaway' garments have contributed to enormous problems with textile waste. Attitudes are slowly changing and shoppers are becoming more educated about purchasing, but the designer has a responsibility to enable the consumer to make better decisions.

The simplest strategy for extending a product's lifespan is to reuse it. This can be done through second-hand retailers such as consignment or charity shops (thrift stores), or by fashion swap organizations, which allow the exchange of garments for items of equivalent quality. If an item is to be reused by several people, it must be constructed to a high standard using durable materials and a stitch structure or fabrication that can withstand wear and tear.

Repairing textiles or garments as an alternative to discarding them also helps to prolong their use. This mending can be purely functional – for example, discreetly patching a moth hole – or can add a new, vibrant feature that is designed to stand out.

Another way of renovating knitwear is to unravel the yarn carefully and reuse it in an updated design. This can also be a great way to use an expensive yarn on a limited budget – for example, unravelling yarn from a cashmere sweater bought at a second-hand shop. Textiles and garments can also be constructed to be multifunctional by being reversible.

Recycling remains a small but important market within knitwear, often through reprocessing existing items, mill ends or by-products into new yarns. Plastic bottles can be transformed into polyester yarn, and discarded fishing nets into nylon yarn. A process to recycle wool involves collecting well-worn woollen sweaters and sorting them into similar colour groupings before shredding the fibre. The coloured wool fibre is then re-spun into yarn, eliminating the need for dyeing.

Chapter 3

Essential Skills

Casting on and casting off is the method in which a fabric is started and ended on the machine; by adding stitches to the needles, and securing them to create a finished edge. It is particularly important to practise and take your time with these techniques. Usually the cast-on serves as the bottom of your fabric or garment, meaning the eye will naturally be drawn to it, so it should look as neat and professional as possible. A successful cast-on and initial courses will also dictate the path of the rest of the knitting. If it is messy or displays problems early on, that may follow into the main body of the fabric. Similarly, an uneven cast-off can distort the rest of the fabric by causing it to gather and tighten at the edge.

Using the machine's tools and working with yarn are also key skills to become comfortable with before moving on to more complex fabrics. Tools are used to move stitches from one needle to another, fix mistakes, and create patterning effects. Simple striped swatches are a good way of practising how to change yarns when knitting, and how to efficiently tidy the ends whether it be on or off the machine.

Needle Arrangement

The number of needles you need to select before you start knitting is determined by the width you intend the finished fabric to be. Small swatches may use only a fraction of the machine's needles, whereas garment pieces or fabric yardage may use the whole needle bed. It is important to note that the number of needles you select for knitting does not equate to the actual fabric width once it is off the machine. Always knit a tension swatch to calculate the fabric tension before embarking on a project that is to be knitted using exact measurements (see page 141).

The stitch pattern will also determine how many needles you should arrange before casting on. When knitting swatches, use enough needles to visualize a colour or pattern repeat within the design, as well as the drape and feel of the fabric. Planning pattern repeats and their placement may require you to adjust the number of needles used to fit in with a stitch sequence. You may also wish to have selvedge needles that knit plain – for example, to border a lace-stitch design. In this case, you may need to add a few extra needles at both ends of your set-up.

The every-other-needle method, which creates space between needles, can be selected when using thicker yarns for your machine gauge. To cast on in this formation, bring one needle to working or holding position (depending on the cast-on method) and leave the next needle in nonworking position. Repeat this for the selected number of needles, making sure the end needle is also in position ready for cast-on. Similar needle arrangements can be used to create openwork structures, by casting on some needles and leaving others out of work. For example, you

Fabrics knit with different needle arrangements. Irregular and regular openwork set-ups with a medium weight yarn (top). Every-other-needle set-up for thicker yarn (bottom).

might cast on every second, third or fourth needle, or even create irregular set-ups for a more organic effect.

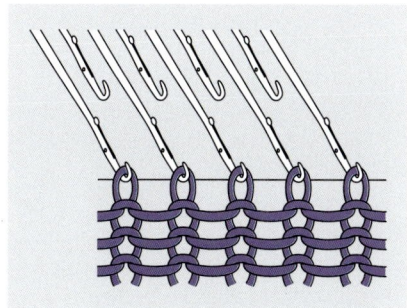

Knitting in the every-other-needle method.

Casting On

Casting on is the process of adding yarn to the needles to begin knitting. Before starting, thread the yarn through the tension unit and place it in the yarn clip. The stitch size that suits the yarn should also be set on the carriage dial.

When securing yarn in the carriage, take time to check that it is firmly situated in the yarn slot. To prevent the yarn from accidentally flying out, you can hold the tail under the carriage, or wrap it securely around the clamp holding the machine to the table.

TIP: *New knitters should start with a yarn that is of medium weight for your machine gauge and in a light colour, so that you can see the stitches easily. While practising, use something inexpensive and with good resilience, such as acrylic or wool. A smooth texture is also more user-friendly, because it shows up stitches and patterns clearly.*

The cast-on you use will depend on the fabric you are creating, and there are broadly two types: open and closed. An open cast-on is often used for quick, small swatches and rough design ideas. When removed from the machine, the cast-on edge is open and thus not protected from unravelling. A closed cast-on will not unravel, and creates a secure, finished edge.

The carriage can begin at either side of the machine bed when commencing the open and closed cast-on methods.

TIP: *A common mistake new machine-knitters make is to pass across the needle bed with the carriage too quickly. This is problematic because if a mistake does occur, such as the yarn not feeding properly, it will affect the knitting much more drastically. Also, if you are passing the carriage at speed from one end of the bed to the other, the working yarn in the carriage can become slack and form unwanted loops at the side of the fabric. Generally, you want to pass the carriage across the working needles and stop just after it clears them.*

Open cast-on methods

Ravel cord or a cast-on comb are used within these open cast-on instructions. Both help to anchor down the fabric after the initial pass of the carriage. When the ravel cord or comb is removed, the first course knitted in your fabric will be a line of open stitches. When using ravel cord, make sure it is free of knots, so that it can be pulled out easily from the knitting.

You can steam the open edge of stitches to discourage them from unravelling, and use a little adhesive tape or a dab of glue along the edge.

Using ravel cord

1. Place the selected needles to working position.
2. Secure the yarn in the carriage and knit one course. If the needles closest to the carriage display small or taut-looking loops, carefully bring them back very slightly. As the needles come back, they take yarn with them.
3. Lay the ravel cord over the stitches just formed, behind the sinker posts, and pull both ends of the cord firmly down towards the ground.
4. Knit between four and eight rows

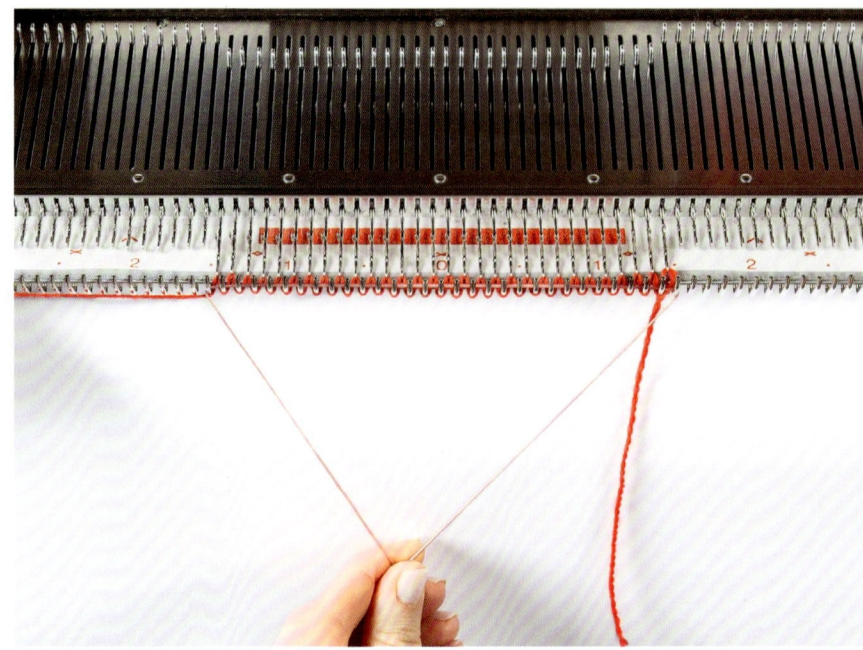

Open cast-on with ravel cord. *Step 3: Lay the cord over the first course of stitches and hold it down before knitting across.*

(more if it is a fine yarn), then slide the ravel cord out by pulling on one end.

5. Add weights to the fabric and continue knitting.

Using a cast-on comb

1. Place the selected needles to working position.
2. Place the yarn in the carriage and secure the tail around the clamp under the knitting table, so that you do not have to hold it in your hand. Loosen the stitch size by a few numbers.
3. With the teeth of the comb facing you, hold it upright and centre it to the selected needles. Bring the comb up so that the base of the teeth are in line with the edge of the knitting machine. Push the comb towards the knitting machine so that the teeth pass through the spaces between the sinker posts.
4. With the comb held as high as it will go, between the sinker posts, slant it slightly towards the base of the knitting bed (so that it is out of the carriage's pathway) and pass the carriage across.
5. Carefully slide the comb down so that it hangs from the machine. The teeth will be resting on the yarn that floats between the needles. If necessary, adjust the yarn coming from the carriage so that it does not get caught under the teeth of the comb in the next step.
6. Adjust the stitch size to the appropriate number. Add weights and keeping the comb slanted for the first few rows, continue to knit. As the fabric continues to grow, move the weights up from the comb to the fabric.

Open cast-on with cast-on comb. *Step 4: Place the comb between the sinker posts and slant it towards the bed.*

Steps 5 and 6: Slide the comb down so that it is hanging from the first row of stitches and then add weights.

Closed cast-on methods

The following methods create a finished, secure edge that is at no risk of unravelling. When first establishing the yarn on the needles, always leave a tail of at least 15–20cm (6–8in) that can be sewn in later. Once completed, make sure the yarn is pushed as far back as possible on the needles, against the sinker posts. After completing the closed cast-on steps, proceed to the instructions for initial courses of knitting for closed cast-on (see page 57).

Weaving cast-on

This is a quick and easy way to get started and another good choice for fast swatching and rough ideas. After completion, there will be a single strand of yarn running through the first course of stitches. If pulled, it can cause the edge to gather.

For machines with weaving brushes

1. Place the selected number of needles to working position, then, starting with the edge needle furthest away from the carriage, place this needle and then every other needle in holding position. If you are using an odd number of needles, the edge needle closest to the carriage will be in holding position; if you are using an even number, it will be in working position.
2. Engage both weaving brushes on the carriage.
3. Secure the yarn in the carriage, then, holding the tail, lay the yarn across the top of the holding position needles.
4. Keep holding on to the tail and pass the carriage across.
5. Disengage the weaving brushes.

Weaving cast-on is complete.

For machines without weaving brushes

1. Place the selected number of needles to holding position.
2. Secure the yarn in the carriage, then hang the tail over the edge needle furthest away from the carriage. Working towards the carriage, weave the yarn under and over the holding position needles.
3. Keep holding the tail and pass the carriage across.

Weaving cast-on is complete.

E-wrap cast-on

This cast-on produces a nicely finished edge with a fair amount of stretch. The tension at which you wrap the needles is important; if it is too loose, the yarn will have a hard time staying on the needles, and if it is too tight, it will be difficult to knit the first row. Make sure you are wrapping stitches with the main yarn coming from the cone or ball, and not the tail.

1. Place the selected needles to holding position.
2. Secure the yarn in the carriage and keep hold of the tail with one hand.
3. Make a slip-knot loop in the yarn 15–20cm (6–8in) from the end.
4. Place the slip-knot loop on the first holding-position needle, furthest away from the carriage, pushing the loop back so that it sits against the sinker posts. Tighten the loop if necessary, but make sure it is not too snug on the needle.
5. Using the yarn coming from the carriage, bring it up between the

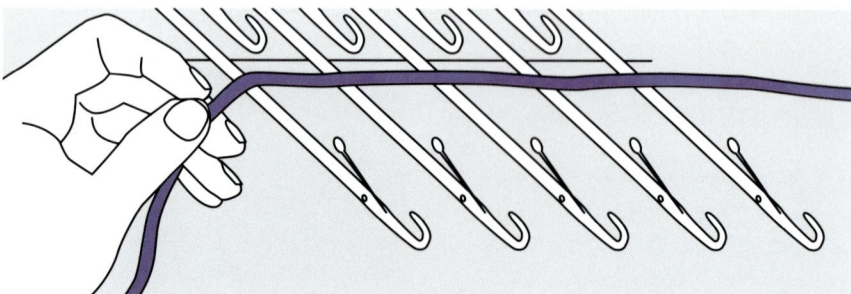

Weaving cast-on for machines with weaving brushes. *Steps 1 and 3: Place alternate needles in holding and working position and lay the yarn over the holding position needles.*

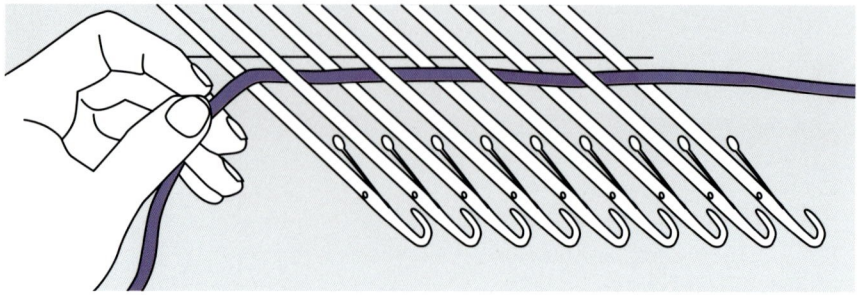

Weaving cast-on for machines without weaving brushes. *Steps 1 and 2: Place needles in holding position, and weave the yarn under and over them.*

second and third holding-position needles, then down between the first and second needles. This creates a loop on the second needle.

6. Bring the yarn up between the third and fourth holding-position needles, then down between the second and third needles. This creates a loop on the third needle.

7. Continue in this manner until the last needle (closest to the carriage) is wrapped.

E-wrap cast-on is complete.

Double e-wrap cast-on

This creates a more decorative and stable edge than the previous e-wrap method.

1. Place the selected needles to holding position, and use a transfer tool to flick open all the latches.

2. Secure the yarn in the carriage and keep hold of the tail with one hand.

3. Make a slip-knot loop in the yarn 15–20cm (6–8in) from the end.

4. Place the slip-knot loop on the first holding-position needle, furthest away from the carriage, pushing the loop back so that it sits against the sinker posts. Tighten the loop if necessary, but make sure it is not too snug on the needle.

5. Using the yarn coming from the carriage, bring it up between the second and third needles and lay it in the hook of the first needle.

6. Manually knit the first needle by placing it to working position (the yarn laid in the hook is pulled through the slip-knot loop).

7. Bring the yarn up between the third and fourth needles and lay it in the hook of the second needle. Manually knit the second needle by placing it to working position

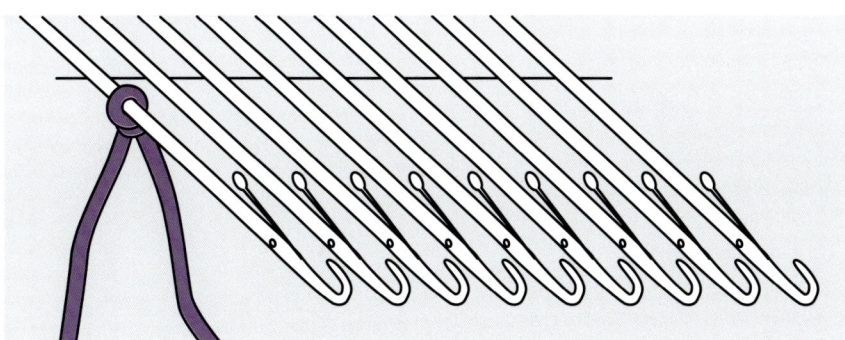

E-wrap cast-on. *Step 4: Place the slip-knot loop on the holding position needle furthest from the carriage.*

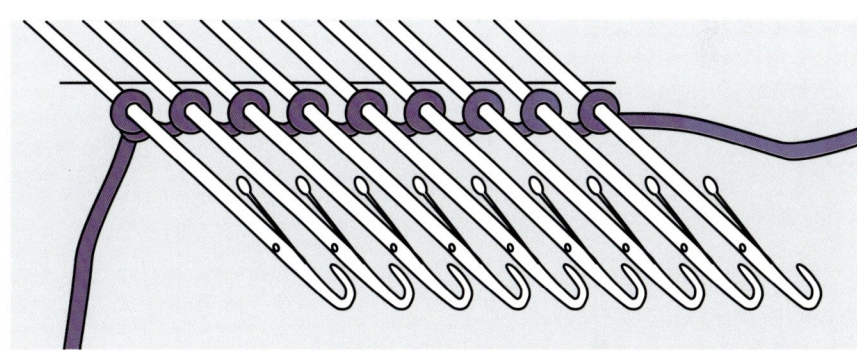

Step 7: Wrap loops of an even tension on the needles and push them against the sinker posts.

TIP: *Making a slip-knot loop*

1. *Leaving a tail of 15–20cm (6–8in), fold the yarn so that it makes a loop.*
2. *Place a finger and thumb into the middle of the loop and pull through the main yarn coming from the cone or ball.*
3. *As you pull the yarn through, it creates a new loop.*

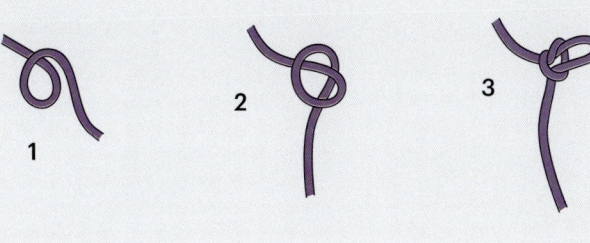

(the yarn laid in the hook is pulled through the loop).

8. Repeat in this way, ending by manually knitting the final needle.

Double e-wrap cast-on is complete.

Latch-tool cast-on

This is also known as chain cast-on, crochet cast-on and tappet-tool cast-on. The result is an attractive edge with slightly less elasticity than the e-wrap methods. Remember when manoeuvring the tool to always keep the loop behind the latch and the working yarn in the hook. Keep an even tension throughout to avoid stitches that are too tight.

1. Place the selected needles to holding position.
2. Do not secure the yarn in the carriage yet. Instead, hold the tail of the yarn and make a slip-knot loop 15–20cm (6–8in) from the end.
3. Place the latch tool in the slip-knot loop. Tighten the loop if necessary, but make sure it is not too snug.
4. Bring the tool up between the two end holding-position needles at the opposite side from the carriage, and place the working yarn under the edge needle. With the slip-knot loop behind the latch on the tool, catch the working yarn in the hook. Pull the yarn through the slip-knot loop by bringing the tool downwards. This forms the first stitch on the first needle, and a new loop on the tool.
5. Bring the tool up between the next two empty needles in holding position. Making sure the loop on the tool is behind the latch, catch the working yarn in the hook. Pull the yarn through the loop to form the next stitch on the needle, and a new loop on the tool.

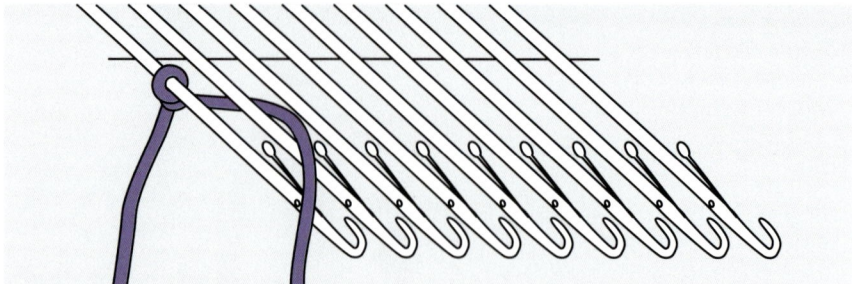

Double e-wrap cast-on. *Step 5: Bring the yarn up between the second and third needles, and lay it in the hook of the first needle.*

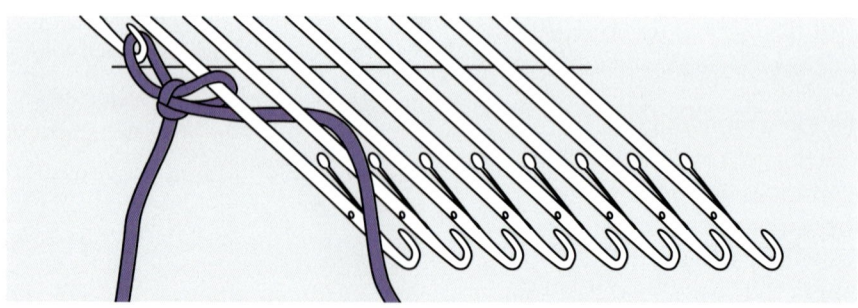

Step 7: Bring the yarn up between the third and fourth needles within the cast on group, and lay it in the hook of the second needle.

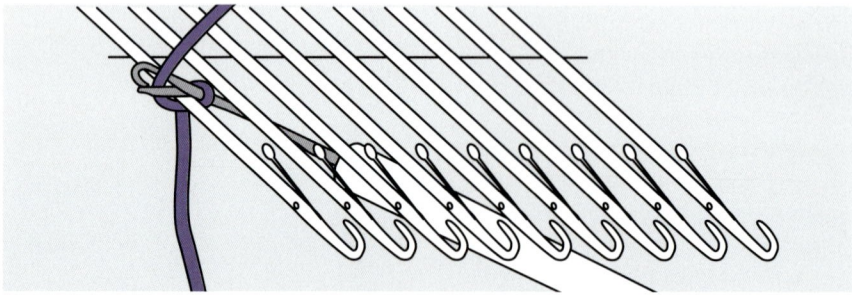

Latch-tool cast-on. *Step 4: Bring the tool up between the first and second needles and pull the yarn through the loop.*

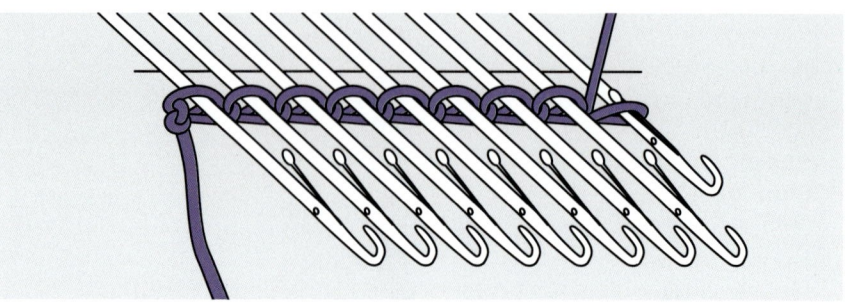

Step 7: Slide the final loop onto the end needle.

6. Continue in this way until you reach the final needle.
7. Slide the loop from the tool onto the final needle. Bringing the needle back slightly helps with this transfer.
8. Place the final needle back in holding position, then bring the working yarn under the needle and secure it in the carriage.

Latch-tool cast-on is complete.

Initial courses of knitting for closed cast-on

Once the closed cast-on method is complete, the machine needs help to knit the first few courses. This is done in one of the following ways:

Hanging a cast-on comb

Once the first row of loops is established on the needles, a comb can be hung to add immediate weight. Needles should be in holding position before hanging the comb.

1. Remove the yarn from the carriage (so that it does not get caught around the edge of the comb).
2. Hold the cast-on comb so that the teeth are facing the machine, centring it to the selected needles. Place the comb up and over the sinker posts so that it sits on the first line of stitches.
3. Place the yarn back in the carriage.
4. Hold the comb down firmly with one hand and use the other hand to pass the carriage across.
5. Give the comb a gentle tug from underneath to make sure it is hanging correctly from the knitting.
6. Add weights to the comb and continue to knit. As the fabric grows, move the weights up from the comb to the fabric.

Using ravel cord

Ravel cord is used in the same way here as for the open cast-on method; see pages 52–53 and follow Steps 3–5. If needles are in holding position after the cast-on, knit one course to place them into working position before Step 3.

Manually pushing the needles out

Needles are placed in holding position each course before passing the carriage. If the needles are already in holding position after completing the cast-on, start at Step 2. If the needles are not in holding position, start at Step 1.

1. Bring the cast-on needles to holding position in small groups using both hands. One hand pushes the butts to bring the needles out, and the other uses a finger underneath the needles to hold the stitches firmly against the sinker posts so that they do not pop off.
2. Pass the carriage across to knit one course.
3. Repeat Steps 1 and 2 for about ten courses, or until you have roughly 2.5cm (1in) of fabric to hang weights on.

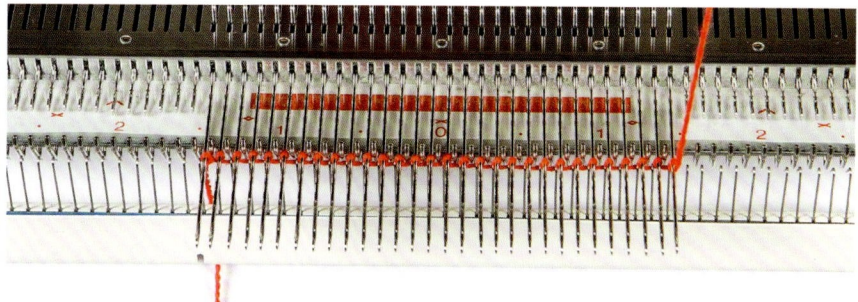

Hanging a cast-on comb. *Step 2: With the teeth of the comb facing the machine, place it up and over the sinker posts so that it sits on the first row of stitches.*

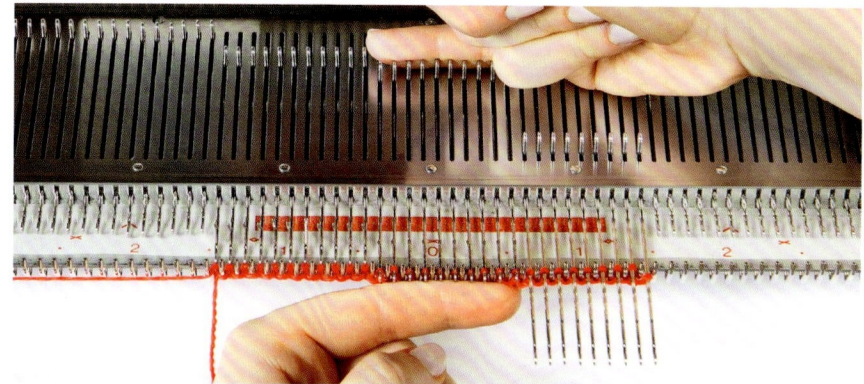

Manually pushing the needles out. *Step 1: Use both hands to carefully bring the needles to holding position.*

Casting Off

Casting or binding off is the means of finishing a piece of knitting securely with a closed edge, so that it does not unravel. Stitches can be cast-off with the carriage at either side of the machine bed.

There is sometimes a risk of uneven tension when casting off, meaning that stitches can mistakenly be pulled too tight and cause the edge to distort. Two common solutions to this are integrated into some of these cast-offs. The first is to use the sinker posts to hold the fabric evenly against the bed as you work across, securing all stitches. The second method can be used on machines without sinker posts (such as some manual machines). This time, empty needles are used as a spacer, ensuring the stitches are equally tensioned. Both these processes use the working yarn to lie around the sinker posts or the empty needles.

For open cast-offs, refer to the ravel cord and waste yarn information on pages 62–63.

Transfer-tool cast-off

This cast-off uses a one-prong transfer tool to secure the stitches one by one. Before beginning, make sure the needles are in working position.

Using sinker posts to tension

1. Using a one-prong transfer tool, move the first stitch (closest to the carriage) to the adjacent needle with a stitch. There are now two stitches on this needle.
2. Use the transfer tool to bring this needle forward so that both stitches slide behind the latch. Remove the transfer tool from the needle hook.
3. Pick up the working yarn and pass it behind the adjacent sinker post

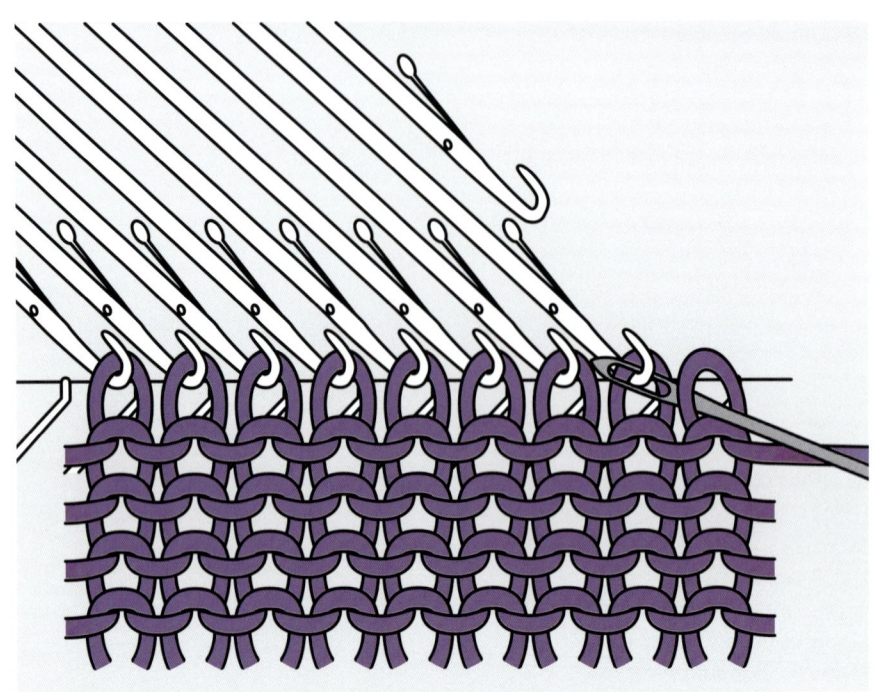

Transfer-tool cast-off. *Step 1: Transfer the first stitch to the adjacent needle.*

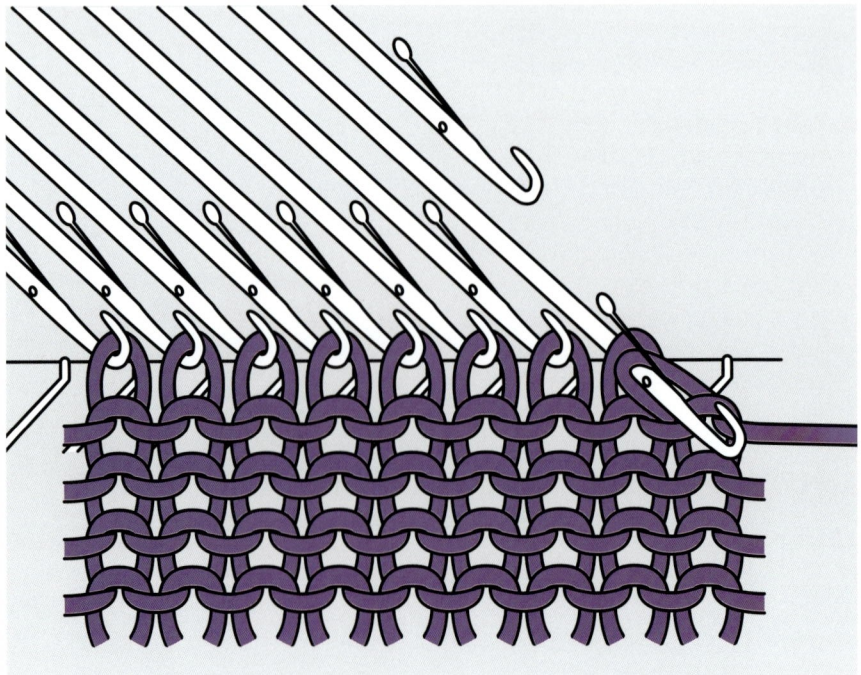

Step 2: Bring the needle with two stitches forward so that they slide behind the latch.

(on the carriage side) and then into the hook of the same needle. (It helps to bring the needle back a little before laying the yarn in the hook.)

4. Bring the needle back to working position. The two stitches slide over the closed latch and the working yarn is pulled through, creating a single stitch on the needle.

5. The single stitch is transferred to the adjacent needle with a stitch, and the same method is continued until there is one stitch left on the final needle.

6. Cut the yarn, leaving 15–20cm (6–8in), and then pull it through the final stitch to secure.

Remove the fabric from the machine by lifting it off the sinker posts.

Using empty needles to tension
Follow the above steps, but do the following for Step 3:

3. Pick up the working yarn and bring the adjacent empty needle to holding position. Lay the yarn over the empty needle and into the hook of the needle with two stitches.

Take the fabric off the machine by removing it from the empty needles.

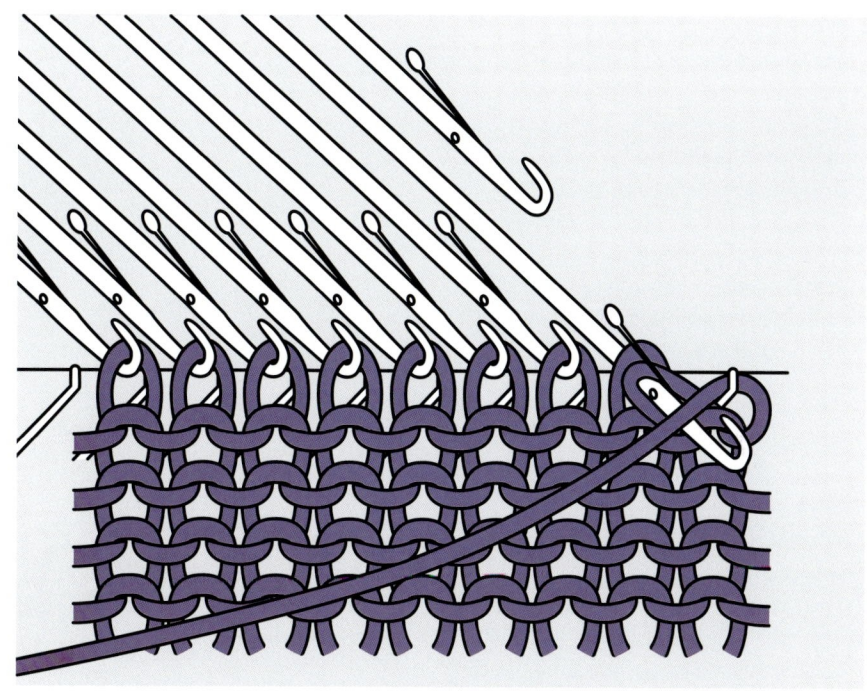

Step 3: Lay the yarn behind the sinker post and into the needle hook.

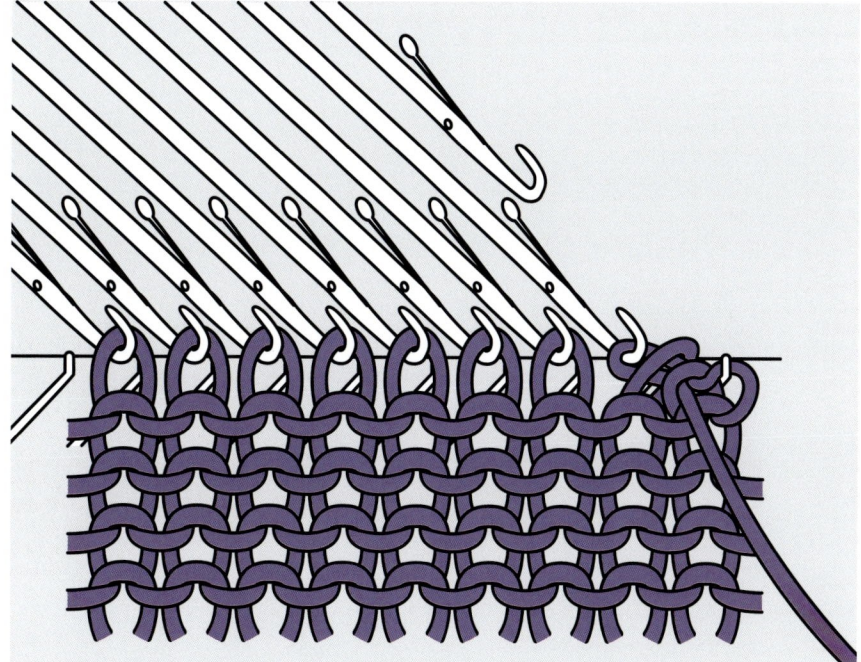

Step 4: Bring the needle back so that the yarn in the hook is pulled through the two stitches.

Latch-tool cast-off

This method mirrors the appearance of the latch-tool cast-on, and creates a horizontal line of chain stitches. Before casting off, knit the final course in a looser stitch size.

Using sinker posts to tension

1. Remove the yarn from the carriage, but do not cut it.
2. Place the needles in holding position and make sure the fabric stays flush with the needle bed.
3. Using one hand to hold the latch tool, place it into the hook of the needle closest to the carriage. With the other hand, bring the needle back to working position so that the stitch slides off the needle and onto the tool. Make sure the stitch sits behind the latch on the tool.
4. Pick up the working yarn and pass it behind the adjacent sinker post (on the carriage side).
5. Catch the working yarn in the hook of the tool and pull it through the stitch that is behind the latch. This forms a new stitch.
6. Bring the next needle back until the tool can easily be placed in the hook. Bring the needle back to working position so that the stitch slides off the needle and onto the tool. Make sure both stitches sit behind the latch on the tool.
7. Pick up the working yarn and pass it behind the adjacent sinker post.
8. Catch the working yarn in the hook of the tool and pull it through the stitches that are behind the latch. This forms a new stitch.
9. Repeat Steps 6–8.
10. Cut the yarn, leaving 15–20cm (6–8in), and pull it through the final loop on the tool to secure.

Remove the fabric from the machine by lifting it off the sinker posts.

Using empty needles to tension

Follow the above steps, but bring the newly empty needle to holding position and lay the yarn over it, instead of behind the sinker post.

Take the fabric off the machine by removing it from the empty needles.

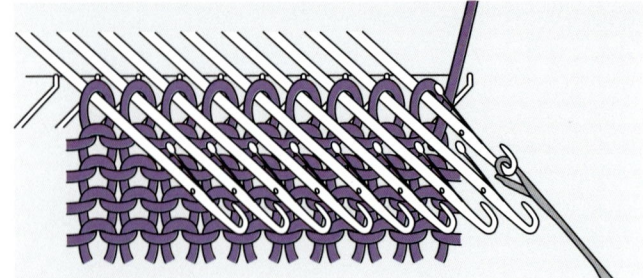

Latch-tool cast-off. *Step 3: With the tool in the hook of the first needle, bring the needle back so the stitch slides onto the tool.*

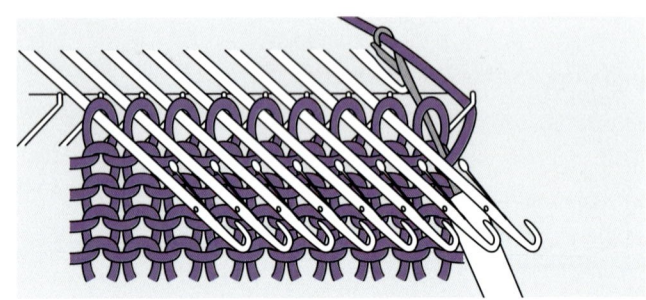

Steps 4 and 5: Pass the yarn around the sinker post, and pull it through the loop situated behind the latch on the tool.

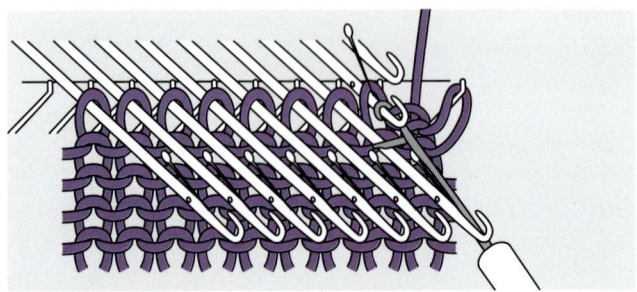

Step 6: Slide the stitch from the next needle onto the tool. Both stitches should be situated behind the latch on the tool.

Backstitch cast-off

This cast-off uses a tapestry needle to sew a line of backstitch through the final course of stitches. The resulting edge is elastic and flexible, with little risk of it distorting, as the stitches remain on the needles while they are secured. Because it creates a more compact finish, it is often used when seaming two fabrics together on the machine.

1. Cut the working yarn, leaving a tail four times as long as the fabric is wide.
2. Thread the yarn into a tapestry needle. Insert it through the first stitch closest to the carriage from the front and out through the second stitch from the back. Pull the yarn up to the surface, keeping an even tension.
3. Insert the needle through the first stitch again from the front and out through the third stitch from the back (leaving out the second stitch). Pull the yarn up to the surface.
4. Insert the needle through the second stitch from the front and out through the fourth stitch from the back. Pull the yarn up to the surface.
5. Insert the needle through the third stitch from the front and out through the fifth stitch from the back. Pull the yarn up to the surface.
6. Continue in this way across all stitches. After the final stitch, insert the needle through the second to last stitch from the front and out again through the final stitch from the back.

Remove the fabric from the needles.

Gathered cast-off

Stitches can be secured by running a length of the yarn through the final course. This can act as a stitch holder if you are undecided about how the fabric will be completed. However, it is most commonly used to gather stitches. Gathered stitches may be incorporated into details such as ruffles and frills, or used to create a tight close, such as at the top of a beanie hat.

1. Cut the working yarn, leaving a tail three times as long as the fabric is wide.
2. Thread the yarn into a tapestry needle and insert it through the middle of all the stitches (from the front), working in groups.
3. After the final stitch, remove the knitting from the machine. When pulled taut, the yarn will gather the fabric.

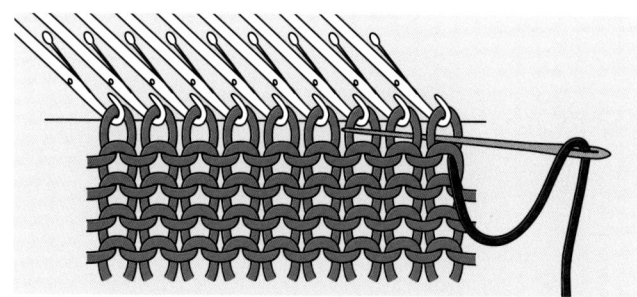

Backstitch cast-off. *Step 2: Insert the needle through the first stitch from the front and out through the second stitch from the back.*

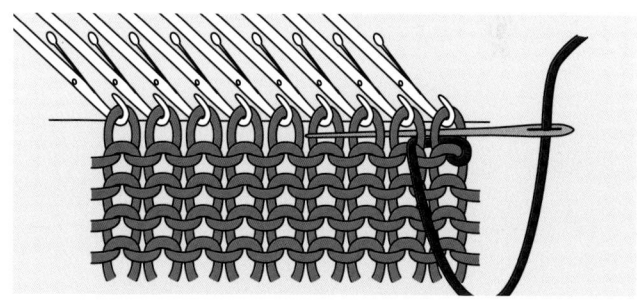

Step 3: Insert the needle through the first stitch from the front and out through the third stitch from the back.

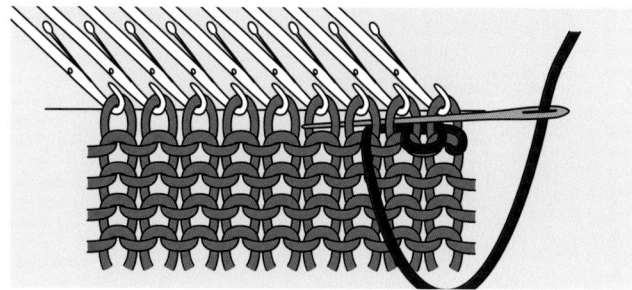

Step 4: Insert the needle through the second stitch from the front and out through the fourth stitch from the back.

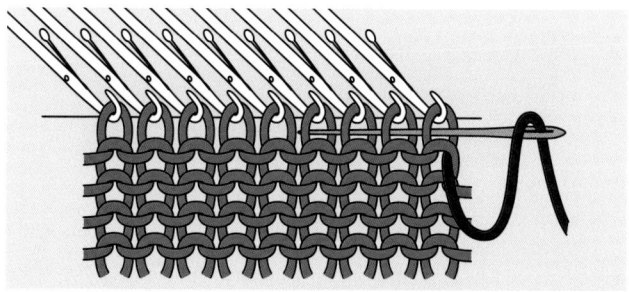

Gathered cast-off. *Step 2: Insert the needle through the middle of all stitches.*

Waste Knitting

Waste (or scrap) knitting is fabric that is knitted in an alternative yarn to the main yarn. This may be knitted for one or several courses, and usually acts as a temporary material that is removed later. When selecting a waste yarn, choose the same weight as the main yarn, but in a contrasting colour, so that you can easily see the separation between the two. A smooth yarn is best; anything too textured can make the stitches difficult to see, and is harder to remove later.

Waste knitting can be used at the beginning or end of your fabric. When beginning with scrap knitting, the first course of main yarn stitches can be open (live) or closed (secured). When ending with scrap knitting, the last course of main yarn stitches is open (live).

Ravel cord for waste knitting. *Step 5: After removing the fabric from the machine* (top), *pull one end of the ravel cord to separate the waste and main knitting* (bottom).

Ravel cord for waste knitting

Ravel cord is fed into the carriage by hand and knitted for one course between the waste and main yarn, enabling a clean and easy separation between the two.

1. Make sure there are no knots in the ravel cord. Place it in the carriage yarn feeder and secure the tail underneath the carriage around the table clamp.
2. Hold the long end between your thumb and forefinger directly above the carriage yarn feeder, and make sure the remaining length is out of the carriage's pathway.
3. Knit across, allowing the long end of the cord to feed from your hand.
4. Remove the cord from the carriage and leave both ends hanging towards the ground, out of the way of the knitting path.
5. Once the fabric is knitted and off the machine, pull one end of the ravel cord to separate the waste yarn from the main fabric.

Beginning with waste yarn

Having a section of waste knitting established on the machine and already weighted can be helpful for stitches or techniques that need extra tension from the first course. Fragile yarns that are prone to splitting, breaking or skipping stitches are also more likely to knit successfully if introduced after several courses of waste knitting.

1. Cast on with waste yarn.
2. Knit at least ten courses.
3. Knit one course with ravel cord.
4. Introduce the main yarn by knitting across (for an open edge) or casting on again over the course of ravel-cord stitches (for a closed edge).

Using the Tools and Hold Function

Ending with waste yarn

This is used, for example, to keep the last course of open stitches from unravelling if the fabric has been removed from the machine without casting off. These open stitches can be re-hung, to display the other side of the fabric, or if you simply need to come back to it later. Alternatively, open stitches can be secured off the machine, such as by hand-seaming or transferring onto a hand knitting needle. In these cases, the waste yarn is essentially acting as a stitch holder that contains the live stitches securely.

1. Knit one course with ravel cord.
2. Knit at least ten courses with waste yarn. Cut the yarn and remove it from the carriage.
3. Take off the weights, then pass the carriage across the work to remove the fabric from the machine.

Moving stitches with a transfer tool

Transfer tools reposition single or groups of stitches. They are used for casting off, for shaping the fabric through increases and decreases, and for techniques such as lace and cables. Exploring simple stitch transfers with the tool is a good way to become comfortable and confident using it.

A single eyelet or lace hole can be created by using a one-prong transfer tool to move one stitch as follows:

1. Hold the tool horizontally, and place the open prong on the hook of the needle where you want the eyelet to appear. (If the needle latch is closed, it will be pushed open once the eye of the tool finds the hook.)
2. Use the tool to bring the needle towards you, until the stitch slides behind the latch. Take care to hold the fabric flush against the bed with your other hand, to avoid adjacent stitches dropping.
3. Use the tool to bring the needle back to working position. As it moves back, the stitch slides over the closed latch and onto the tool.
4. With the stitch on the tool, move over to the adjacent needle to the left or right and place the open prong on the hook of this needle. (To avoid the stitch falling off the tool when moving, hold it upright so that the stitch sits towards the handle.)
5. Transfer the stitch from the tool into the needle hook. Using the tool to bring the needle slightly towards you and wiggling the stitch onto it can help. This needle will now have two stitches in the hook, and the original needle will be empty.
6. Align any shifted needles back to working position. When the carriage passes across, a new stitch will form on the empty needle, and it will continue to knit as normal.

Repairing a column of dropped stitches

Latch tools are designed to duplicate the function of the machine's needles. Because of this, they are the ideal tool to repair dropped stitches. Use as follows:

Note: it is easier to handle the fabric if you remove the cast-on comb and weights first.

1. Find a stitch just below the one that has dropped and insert the tool into it from behind (the knit side of the fabric). Drop any stitches above until you reach the one secured on the tool.
2. Bring the tool towards you, so that the stitch slides behind the latch.
3. Bring the tool away from you, catching the float above in the hook. As the tool travels back, the float pulls through the stitch.
4. Repeat Steps 2 and 3, bringing the tool into the space under the next float.
5. At the top of the column, place a one-prong transfer tool in the last stitch and slide the latch tool out. Use the transfer tool to place the stitch back onto the empty needle hook.

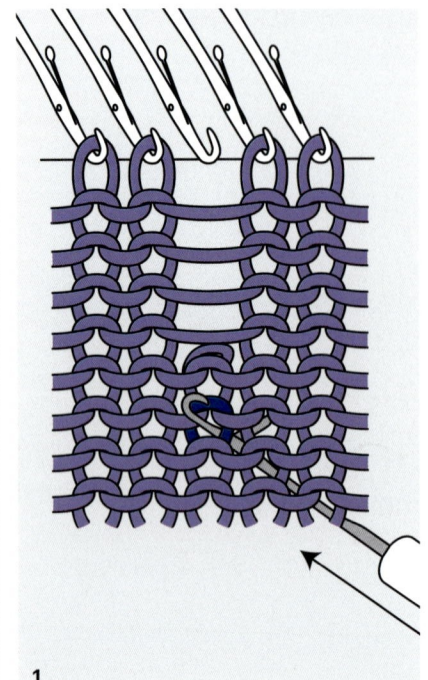

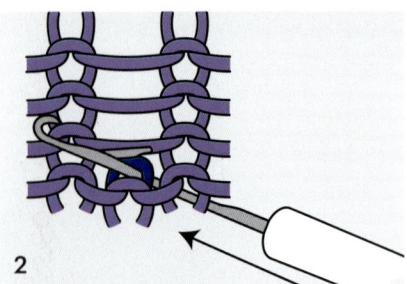

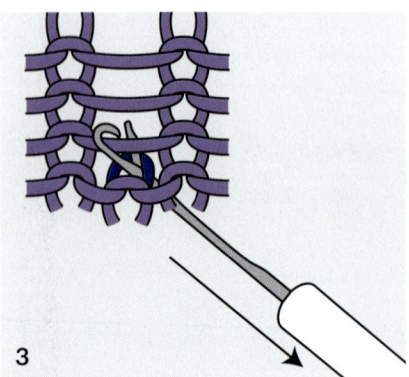

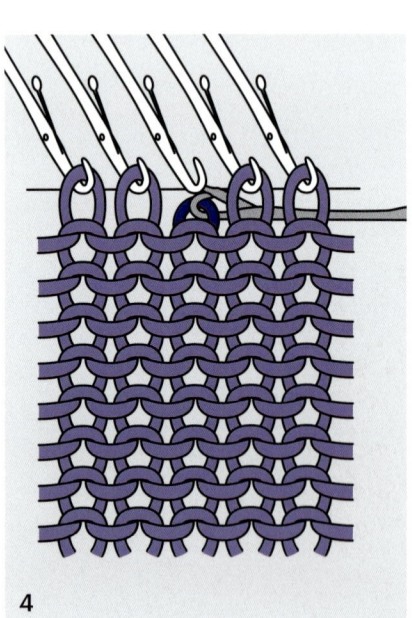

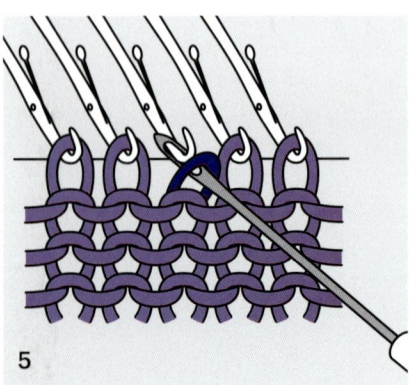

Using a latch tool to repair dropped stitches.

A latch tool can be used to create fabrics with knit and purl stitches on the same side.

Reconstructing a column of stitches

Using a latch tool to reconstruct stitches allows you to create a knit stitch on the purl side of the knitting, and a purl stitch on the knit side. Use as follows:

1. Locate the stitch where you want the reconstructed column to begin, and insert the tool into it from the front (the purl side of the fabric).
2. Drop the stitch from the needle above until it runs down and stops on the tool.
3. Making sure the stitch is behind the latch, catch the float above and bring the tool towards you so that the float pulls through the stitch.
4. Slide the stitch behind the latch, and catch the next float in the hook before pulling through.
5. Repeat to the top of the column, then place a one-prong transfer tool in the last stitch and slide the latch tool out. Use the transfer tool to place the stitch back onto the empty needle hook.

Holding stitches

When the hold function is selected on the carriage and needles are placed in holding position, the stitches remain live but do not knit when the carriage passes across. Needles that are in working position, however, continue to knit. This results in a fabric that grows in length in some places (under the working-position needles) but not in others (under the holding-position needles). It is for this reason that the hold function is also known as short-row or partial knitting.

Fabrications can be both two- and three-dimensional. Examples include multicoloured intarsia effects, tuck-stitch surfaces and sculptural stitch structures. Holding position is also used in the construction of shaped items such as garments and accessories – for instance, knitting the heel of a sock, making a dart or curving a hem.

When the carriage is set to hold, and it passes over a needle in holding position, it leaves a float of yarn. There is a limit to the number of floats a needle can collect, since they must eventually be knit. While floating yarn adds to the decorative nature of tuck patterns, it is avoided for three-dimensional or shaped fabrics. To achieve this, needles are always brought to holding position at the opposite side of the work from the carriage.

Because the fabric grows in length through separate groups of stitches, slits or holes can occur. Unless they are required for a deliberate design, such openings are avoided using a technique called wrapping. Wrapping uses the yarn coming from the working position needle on the carriage side, and places it under the adjacent held needle. The yarn must only pass under this one needle when wrapping, and should lie over the remaining held needle(s).

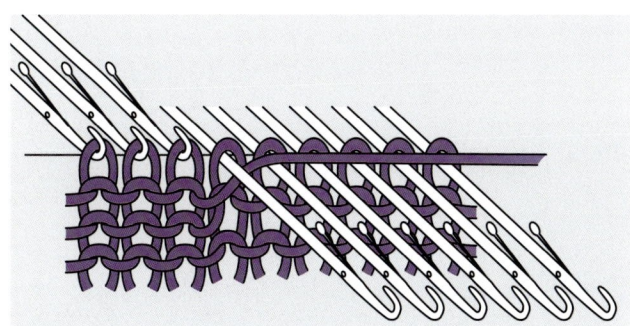

Wrapping a needle prevents a hole from occurring when knitting in holding position.

Methods to Ease Knitting

Example: Knitting using holding position and wrapping

1. Begin with the carriage on the right. Cast on 30 stitches and knit 10 courses. Make sure the knitting is weighted well.
2. Set the carriage to the hold function.
3. Bring the working needle furthest away from the carriage (on the left edge) to holding position.
4. Knit one course (carriage is now on the left). Wrap the held needle by bringing the working yarn underneath it.
5. Knit one course (carriage is now on the right).
6. Bring the next working needle furthest away from the carriage to holding position.
7. Knit one course (carriage is now on the left) and wrap the most recently held needle by bringing the yarn underneath it. Lay the yarn over the remaining held needle.
8. Repeat Steps 5–7, wrapping the last held needle and letting the yarn lie over the previous held needles. Pay attention to the weight, especially underneath the needles in working position.
9. When just one needle remains in working position, and the carriage is at the right-hand side, disengage the holding function and pass it across to knit all needles.

Moving the carriage across without knitting

There are times when you require the carriage to be on the other side of the bed, but don't want to knit a course – for example, after unravelling one or more rows of knitting. There are a few different ways to do this, all of which involve removing the yarn from the carriage beforehand.

1. The carriage can be slid off the needle bed on one side and moved to the other side. Take care that the carriage is set correctly, by making sure the underneath groove slides properly onto the needle-bed rail. If it does not glide easily, take it off and reposition it.
2. Alternatively, set the carriage to the hold function, then place all needles in holding position. As the carriage goes across, it skims past every needle. Once it is on the correct side, disengage the hold function. Keep in mind that this solution is not ideal if you already have some needles in holding position, as the repositioning of needles can require extra attention.
3. The final solution is to use the miss setting on the carriage to knit a free pass across the needles. Set the carriage to this function, keep the needles in working position and pass across. On the other side, release the miss setting. To avoid stitches dropping, make sure there is no punchcard in the machine before using this method.

Remember to adjust the row counter to account for the non-knitted course, and thread the yarn back into the carriage before resuming knitting.

Manually knitting stitches

Forming a stitch by hand gives you control over how much yarn is pulled through to create it. This allows you to make far larger stitches than those produced by loosening the stitch size. An entire course can be knitted in this way, by removing the yarn from the carriage and using it to manually form each stitch. To knit a course by hand:

1. Remove the yarn from the carriage.
2. Bring all needles to holding position.
3. Lay the yarn in the open hook of the needle closest to the carriage, and bring this needle back to working position. At this point the new stitch, formed from the yarn in the hook, can be stretched by bringing the needle back further than it is usually led by the carriage. The further it is pulled back, the larger the resulting stitch.
4. Repeat this for each needle.
5. Carefully realign all needles to working position. Gently tug the fabric down and make sure it is weighted so that the newly formed larger stitches are tensioned correctly.
6. Return the carriage to the other side of the machine bed and rethread the yarn before passing it across (see 'Moving the carriage across without knitting', opposite).

To enlargen only certain stitches within the course, a separate strand of yarn is used. To knit isolated stitches by hand:

1. Bring the selected needles to holding position.
2. Using a separate strand of the main yarn and leaving a tail to finish later, lay it in the open hook of the first needle, and bring this needle back to working position. At this point the new stitch can be stretched by bringing the needle back. The further the needle is pulled back, the larger the resulting stitch.
3. Repeat this for all needles in the group, then carefully realign them to working position.
4. Ensure the ends of the strand are hanging down towards the floor, out of the carriage's pathway, then knit across.

Multicoloured stitch designs, such as a hand-formed Fair Isle pattern, can also be created by manually laying in separate strands of yarn. In this case, the yarn is used for contrasting colour or texture, rather than stitch size, so the stitches should be knitted with as close a tension as possible to the main fabric.

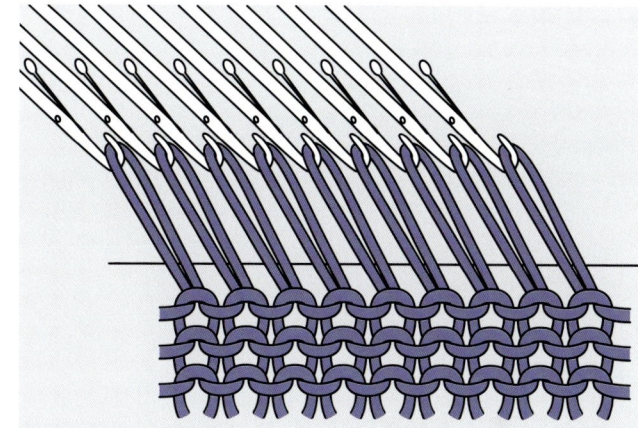

A row of large stitches can be created by manually knitting each needle with the working yarn.

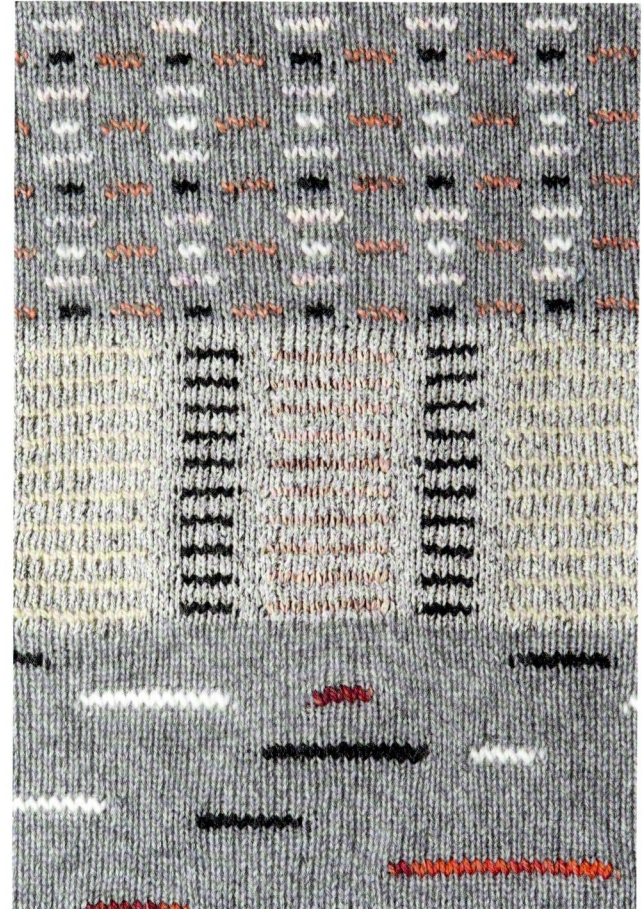

Manually knitted groups of stitches using a contrasting yarn to create multi-coloured patterning.

Working with Yarn

Changing yarn

Depending on the machine model, there is typically space for between two and four different yarns to be threaded through the tension unit at the same time. Each one is threaded separately, in its own pathway, and is held securely on the yarn clip until it is selected for use. When a new yarn is added or an old one is removed, always leave a tail of about 15–20cm (6–8in). To change from one yarn to another:

1. Remove the current yarn from the carriage and cut it, leaving a tail.
2. Place the next yarn in the carriage. Hold the tail underneath or wrap it firmly around the table clamp, then pass the carriage across to knit.

If you are using more cones of yarn than can be threaded through the tension unit, they should be swapped out as necessary. Rather than removing one yarn entirely, you can cut it below the first threading point and tie it to the new one. The new yarn can then be quickly pulled through. Before securing it in the carriage, cut above the knot to remove the previous yarn tail.

Hand-feeding is useful when making frequent yarn changes (such as for stripes), knitting ravel cord (as for waste knitting) or using a strand that may be too short to thread through the tension unit. To hand-feed cut strands, follow the process described for ravel cord on page 62.

TIP: *When hand-feeding from a cone or ball of yarn, keep it at your feet in front of the machine.*

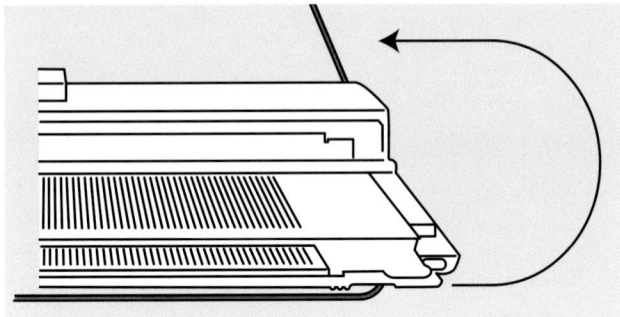

When making frequent yarn changes, place the one not knitting at the rear of the machine.

If you are working with two yarns that are changed frequently – every two to six courses – it is not necessary to cut them each time. Instead, the yarn not in use is removed from the carriage and placed at the rear of the machine or, if there is one, in the clip at the edge of the machine. Then, the next yarn is placed in the carriage to knit. This sequence is repeated, and each yarn carries up the side of the fabric as it alternates. Make sure the two yarns do not get twisted when you switch them.

Finishing yarn ends

Yarn tails must be finished so that they are secure in the knitting, and to give the fabric a professional look. This can be done on or off the machine.

Securing on the machine

Loose ends can be secured by being woven over and under the needles. When the carriage knits the next course, it binds the tail to the purl side of the fabric. This is a quick solution that eliminates the extra time needed to finish ends by hand. Bear in mind, however, that it is suitable only for fabrics that use the knit side as the face. It is not always a good idea to secure the ends of thicker yarns in this way, because they can add bulk to the fabric or become visible from the face.

Since this method involves bringing a group of needles to holding position, make sure the carriage is set so that it knits needles in hold. If the carriage must be set to holding position for a stitch pattern or technique, bring the needles to upper working position after weaving the tail.

1. Remove and cut the yarn in the carriage, then bring approximately 11 needles (more if the yarn is slippery) to holding position on the edge where the tail of this yarn is hanging.
2. Weave the tail over and under the holding-position needles. Make sure the yarn lies against the sinker posts.
3. Knit one course with the next yarn.
4. Bring approximately 11 needles to holding position on the edge where the starting tail of the new yarn is hanging.
5. Weave the tail over and under the holding-position needles.
6. Knit the desired number of courses in this yarn.
7. Work Steps 1–6 to continue securing ends as you change yarn. Excess yarn can be trimmed as you work. Knit several courses before doing this, so that the cut end does not get caught in the current row's stitches.

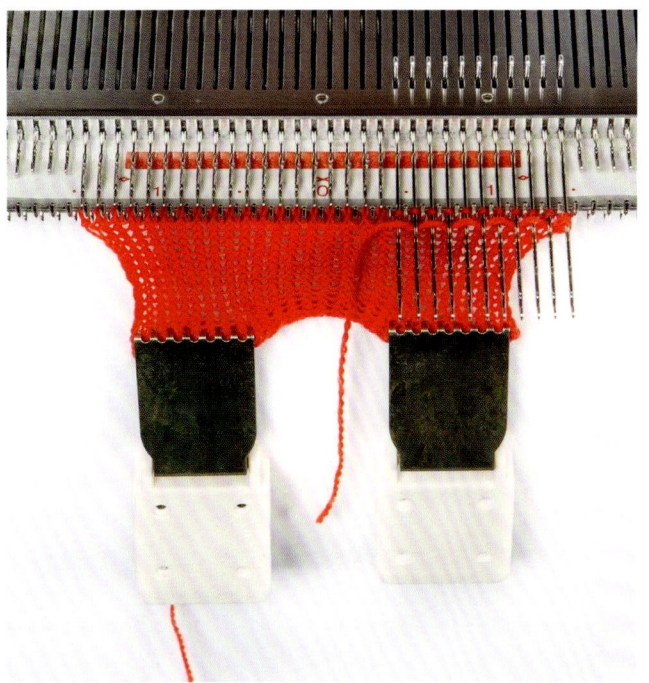

Securing yarn ends on the machine. *Step 2: Weave the ending tail of the old yarn over and under a group of needles.*

Securing off the machine

There are many methods of finishing yarn ends by hand, and each knitter will have a preference. Regardless of the approach, the most important factor is to secure yarn tails in the least visible way possible. Knots should always be avoided, since they are not strong enough to hold the fabric secure and can cause unwanted bulk. Most techniques use a tapestry needle to weave or integrate the tail into the reverse of the fabric.

Duplicate stitch or Swiss darning can be worked on either side of the fabric, and mimics knit or purl stitches that blend flawlessly with the background. Alternatively, on the purl side ends can be woven in horizontally (under and over the purl bumps) or diagonally (under a line of purl bumps). On the knit side, tails can be woven vertically (by running the needle under alternate horizontal strands between the Vs of knit stitches). Ends should be fastened into the fabric for approximately 2.5cm (1in), or until you feel they are secure. The remaining yarn tail can be trimmed carefully, close to the fabric.

Step 5: Weave the starting tail of the new yarn over and under a group of needles.

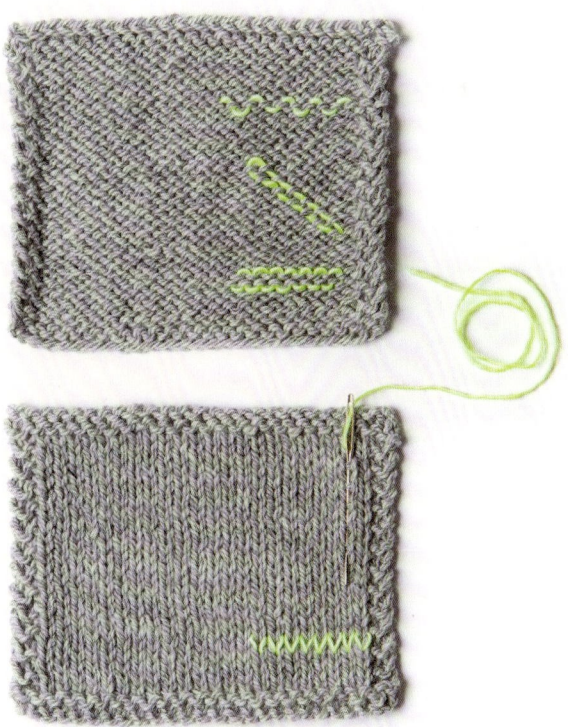

A contrasting colour yarn highlights the techniques used to secure yarn ends off the machine.

Part 2

Materiality

Drew McKevitt's mixed technique
textile balances positive and negative
space beautifully.

Chapter 4

Colour and Pattern

Working with colour opens up a plethora of possibilities in knitting. Yarns can be knitted one at a time, as for stripes, or combined with additional ends for blends or mélanges. The fibre, structure and tone of several yarns can be mixed as barely there, subtle harmonies or bold, eye-catching contrasts. They can form small, symmetrical patterns, as in Fair Isle knitting, or large pictorial representations, as in intarsia knitting. Punchcards are particularly helpful in exploring creative colour and pattern effects. For manual machines, the technique to create a particular stitch or pattern can be translated and carried out by hand.

Yarn Effects

Marling

A mottled or mélange effect is created when two or more yarns are threaded through the same tension-unit pathway and knitted together as if they were one. The yarns twist and change position as they are knitted, and as they fight for dominance, one may be more prominent on the face and the other on the reverse. If you are using yarns that are similar in weight, texture and colour, the overall effect may look well blended. However, if these elements are different, the result will be more striking, often resembling a high-contrast space-dye look.

Gradients

A gradient is a gradual fade or transition from one colour to the next, either between tones or into other hues. This can be achieved by the same process as marling – threading two or more yarns into the same feeder to knit as one.

For instance, a simple gradient can be knit using six tones of pink with one end of yarn changing for another after the desired number of courses:

Begin with: two ends of tone 1
Change to: one end of tone 1, one end of tone 2
Change to: two ends of tone 2
Change to: one end of tone 2, one end of tone 3
Change to: two ends of tone 3
Change to: one end of tone 3, one end of tone 4
Change to: two ends of tone 4
Change to: one end of tone 4, one end of tone 5
Change to: two ends of tone 5
Change to: one end of tone 5, one end of tone 6
Change to and end with: two ends of tone 6

This example involves just two ends of yarn, but a gradient could also be worked with three or more finer ends to create an even more intricately blended fade.

Marled fabrics can appear well-blended or high-contrast depending on the colour of yarn and the number of ends used.

Gradient effect created by transitioning from different tones of blue and green yarn.

Plating

In this effect, a main and a plating yarn are threaded through the yarn tension unit separately, and into individual slots in the carriage yarn feeder. The division of slots in the yarn feeder keeps the ends separate and means that the main yarn is always in front of the plating yarn as the stitches form. In the resulting fabric, the main yarn lies on the knit side, and the plating yarn on the purl side.

Apart from creating aesthetically unique textiles, plating can help to:

- **Balance form with function.** Not only are two-sided fabrics visually interesting, but also they can improve the practicality of a textile. For example, wool may provide excellent stitch definition and the desired look for the garment, but may feel scratchy when worn. Plating the wool with a skin-friendlier yarn such as cotton will provide comfort without sacrificing the garment's visual appeal.

- **Increase the versatility of fine yarns.** Since plating knits with two yarns together, different coloured fine yarns can be doubled to make a more substantial fabric. Compared to marling, the two ends will not appear as 'mixed' when they knit.

TIP: *Several of these colour and pattern techniques use more than one end of yarn in the carriage yarn feeder. Sometimes these yarns are threaded into the same main yarn feeder (as for marling or gradient effects), and other times an additional yarn is placed in a different area or slot in the yarn feeder (as for plating and Fair Isle). Whenever an additional end of yarn is used, the stitch size must be adjusted to reflect the combined thickness. Remember not to exceed the total weight the machine can knit with ease.*

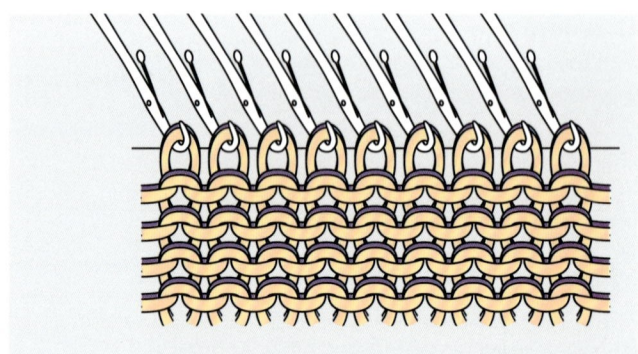

During plating, the main yarn is more visible on the knit side and the plating yarn on the purl side of the fabric.

Plating can add unexpected detail to simple fabrics.

Stripes

These horizontal bands of pattern are created by alternating yarns that differ in fibre, colour, texture or weight, or varying the stitch size or type between courses. Stripes are one of the most versatile patterns to knit, and the ease with which they can be reinterpreted is endlessly alluring to designers.

Stripes in textiles have an intriguing history. In medieval Europe, bold, broad contrasting stripes were associated with deviance and were assigned to servants, jesters and criminals as a form of visible humiliation – a tradition that continued for centuries. In the nineteenth century striped clothing was worn by French sailors and fishermen, allegedly to help them stand out in rough waters if they met with danger. Stripes later adorned the undergarments of the lower ranks of the French Navy, and were subsequently introduced to the uniforms of other nationalities. This nautical pattern, also known as the Breton or marinière stripe, was famously reinterpreted in a fashion context by Coco Chanel, helping it to spread far and wide.

When knitting stripes through yarn changes, patterns composed of an even number of courses can be simpler to knit than those formed from an odd number of rows. With the former, yarn changes occur at the same side of the fabric throughout the knitting, whereas the latter calls for them to be made on both sides of the work. Odd numbered row patterns can also require the carriage to be repositioned to the other side of the needlebed (without knitting) depending on if the yarn change is to occur on the left or right side of the fabric.

TIP: *With striped compositions, the number of yarn ends to finish can be very high. To save a lot of unwanted finishing time, and if you have chosen to use the knit side of the fabric as the face, it is a good idea to weave the yarn ends in as you knit.*

Designing stripes

Inspiration for stripes is abundant in both the natural and human-made worlds. Parallel lines can be found on everything from fingerprints to football shirts, badgers to barcodes and mushroom gills to machine wires. Sometimes the impact is bold and optical, playing tricks on your eyes if clever use of colour and scale is integrated; the stripes used in Op art designs can appear to move or pulsate before your eyes. On the other hand, the pure simplicity of horizontal lines can also be celebrated.

A collection of striped fabrics (from left to right): knit side pattern with bands of brushed mohair, colour changes and pintucks within an openwork structure, purl side pattern, contrasting weight yarns with Fair Isle, and horizontal and vertical lines.

Textured stitches add interest and depth to 1X1 Studio's striped knitwear compositions.

Numerous explorations can give way to striped outcomes:

- Colour effects can be explored by adjusting the number of courses knitted in one hue before moving on to the next.
- Stripes can be formed from tactile, openwork or patterned stitches to create fresh interpretations and intricate surface effects.
- Vertical and diagonal stripes can be established using automated knit patterns as well as by knitting a garment sideways or through creative seaming.
- Contrasting or opposing yarn weights can be mixed. Yarns of similar weight tend to produce flatter, more graphic stripes, whereas varying thicknesses can create dimensional stripes.
- Striping with a transparent or fine, pale yarn can lead to the appearance of floating lines.
- The stitch size can be adjusted for a number of courses. A larger stitch size than recommended for the yarn, striped with areas that are knitted more tightly, creates bands of lace-like openwork.

Machine Patterning

All types of knitting machines are capable of creating an inspiring and diverse range of stitches, but the manner in which patterns are created varies according to the category of machine. Patterning for manual machines must be completed entirely by hand through the use of tools or selecting needles and configuring the carriage settings. Easy-to-remember patterns can be carried out fairly quickly, but detailed or very complex compositions can take much longer.

Punchcard machines can select needles automatically instead of by hand, and thus knit patterns much faster than manual models. The punched and un-punched spaces in the punchcard communicate to the machine the role of the needles in the pattern. Punchcards are a specific size, and so certain design requirements must be followed.

For electronic machines, designs are built into the computer memory, meaning they can be selected and changed quickly and easily. New designs can also be stored in the memory, allowing the knitter to build up a large library of stitch options. The greatest potential for pattern-design is available with these machines, and their requirements are more flexible than those of punchcard models.

Because of their popularity and ease of use, we will focus on punchcard machines here. Being simpler than their electronic counterparts, they are often the first port of call for students and novice designers. However, each technique is also explained and detailed so that it can be carried out using hand-tooled methods on a manual machine.

Punchcard patterns

Punchcards are sturdy but pliable plastic cards with a series of punched holes in a pre-designed pattern. When the card is inserted into the machine, the machine reads it and selects needles according to the punched and un-punched areas.

The punched and un-punched areas may dictate a different kind of stitch – for example knit and tuck – or a different yarn – for example a main and a contrasting yarn – in the same course of knitting. This is determined by a carriage cam setting, which can be set to Fair Isle, miss or tuck. Another category of stitch pattern, known as knit-weave, is also achievable through punchcard patterns. For this, the weaving levers on the carriage sinker plate are used.

Because the machine forms patterns in different ways, punchcards must usually be designed according to the individual requirements of a particular stitch. For example, designing a Fair Isle punchcard would require a different approach from a tuck punchcard. On some occasions, however, the same punchcard design is interchangeable among two or more pattern structures. In that case, it is possible to knit two very distinct fabrics with one punchcard design – one textile in a tuck stitch and the other in a Fair Isle stitch. The reason the two fabrics look different is because of the carriage setting, which communicates the desired stitch structure to the machine.

A small scale punchcard pattern is used to knit distinct fabrics within the four stitch types. Clockwise from top left: Fair Isle, tuck, knit-weave, and miss.

Punchcard knitting directions

A pre-punched set of cards, which can be used to practise and explore stitch types, is included with most punchcard machines. Although the punchcard is produced to a certain dimension, it can be used to knit a fabric of any size. This is because the punchcard will automatically repeat the pattern when it knits, adjusting to as few or as many stitches and courses as are required.

A punchcard can knit a design in four orientations, depending on how it is inserted into the machine, labelled on the card as A, B, C and D:

- Direction A is the standard pattern orientation.
- Direction B flips the pattern horizontally.
- Direction C flips the pattern horizontally and vertically.
- Direction D flips the pattern vertically.

It is recommended to have 2.5–5cm (1–2in) of knitting on the machine after casting on before proceeding into a punchcard pattern. If you want to knit the pattern directly after the cast-on, you should begin with waste yarn and ravel cord to ensure that you have enough fabric to hang weights from.

Inserting the punchcard into the machine

The punchcard lever, next to the slot into which the card is inserted, can be set to lock the punchcard stationary (so that it does not knit), or set to allow it to feed through the machine every time the carriage passes it (so that it does knit). To insert the card:

1. Ensure the lever is in the feeding position and hold the card straight, with the chosen orientation letter displaying on the bottom right edge.
2. To help the card feed, there is a knob or wheel (depending on the machine model) that can be turned. The card must be completely straight and parallel to the slot as it enters the machine. If it becomes misaligned, take it out of the slot and start again.
3. Feed the card until the other half is visible, then use the designated plastic clips to secure the ends together, overlapping the front end onto the back so that it can rotate continuously in a loop.
4. Set the card at the course number from which you want to start the pattern.
5. Set the lever to lock until you are ready to start knitting the pattern.

Punchcards can be used to knit a fabric of any size, as the pattern automatically repeats within any number of stitches and rows.

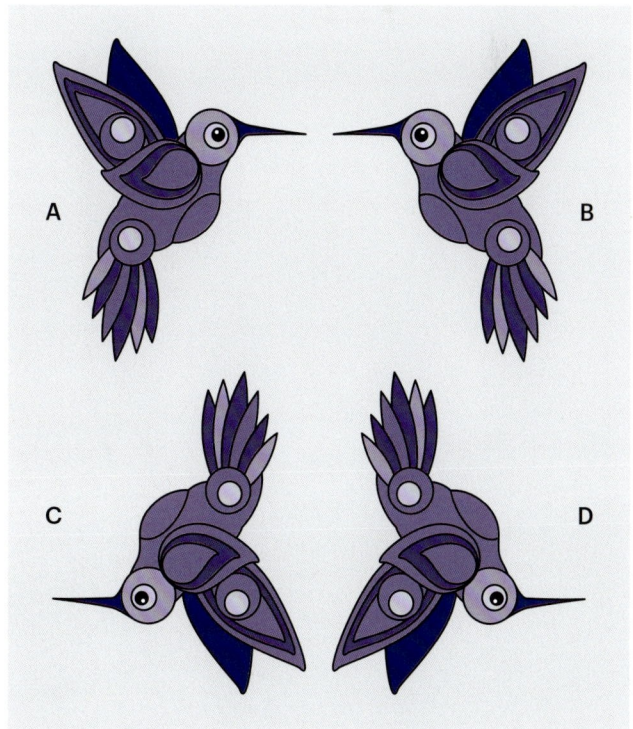

Depending on how the card is inserted in the machine, it can knit the pattern in four different orientations.

Inserting the punchcard into the machine. *Step 2: Hold the card straight as you feed it into the machine.*

Step 3: To prevent the edge getting chewed up, clip the card together with the front end overlapping the back end.

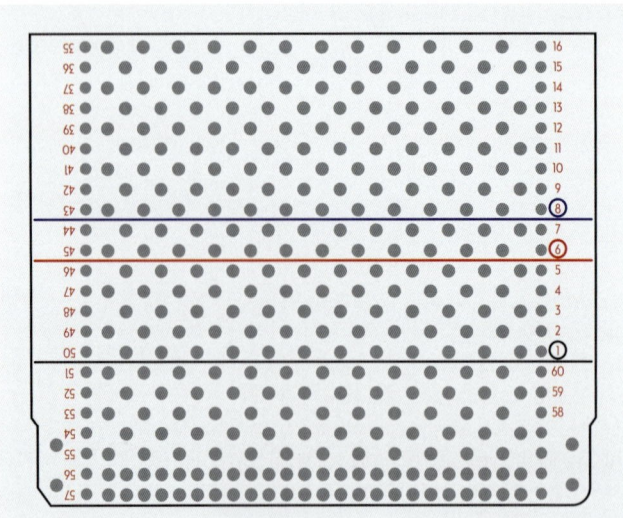

To start knitting from row 1 of this pattern, the punchcard is set to the red line (Row 6) for Silver Reed machines, and the blue line (Row 8) for Brother machines.

TIP: *It is important to note that the pattern course number displayed is not actually the one being knitted, because the card is inserted into the machine deeper than what is shown. This varies between machine brands: Brother machines read the pattern seven courses below the number displayed, and Silver Reed machines read the pattern five courses below. Therefore, to start knitting the pattern from course number 1 on the punchcard, the number displayed would be 8 for Brother machines and 6 for Silver Reed machines.*

Knitting a preparation course

A preparation course is knitted immediately before you knit the first course of the punchcard pattern.

1. If it isn't already, set the punchcard to the lock position.
2. Set the carriage to read the pattern by positioning the side levers (on Silver Reed machines) or change knob (on Brother machines) for punchcard knitting.
3. Knit one course.

After this course, some machines will position the needles in a mix of upper working and working position, and other machines will keep the needles in working position throughout the pattern knitting.

Knitting the punchcard pattern

After the preparation course, the punchcard pattern is ready to knit. The card can now be set to the feeding position.

Selecting the stitch type

The carriage is then set according to the stitch type: Fair Isle, tuck, miss or knit-weave.

Adding a second yarn

Fair Isle and knit-weave patterns require a second yarn to be introduced while the main yarn remains in the carriage's main yarn feeder slot. This additional yarn should be threaded through its own pathway in the yarn tension unit and held on the yarn clip until needed. For Fair Isle patterns, the second yarn is inserted into the carriage yarn feeder without opening the guide pin, but instead to the left of it, into an additional slot. The second yarn used for knit-weave patterns is placed in the weaving yarn holder on the left or right side of the carriage (depending on which direction the carriage is about to knit).

Knitting

After the set-up is completed, the punchcard pattern will begin knitting with the next pass of the carriage, automatically repeating the pattern sequence for the designated number of courses.

Ending the pattern

To stop knitting the pattern, the card should be set to the lock position and the carriage returned to the settings for single jersey.

Selecting the stitch type

Stitch pattern	Silver Reed machine	Brother machine
Fair Isle	Cam setting 'F'	Cam setting 'MC'
Tuck	Cam setting 'T'	Both 'Tuck' buttons
Miss	Cam setting 'S'	Both 'Part' buttons
Knit-weave	Drop weaving knobs/levers	Drop weaving knobs/levers

Quick reference directions

1. Cast on the required number of stitches with the main yarn or with waste yarn and ravel cord before commencing into the main yarn. Once enough courses have been knitted, hang your weights.
2. Select the punchcard to be used.
3. Decide on the pattern orientation (A, B, C or D).
4. Set the punchcard lever to the feed position.
5. Hold the card straight, with the appropriate orientation mark (A, B, C or D) at the bottom right. Insert the card into the slot and use the knob or wheel to feed it into the machine. Continue until the other half of the card is visible.
6. Clip the card ends together, with the front edge overlapping the back edge.
7. Set the card to the designated beginning pattern row, then lock it in the stop position.
8. Set the carriage to read the punchcard, then knit the pattern preparation row.
9. Engage the punchcard to the knitting setting.
10. Select the pattern stitch type on the carriage.
11. Insert an additional yarn into the carriage if required (for Fair Isle or knit-weave).
12. Adjust the stitch size if necessary.
13. Knit the pattern for the desired number of courses, changing yarn (if required) as dictated by your design.
14. To return to single jersey, stop the punchcard and return the carriage settings to those for plain knitting. If necessary, remove the second yarn and readjust the stitch size.

Designing punchcard patterns

Once you are familiar with the basic method of knitting with punchcards, you can use blank cards and a punch tool to create your own designs. Depending on the stitch type, the areas you punch on the card and the areas you leave blank will be read by the machine differently. It is important to understand how the machine will read the punched areas versus the unpunched areas when you are designing with a particular stitch.

For example, when designing a tuck-stitch pattern, the unpunched holes will correlate to the stitches that tuck (pattern stitches) and the punched holes to the stitches that knit (plain stitches). On the other hand, Fair Isle cards display the unpunched holes in the main colour (plain stitches), and the punched holes in the contrast colour (pattern stitches).

Designing within the repeat

Blank cards are produced in standard sizes according to the machine gauge. Standard-gauge punchcards, for example, are 24 stitches wide and 60 rows tall. (Fine-gauge machines are 30 stitches wide, and bulky machines are 12 stitches wide, while both are also 60 rows tall.) These numbers set the boundary within

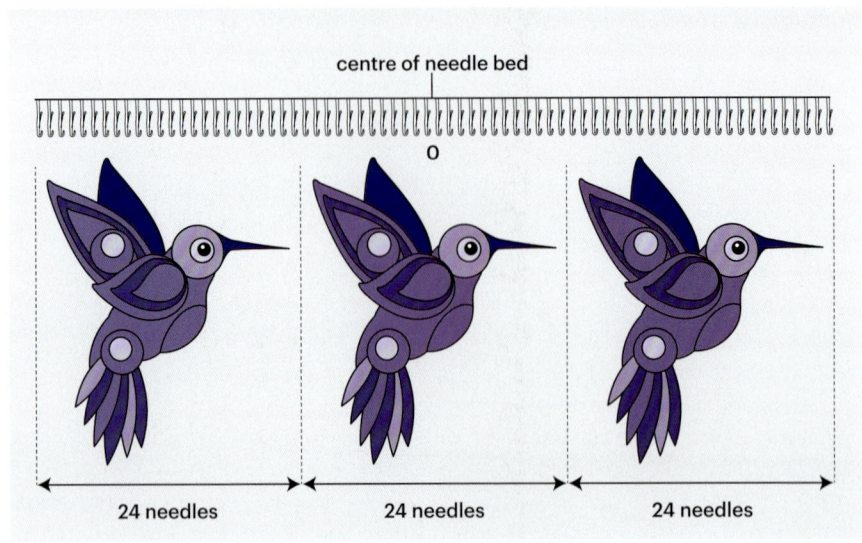

centre of needle bed

0

24 needles   24 needles   24 needles

The punchcard pattern is centred on the middle of the machine bed, with further repeats forming either side. This example illustrates a pattern repeating on a standard-gauge machine.

which you must design to create a pattern that can repeat seamlessly across any number of stitches and courses.

When the punchcard knits, the pattern is automatically centred on the bed, with the first repeat knitting on 12 (or 15, or 6) needles either side of the centre mark '0'. Further repeats are then made on consecutive groups of 24 (or 30 or 12) needles to each end of the bed. Regardless of the number of needles selected, the pattern will

automatically repeat to fill them. If you do not want the pattern to repeat, it can be knitted as a 'single motif', which creates an isolated pattern.

Stitch repeat

It is important to note the following:

- One full pattern repeat cannot exceed the width of the punchcard – that is, 24 (or 30 or 12) stitches.
- Smaller pattern repeats must be formed of stitch combinations that are divisible by the total width of the card. For example, for a standard-gauge stitch repeat of 24, a design can be made up of motifs measuring 2, 3, 4, 6, 8 or 12 stitches.
- Single-motif designs can be as wide as the punchcard or made up of any smaller number of stitches.

Row repeat

There is more flexibility when designing the vertical repeat:

Designing punchcards for each stitch type

Stitch pattern	Punched holes in punchcard	Unpunched holes in punchcard
Tuck	Knit	Tuck
Miss	Knit	Miss
Fair Isle	Pattern colour/contrast colour	Background colour/main colour
Knit-weave	Yarn weaves over	Yarn weaves under

- Patterns that exceed 60 rows can be created by joining two punchcards with plastic clips, or using blank cards that are bought on a continuous roll.
- Patterns that are less than 60 rows can be created, so long as the punchcard can easily have its two ends clipped together (and rotate in a loop). For these designs, you must punch two full lines on the card above your final pattern row. The card can then be cut directly above these two lines to discard the unpunched area.

Extending the pattern

It is possible to lengthen the pattern vertically, by setting the punchcard to move only every other row, thus knitting each course twice. Knit the first pattern row (after the preparation row) with the punchcard still in the lock position, but with the stitch type selected on the carriage and a second yarn added, if applicable. For all following rows, engage the punchcard and set the machine to stretch the pattern.

Most patterns can be extended in this way, but be mindful of tuck stitches, which can build up too many floats to knit back in.

Planning your design

It is always best to draw your design on graph paper before transferring it to the punchcard. This allows you to edit and rework the design, particularly if adjustments have to be made to the scale and repeat of the pattern.

TIP: *Use proportional graph paper, also known as knitter's graph paper, to avoid distortion in your knitted design. Distortion occurs because a knitted stitch is wider than it is tall, and knitter's graph paper reflects this scale, whereas regular graph paper does not.*

Some designs, such as multicoloured Fair Isle patterns, require the yarn to be changed frequently. Having this mapped out on a piece of paper is useful as you knit so that you do not lose track of what yarn or colour goes where.

When integrating a tuck or miss-stitch punchcard pattern into a knitted fabric, it is always useful to plan for at least one plain knitting stitch at each edge. This helps to keep the sides of the fabric even as they knit, and makes finishing processes such as seaming easier. To do this, place the edge stitches in holding position before you knit each course.

TIP: *If you notice you have punched a hole in error, stick a small piece of Scotch tape over the hole on one side, then place the loose punch circle back in place and tape over the other side too. Carefully remove any excess tape.*

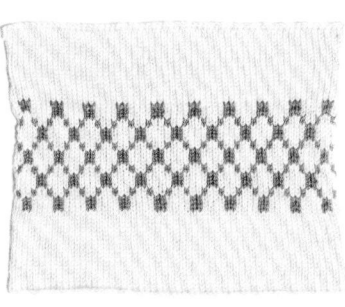

The same Fair Isle punchcard pattern knit in the standard setting (top) and the extended length setting (bottom).

Fair Isle

Also known as 'stranded knitting', this multicoloured pattern technique is named after the small island in the Shetlands (north of the Scottish mainland) where it originated. There, easy access to high-quality wool from the native breed of sheep, as well as the fibres' inherent ability to resist the damp climate, no doubt contributed to its popularity.

In the twentieth century Fair Isle-patterned sweaters became fashionable more widely after the style was worn by Charles, Prince of Wales. As with many heritage knitting techniques, the versatility and creative potential of Fair Isle make it an exciting prospect for designers, who can reinvent and innovate in their own way.

This method of creating multicoloured patterns employs two yarns in one course of knitting. During that course, the yarn that is not in use is stranded along the reverse (purl side) of the fabric, resulting in short floats. The added thickness of the floats makes it effectively a double-weight fabric.

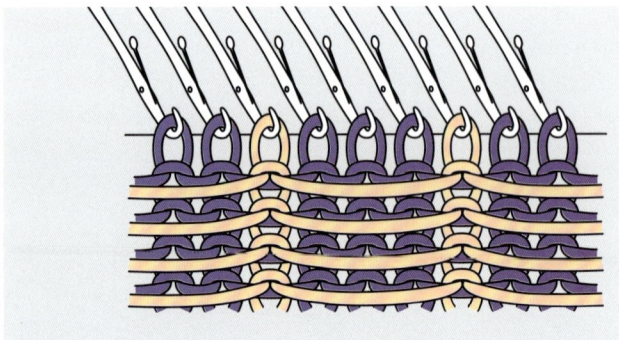

A Fair Isle knitted structure, with two different yarns forming stitches in the same course.

Fabrics are recognizable for their multicoloured patterns on the face, and floats of yarn on the reverse.

Fair Isle for punchcard machines

The holes punched in the card knit the pattern or contrasting colour stitches, and the unpunched holes knit the background or main colour stitches.

The two yarns are inserted into the carriage yarn feeder in separate slots, and they knit the pattern stitches and the background stitches simultaneously. The background yarn is placed in the main slot in the feeder, and the pattern yarn in the second slot.

Fair Isle for manual machines

Manual machines are capable of creating Fair Isle fabrics by hand using the miss-stitch function. Instead of the two yarns knitting the same pattern course simultaneously, each one knits the pattern course separately. This means that each row of the Fair Isle pattern requires two passes of the carriage – one with the background yarn and one with the pattern yarn.

1. Draw out your pattern repeat on knitter's graph paper and set it clearly in view while you sit at the machine.
2. Knit to the course where you want the pattern to begin, ending with the carriage on the right.
3. Thread the background colour yarn into the right side of the tension unit, and the pattern yarn into the left side.
4. Set the carriage to the slip function.
5. Following the first row of the chart, place the background colour stitches in holding position and knit across with the background colour yarn (carriage is on the left side). Since the carriage is set to slip, only the needles in holding position will knit. Remove the yarn from the carriage and secure it at the left side of the machine (at the rear or in the clip at the edge of the machine).
6. Thread the pattern yarn into the carriage, bring the pattern colour stitches to holding position and knit across (carriage is on the right side). This completes the first pattern course of the Fair Isle graph.
7. Following the second row of the chart, place the pattern colour stitches to holding position and knit across (carriage is on the left side). Remove the yarn from the carriage and secure it at the left side of the machine.
8. Thread the background yarn into the carriage, bring the background colour stitches to holding position and knit across (carriage is on the right side). This completes the second pattern course of the Fair Isle graph.
9. Continue knitting in this way, remembering that

whichever colour was used to end the pattern course will also be used to begin the next course.

Designing Fair Isle patterns

Before embarking on your own stranded pattern, it is worth looking at traditional Shetland motifs to gain an understanding of their visual and practical approaches to design. You can study original Fair Isle sweaters, as well as hand-knitting books that contain examples of popular styles and arrangements. These patterns tend to follow guidelines:

- Most designs are simple in shape, and symmetrical and geometric patterns are more prevalent than representational motifs. This regularity traditionally stems from the needs of hand-knitters, as it made the pattern easy to remember and follow once the first sequence had been established.
- Small pattern repeats are favoured because they result in short floats (classified as five stitches or fewer) when one yarn changes to another. Patterns resulting in long floats are usually avoided, as they can snag and catch easily.
- Diagonal lines, which give the textile elasticity, are preferred to strong vertical lines, which can pull the fabric and cause it to tighten.
- Patterns often have an odd number of courses, allowing the centre course to be emphasized in a contrasting or bright colour.

While keeping your own design concept in mind, other textile techniques – including weaving and tapestry samples, simple embroidery and lacework – can also provide a starting point for shapes and compositions.

Pattern placement, colour use and yarn choice

Consider the arrangement of your pattern on the fabric, the colours you wish to inject and the yarn type you will use. An all-over repeat pattern could feature a small motif dotted throughout, or a more complex, larger motif which creates a busier-looking outcome.

Stacked Fair Isle arrangements featuring bands or borders of pattern are perfect for creating designs with numerous colour changes. The bands need not be uniform; wide repeats spread over numerous courses can be juxtaposed with narrow, smaller ones, and patterns could blend and synchronize with one another or appear contrasting.

For a subtler look, the detail can be inserted into just a section of the fabric, such as along the hem of a simple plain knit garment. Single-motif designs can also be used when you want a focussed area of stranded pattern.

The interplay of colour in Fair Isle patterns is fascinating and can give a vast range of possibilities to a single pattern. A design knitted in two or three colours will feel entirely

Shetlander wearing a Fair Isle pullover that displays traditional stranded knitting patterns and motifs.

Fair Isle pattern placement (clockwise from top left): larger scale all-over design, single motif, smaller scale all-over design, border detail, and stacked bands of pattern.

The same Fair Isle pattern knitted with (from left to right): three colours, two colours, regular and stretch yarn, purl-side floats as the face, and textured yarns.

different from one knitted in several colours. Similarly, a monochrome design will look unique from the same design knitted in two shades of green.

The texture and type of yarn will also contribute greatly to the textile. Two plain, smooth yarns will yield a very distinct fabric compared to two textured fancy yarns. Stretch yarns, or those that can be altered during the finishing processes, can also produce unexpected results.

The combinations and iterations are endless, and by exploring them through knitted samples you can produce a vast array of fabric types from just one pattern design. The weight, sharpness of pattern and hand feel created by various yarn permutations can inform your ideas for garments or other products.

Floats

Larger scale patterns present longer floats (spanning five stitches or more) that can pull and catch, making a garment more difficult to wear and care for. There are, however, several ways to manage them:

1. If your pattern has large areas of knitting in a single colour, you can break them up by adding one or more additional 'filler' stitches in the other colour. For example, if 11 stitches are to be knitted with Colour 1, you could adjust the pattern so that the sixth stitch knits with Colour 2. This would result in five stitches knitted in Colour 1, one stitch knitted in Colour 2 and five stitches knitted in Colour 1. The filler stitch is unlikely to detract much from the pattern, and contributes to a fabric with shorter floats.

2. If you do not want to alter the design, you can use a latch tool to latch floats up in stages as the fabric is knitting, or once the fabric is off the machine. The last float can be secured on a central needle if on the machine, or sewn in place with thread if off the machine. Latching works best with patterns that create floats that are stacked on top of one another.

3. An isolated long float can be lifted onto a central needle on the course immediately after it is knitted.

4. Groups of floats that vary in length and position can be managed by using a small piece of yarn to tie them together once the fabric is off the machine.

Adding additional colours

Additional colours can be introduced into the same pattern course as a highlight or accent.

On the machine

For manual knitting:

Highlight the extra colours on the graph paper chart and keep in mind that every extra colour added per pattern repeat row will require an additional pass of the carriage.

For punchcard knitting:

It is possible to add extra colours through manual manipulation. This example adds a third colour to the pattern course:

1. Draw your design out on knitter's graph paper, with the three colours clearly highlighted.
2. Keep the third colour on the floor in front of the machine. Knit to the pattern course where the third colour is to be introduced, and set the carriage to the hold function.
3. Bring the needles corresponding to the third colour into holding position.
4. Pass the carriage across to knit the pattern course with the two yarns in the carriage feeder, then hand-knit the needles in holding position using the third colour (see page 67). Use one continuous strand of yarn to do so, and match the tension of the stitches and floats formed by the yarns in the carriage. These needles will now be back in working position.
5. Repeat Steps 3–4 for each row that features a third colour.

Off the machine

A simple embroidery stitch known as Swiss darning or duplicate stitch can work very well to add additional colours to the design. It mimics the appearance of a knitted stitch, and can even be a useful way of correcting colour mistakes in a Fair Isle pattern. Since the aim of the embroidery stitch is to cover the knitted stitch in the fabric, the yarn you use should be of equal weight.

Thread the embroidery yarn onto a tapestry needle and, coming from the back (purl side) of the fabric, bring the needle to the front, pulling it through so that it is in the space below the stitch to be worked. Insert the needle under both sides of the stitch that is one course above the stitch to be worked, and pull through. Bring the needle back down into the space below the selected stitch (where you started).

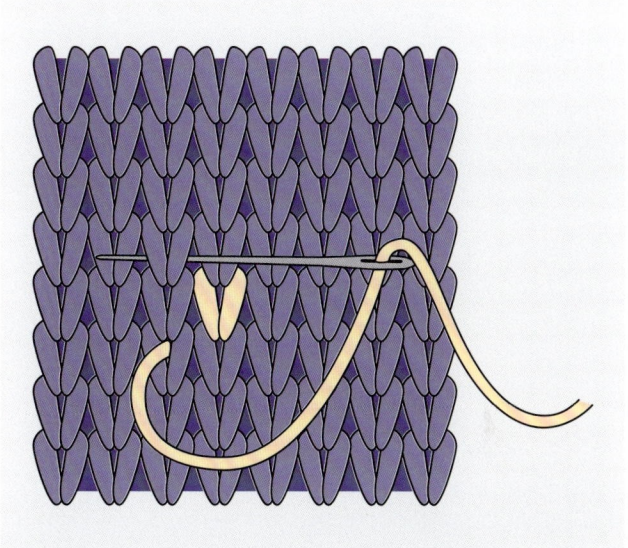

The Swiss darning embroidery stitch appears as a knitted 'V'.

A simple Fair Isle pattern adorned with numerous pops of colour incorporated through duplicate stitch embroidery.

Tuck- and Miss-stitch Colour Patterns

Mosaic Patterns

This category of patterns is essentially formed by combining yarn changes with tuck or miss stitches. Separately, plain stitch yarn changes appear as stripes, and single-colour tuck or miss-stitch fabrics are textured and dimensional. When united, however, the tuck or miss stitches 'distort' the stripes so that two colours appear to be knitting on the same row. The resulting fabric can be likened to a lighter-weight Fair Isle and while simple to knit, can look very complex.

A single tuck- or miss-stitch arrangement can yield distinct iterations depending on the number and frequency of yarn changes and if they follow, or do not follow, the stitch pattern. When the stitch structure is not used to guide the use of yarn, the results tend to be more unpredictable. Try exploring this concept by knitting small swatches in the same tuck- or miss-stitch pattern using different colour layouts. You could start by using just two colours and then increase to a three- and then four-colour palette. Vary the order in which you place the colours and the number of rows each one knits to add to the complexity.

Both manual and automatic patterning machines can be used to knit these patterns. See pages 93–96 for instructions and guidelines on knitting and designing tuck- and miss-stitch fabrics.

Identifiable by interconnecting lines that form maze-like arrangements, this knitting technique is a special type of tuck/miss-stitch colour pattern. Mosaic fabrics are created when these stitch patterns are knitted using dark and light (or other contrasting) yarns, alternated every two courses throughout the fabric. They are constructed so that the pattern changes (i.e. different needles are selected to tuck/miss and to knit plain) every two rows, meaning that Rows 1 and 2 knit the same pattern, as do Rows 3 and 4, Rows 5 and 6, and so on. This sequence is mirrored by the yarn change: knit Colour 1 for Rows 1 and 2, knit Colour 2 for Rows 3 and 4, knit Colour 1 for Rows 5 and 6, and so on.

It is important to practise and get into a rhythm when making the frequent colour changes that a mosaic pattern requires. Because the yarn is alternated every two courses, there is no need to cut it each time.

Mosaic knitting for punchcard machines

When using a mosaic punchcard pattern, the punched holes dictate the designated needles to knit, and the unpunched areas the needles to tuck or miss. To knit a mosaic pattern using a punchcard machine:

1. Thread the two contrasting yarns to be used for the pattern separately through the tension unit.
2. Set the machine up for pattern knitting (see page 79), with the carriage set to the tuck or miss setting.
3. Knit two courses with the first colour.
4. Knit two courses with the second colour.
5. Repeat Steps 3 and 4 for the desired number of courses.

Mosaic knitting for manual machines

For manual machines the needles are selected by hand according to a chart, which you should keep in clear view by the machine.

As with automated machines, mosaic can be knitted as tuck or miss, but on manual machines the tuck setting requires less work. Each setting requires needles to be placed in holding position according to the chart. With tuck, it is the pattern needles that are hand-selected to holding position, and with miss the background needles are pushed to holding position. Because there are typically fewer pattern stitches (that tuck or miss) in a design than background stitches (that knit), fewer needles have to be selected with the tuck setting.

Furthermore, with tuck, needles only have to be selected once every pattern change (i.e. every two rows), rather than twice every pattern change (i.e. every row) in the miss

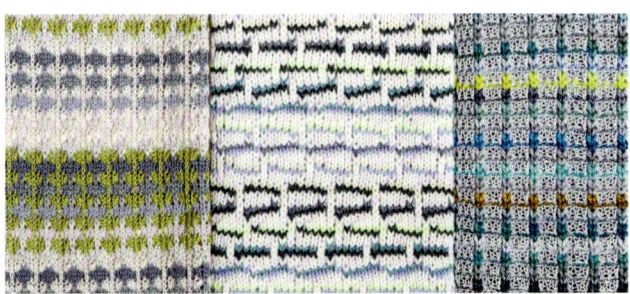

Tuck-stitch (top) and miss-stitch (above) colour patterns. While each colour is knitted separately, they appear as if they are knitted together on the same row.

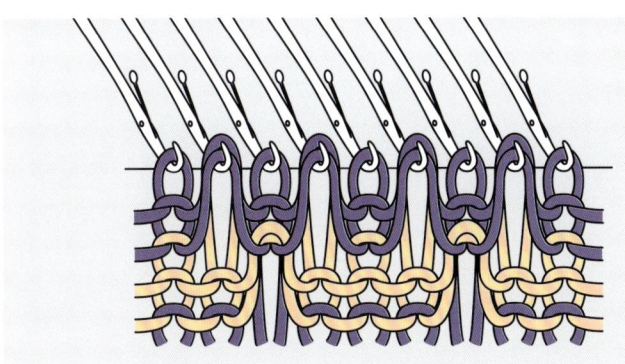

Knitting a mosaic pattern with the tuck-stitch setting.

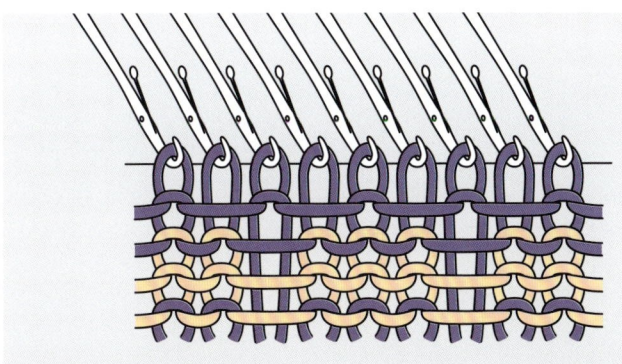

Knitting a mosaic pattern with the miss-stitch setting.

Tuck-stitch mosaic fabrics (left) possess no floats on the purl side whereas those knit with miss stitch (right) do.

setting. This is because when the carriage is set to the hold function, it won't knit needles in holding position back to working position until it is instructed to do so. On the miss setting, however, the needles move from holding position to working position with the first pass of the carriage.

The following instructions assume the mosaic pattern is to be knitted using the tuck setting.

1. Thread the two contrasting yarns separately through the tension unit.
2. Set the carriage to the hold function.
3. Following the first pattern change of your design, place the pattern (tucking) needles in holding position.
4. Knit two courses with Colour 1, then place the pattern needles in upper working position so that they are ready to knit on the following course.
5. Following the second pattern change of your design, place the pattern (tucking) needles in holding position.
6. Knit two courses with Colour 2, then place the pattern needles in upper working position.
7. Continue alternating yarns and selecting needles in this way, placing the recently tucked needles in upper working position, and the next pattern (tucking) needles in holding position.

Designing mosaic patterns

Patterns or motifs such as those founds in ancient artifacts or artworks around the world lend themselves well to the multidirectional lines that make up mosaic knitting, but you can adapt ideas from a wide range of fields. Designs in hand-knitting books can also be useful for visualizing the potential of the technique.

Whereas the charted design of a Fair Isle pattern clearly correlates with the resulting fabric, this is not the case for mosaics, which can look very different before and after knitting. In order for the knitted outcome to reflect the intended design, it must be charted in a specific way as follows:

1. Use knitter's graph paper to chart out the mosaic design (Chart 1, overleaf). A repeat pattern must be made up of an even number of pattern changes so that it can knit seamlessly using two colours. If the design is not symmetrical, use a photocopier or computer to flip the orientation before moving to the next step.
2. Mark Colour 1 next to the first pattern change row. Then, mark Colour 1 next to every other pattern change row.

3. Mark Colour 2 next to the second pattern change row and every other pattern change row.
4. Create a new chart (Chart 2, right) with the same amount of squares as the first one. Chart 2 is used to communicate the knitting instructions, so that once followed, the knitted pattern will appear as designed in Chart 1.
5. Starting at the first pattern change row on the first chart, identify the squares made up from Colour 1 and mark these on the second chart. Repeat this for every Colour 1 pattern change row.
6. Starting at the second pattern change row on the first chart, identify the squares made up from Colour 2 and mark these on the second chart. Repeat this for every Colour 2 pattern change row.

After completing Step 6, evaluate if Chart 2 can be successfully knit according to the tuck- or miss-stitch design guidelines (see pages 94 and 96). If it is not within the guidelines – too many courses assigned to tuck, for example – modifications may need to be made to the original design and second chart.

When transferring Chart 2 to a punchcard, you can punch two identical courses to display every pattern change or punch one course and set the machine to the elongation feature, which knits each course twice. The latter option allows more space in the punchcard for larger designs. For manual machines, it is probably easier and more intuitive to adapt Chart 2, illustrating each pattern change twice, to reflect the actual knitting procedure.

Chart 1

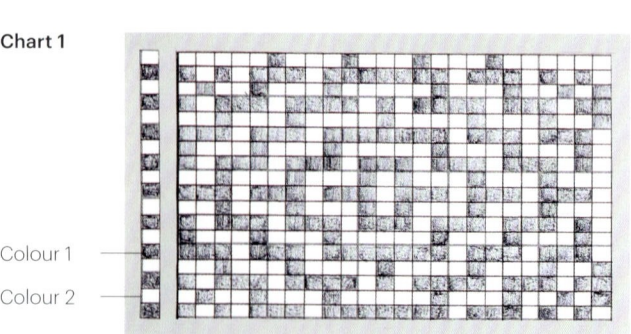

Colour 1
Colour 2

Chart 2

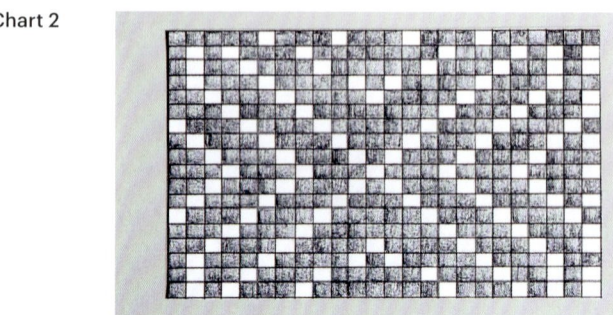

Chart 1 displays the mosaic design, formed from an even number of pattern changes. To the left, each pattern change row is alternately marked as Colour 1 and Colour 2. The design is then translated into knitting instructions in Chart 2 by marking the squares according to if they are within a Colour 1 or Colour 2 pattern row. To knit the pattern, using Chart 2, the white squares tuck/miss and the dark squares knit. Each charted pattern row represents two courses of knitting. The fabric on the right was knitted using the miss stitch function.

Intarsia

Intarsia is a very creative technique in which patterns can be built in an unlimited number of colours, much as an artist paints a picture. The resulting fabrications can exhibit outcomes that range from minimalist geometric compositions to pictorial and even figurative works.

The different yarns that make up the design knit in separate blocks of pattern that can be as small as one stitch wide. No yarn has to travel to any other blocks of pattern within the design, even if they are knitted in the same one. As a result, intarsia fabrics do not have floats on the reverse side. This lack of floats, the ability to knit several colours in the same course and the potential to produce large-scale patterns are the main ways that intarsia differs from Fair Isle.

A knitting machine may have a built-in intarsia setting on the main carriage, or it may require a separate carriage specific to this technique. Regardless of this, the method for creating these fabrics remains the same:

- Needles remain in upper working position throughout, so that the yarns can easily be laid onto them.
- Instead of threading yarn through the carriage, it is laid by hand across the open hooks of the needles, according to the design.

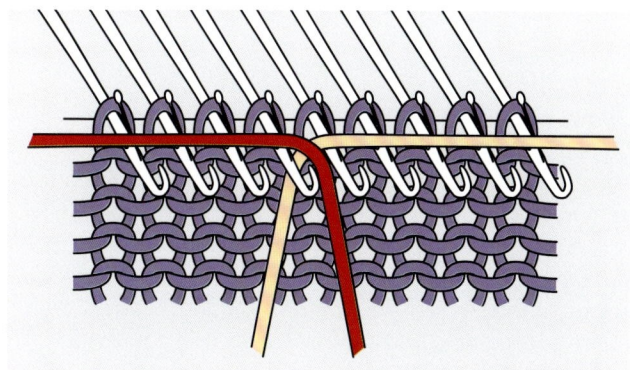

Needles are positioned in upper working position throughout intarsia knitting, with the old course of stitches behind the latches, and the yarn for the current course laid across the open hooks.

- When the carriage passes the needles with the yarn laid across the open hooks, it knits this course and returns the needles to upper working position, with their latches open ready to receive the next course of yarn.
- The stitches from the previously knitted course should always be behind the open needle latches, and the hand-laid yarn should always be in front of the open latches.

Preparing yarn

Before starting to knit, calculate the yarn you will need for the design. Each pattern block within a course requires its own source of yarn, even if the same one is repeated. For example, if the first pattern course is made up of one block of yellow, one block of red, one block of yellow, one block of blue and one block of yellow, you must prepare three separate quantities of yellow yarn, one quantity of red and one of blue.

Yarn is always set up in front of the machine so that it can be fed from the floor, and it can be prepared in a few different ways, depending on how much is needed for each block:

- If there are only a few pattern blocks across the whole course, you may be able to work from the cone or smaller balls.
- If there are several pattern blocks across the whole course, it is best to wind yarn onto bobbins. Bobbins keep the many yarn ends more manageable and add weight to the strand, keeping it in place as it is laid on the needles.
- For very small areas of colour, you can simply wind yarn around your finger to make a 'butterfly'. These small

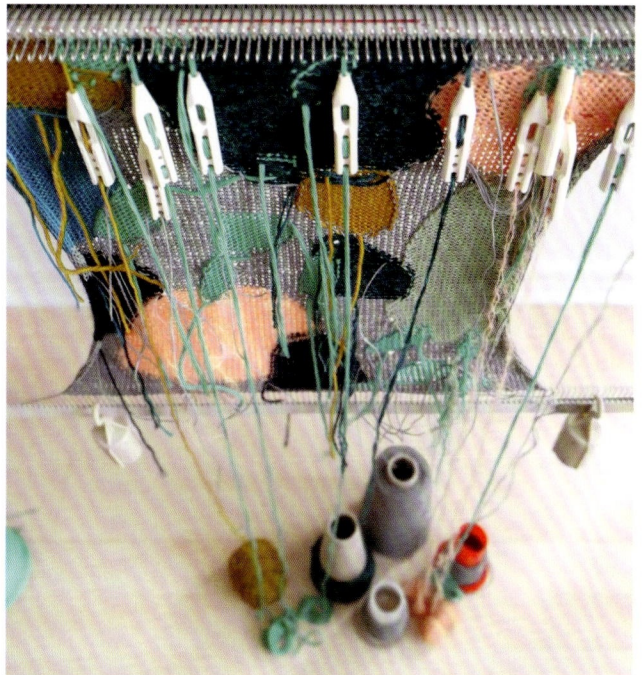

Abstract patterned intarsia knitting in progress by Anna Husemann.

pieces of yarn must be tensioned with a clothes peg or bulldog clip.

TIP: *To make a yarn butterfly, lay the tail end of yarn coming from the cone or ball across the palm of your hand. Holding the tail in place with your thumb, wrap the yarn in a figure of eight, alternating between your thumb and one of your fingers. Once you have wrapped enough, cut the end of yarn coming from the cone/ball and wrap it around the back of the strands collected on your hand, making sure to include the first tail end. Bring this cut end around the strands a few times (not too tightly) and secure it by pulling it through one of the wraps you just made. Trim the cut end. When using the butterfly, pull from the first tail end.*

Knitting instructions

1. Knit to the course where you want the intarsia to begin.
2. Remove the yarn from the carriage. If it is being used in the pattern, cut it, remove it from the tension unit and place it on the floor in front of the machine.
3. Place all other yarns needed on the floor in front of the machine.
4. If using a separate intarsia carriage, remove the main carriage from the machine bed and replace it with the intarsia one (setting the stitch dial to suit the yarns). If the main carriage is able to knit intarsia, configure it to this setting.
5. Pass the carriage across the needles. They are now all in upper working position with their latches open. If any latches have closed, manually flick them open to avoid the risk of dropped stitches. The latches must remain open throughout.
6. When introducing yarns across the needles for the first pattern course, leave a 15–20cm (6–8in) tail and lay the main end of the yarn (coming from the cone, ball or bobbin) in the direction that the carriage is about to take. That is, if the carriage is on the right side, start with the closest yarn and lay it towards the left.
7. Pass the carriage across the needles slowly, making sure the loose ends are lightly tensioned to keep them from jumping up.
8. When laying yarns for the next pattern course, twist them together to prevent holes or slits occurring between pattern blocks. Starting at the carriage side, lay the first yarn across the needles, then pick the second yarn up from behind the one just laid. If it is not already behind, simply place it in the right configuration. As the

second yarn is laid across the needles, you will see it twist and secure the first one. Repeat across the course.
9. Repeat Step 8, always keeping the strands lightly tensioned.

If you are using an intarsia carriage, large areas of a single colour are much quicker to knit with the main carriage. Be aware that the tension between the two will vary, because while the yarn is threaded through the tension unit for the main carriage, it is not for the intarsia carriage. A discrepancy in tension may not be hugely important when knitting swatches in no set size, but it can be a problem when knitting garments or pieces that must adhere to specific measurements. In that case, knit two tension swatches: one using the main carriage and one using the intarsia carriage.

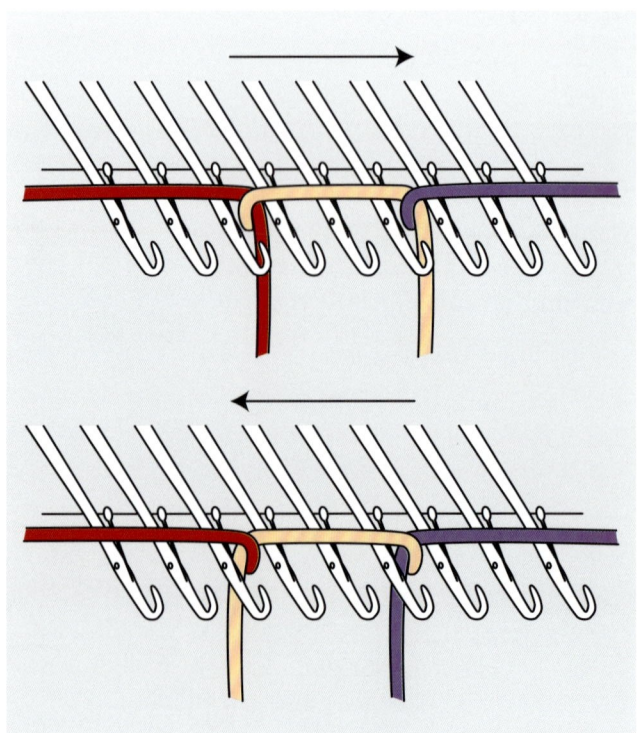

Step 8: When knitting to the right side of the bed, lay yarns from left to right. When knitting to the left side of the bed, lay yarns from right to left. Make sure yarns are twisted to prevent holes occurring.

Introducing new yarns

When introducing a new yarn in the intarsia pattern, it is useful to clip a clothes peg to the end so that it stays in place. This can be removed after a few courses, once the yarn is integrated. To secure the new yarn further on the first course:

1. Manually knit the first stitch of its pattern block and leave this needle in working position.
2. Lay the yarn over the remaining needles in that block, keeping them in upper working position throughout.
3. Repeat this for any blocks where a new yarn is being introduced.
4. When the carriage passes, it will not knit the edge needle in working position, but will instead bring it back to upper working position along with the other needles that have been knitted.

Tidying yarn ends

This technique results in numerous ends of yarn and so it is advisable to finish the ends as you go by weaving them under and over the needles.

- Make sure the end is woven behind the open latches and held against the sinker posts so that it does not interfere with the yarn that is to be laid over those same needles.
- If the needles shift out of place or the woven yarn causes the latches to close, adjust them before laying the intarsia yarn.
- Once the fabric is off the machine, trim the woven ends.

Designing intarsia patterns

The possibilities are endless when creating intarsia. Geometric patterns are often an approachable category to explore first, since the most common shapes tend to flow more intuitively. But photographs or other artworks may inspire you, and letters, numbers or symbols can also be incorporated.

To get the scale right, use knitter's graph paper to sketch and chart out your designs. Remember that each square represents one stitch, and every time a new section of pattern is introduced in the same line, a yarn will have to be added to the work. You may start with a complex design that you simplify through edits, especially if you want to keep to a certain number of yarns knitting at any one time. If you are using images with a certain orientation, such as letters or numbers, they must be charted in reverse before you work from them.

Scenic landscape intarsia knit by Gareth Wrighton. Simple garment shapes provide a blank canvas perfect for highlighting complex pictorial compositions.

TIP: *For very small areas of repeated pattern – such as a chequerboard that switches between black and white every two stitches across the whole course – it may become unwieldy to knit using intarsia. Making a punchcard for this pattern and knitting it with the Fair Isle technique will be much quicker, although an additional tension swatch may be required for this stranded section. Alternatively, very small areas of colour can be added once the fabric is off the machine using Swiss darning or duplicate stitch (see page 85).*

You can create intriguing surfaces using yarns that are diverse in texture and weight. Blocks of a finer yarn can be carefully incorporated to mimic burnout (devoré) or lace-like surfaces. Openwork structures can be formed by foregoing the process of twisting yarns together from each progressing pattern block, and instead using the holes and slices as a design detail.

Additional surface interest, such as cables or lace stitches, may be incorporated into the design through manual manipulation. When combining methods in this way, always make sure you return the needles to upper working position, with the stitches behind the open latches.

Chapter 5

Texture and Structure

Knitted fabric is inherently tactile; it welcomes our touch. Fabrics built with extra dimension and structural foundations are particularly good at making you want to handle the stitches and layers. Those in this category best exemplify the advantages of knitted structures: their infinite versatility and ability to transform through subtle changes.

This chapter examines how stitch arrangements, machine settings and hand-manipulation can yield fabrics that celebrate the temptation to touch. The stitches included here are chameleon-like, producing fabrics that are subtle and nuanced or wonderfully sculptural. The full final effect can be unpredictable – to the delight of the designer.

TIP: *Persevere with a method or stitch arrangement even if the results are far from perfect at first. As with many things that are worth pursuing, sculptural knits sometimes demand extra attention and concentration. Be sensitive to the yarn type and stitch size, and keep the fabric adequately weighted. Your yarn choice will have a huge impact on the amount of structure that can be achieved, and you should explore this if you wish to create architectural attributes.*

Tuck Stitch

These fabrics are made by mixing two types of stitch in one knitted structure; some that tuck and others that knit plain. The arrangement of these stitches, as well as the choice of fibre, yarn and gauge, can have a big impact on the resulting textile. Patterns will exhibit differently on each side of the fabric; typically, as softer waves, bumps and bubbles on the knit side, and raised honeycomb-like folds on the purl side.

TIP: *Keeping the fabric sufficiently weighted during knitting is of paramount importance with tuck stitches. Weights should be moved up the fabric frequently. Loosening the stitch size by at least a full number also makes knitting easier; loosen it even more for dense arrangements of tuck stitches with thick yarns or those that possess little elasticity.*

Machine type
Tuck-stitch fabrics can be knitted on both manual and automatic patterning machines.

Automatic patterning machines
Plain knit stitches are dictated by the punched areas in the card, and tuck stitches by the unpunched areas. The machine is set up according to the automated pattern-knitting instructions, with the tucking cam selected on the carriage.

Manual machines
To replicate these patterns for manual machines:

1. Place the tucking needles in holding position and leave the plain knit stitches in working position.
2. Set the carriage to the hold function. As the carriage knits a pattern course, the needles in working position will knit plain, while those in holding position will tuck.
3. To select needles for the next pattern course, place the holding position needles to upper working position, and the next set of tucking needles to holding position. If the same needle arrangement is repeated for more than one course, the needles may stay in their existing positions until it is necessary for them to be changed.

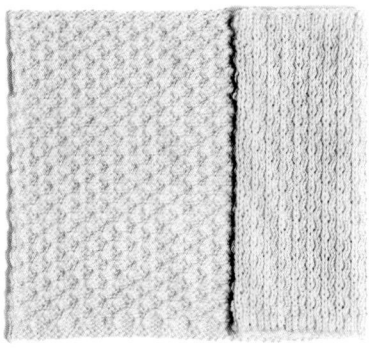

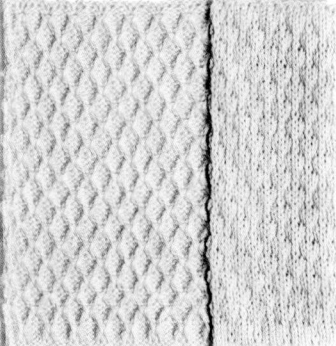

Fabrics with the same stitch arrangement in which needles tuck for (clockwise from top left): 2, 3, 5, and 4 rows.

Tuck-stitch fabrics (from left to right): lightweight two-colour pattern, bubbly surface effect formed from mixing yarn weights, and pattern arrangements inspired by cable and rib stitches.

Designing with tuck stitch

Tuck-stitch compositions must abide by certain guidelines:

- Tuck stitches can never be placed directly next to one another in the same course of knitting; neighbouring plain stitches are required to anchor the tucked yarn. There is, however, no limit to the number of tuck stitches in a course of knitting, as long as plain stitches are sandwiched in between.
- Selvedge needles should always be knitted as plain. If the edge needle is selected as a tuck stitch, it will not form properly, because it requires an adjacent plain stitch to secure its float. Besides keeping the stitch pattern consistent, plain edge stitches contribute to a professional-looking finish and make seaming easier.
- It is possible to tuck a stitch over several successive courses of knitting, depending on factors such as the yarn type and thickness and the stitch size. Up to six courses is generally an advisable standard; it may be fewer if you are using a thicker yarn and tighter stitch size, or more with a finer yarn and looser stitch size. Fabrics that tuck stitches over the higher range of courses will yield more exaggerated effects than those tucked for fewer rows.

TIP: *Starting a tuck-stitch pattern directly or soon after the cast-on may result in a scalloped effect. This may be desired for certain designs, but if not it can be avoided by knitting at least a few courses of single jersey before beginning the tuck arrangement.*

The same tuck-stitch pattern will yield varied results when knitted in yarn of differing weights. Fine yarns can create beautifully airy and ethereal fabrics that are surprisingly substantial; medium-weight yarns show off the tuck's tactile hand and waffle-like framework; and heavier yarns bring body and transform the tuck stitch into something more constructed.

Mixing yarns of diverse gauge in one fabric generates fascinating alignments of texture and form. This can be done to push the machine to create more heavily tucked fabrications, since you can tuck more rows with a thin yarn than with a medium-weight or thick one. For example, a very fine yarn can be used when tucking occurs over several courses, followed by a heavier yarn to knit one or two courses of plain.

Miss Stitch

Miss-stitch structures are formed from a combination of stitches that either miss or knit plain. Wide-ranging fabrics may be created according to the number of missed stitches across a course, the pattern they follow and the number of courses they are missed for. Mixes where proportionally only a few stitches are missed, can be subtle and delicate. Larger-scale patterns, in which a stitch is missed over several courses, can contribute to origami-like outcomes. As the stitch stretches, it pulls the fabric up like a drawstring, forming gathers and folds.

Purl-side floats lend strength, making this a wise contruction choice when harder-wearing textiles are required.

TIP: *Miss-stitch fabrics should be knitted using a stitch size at least one number looser. This number should rise as the extent and intensity of stitch-missing increases, and may vary according to the attributes of the chosen yarn.*

Machine type
Both manual and automatic patterning machines can be used to knit miss-stitch fabrics.

Automatic patterning machines
Automated machines are set up according to the pattern-knitting instructions, with the miss-stitch cam selected on the carriage. The plain knit stitches are represented by the punched areas of the card, and the miss stitches by the unpunched areas.

Manual machines
1. Place the plain knit needles in holding position and leave the miss-stitch needles in working position. The carriage should be set so that it knits needles in holding position back to working position.
2. Configure the carriage to the miss-stitch setting. As the carriage passes, it skips the needles that are in working position and knits those in holding position before returning them to working position.
3. Position needles in this way for each subsequent miss-stitch pattern course. You will find it helpful to work from a chart that indicates which needles should be in holding position.

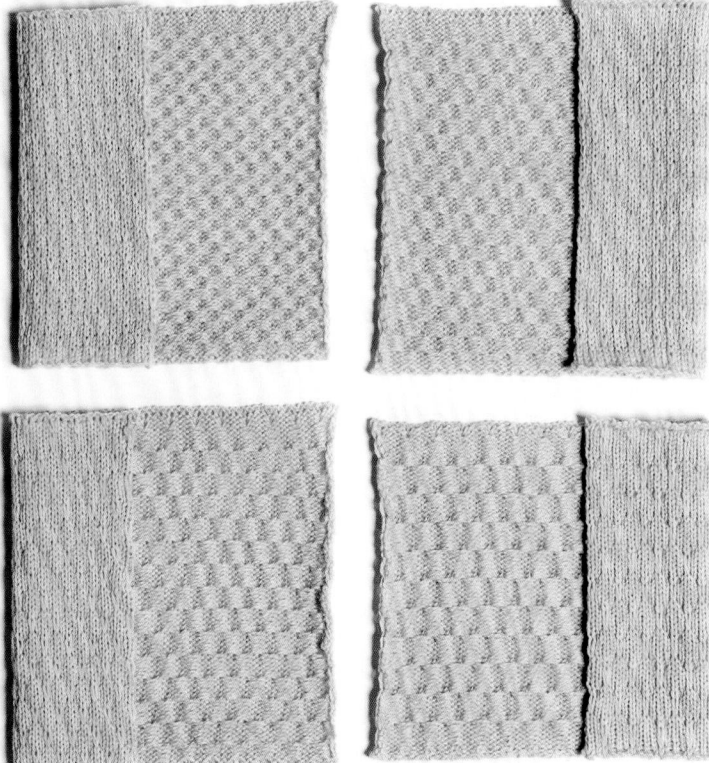

Fabrics with the same stitch arrangement in which needles miss for (clockwise from top left): 3, 4, 8, and 6 rows.

Ridges and Ruching

Designing with miss stitch

Adhere to these guidelines when designing miss-stitch patterns:

- The greater the number of adjacent miss stitches along a course, the larger the resulting float of yarn. For this reason, usually no more than six neighbouring stitches are selected to miss.
- Needles may miss consecutively for numerous courses – typically up to twelve. The yarn type, weight and stitch size will affect the ease with which this can be performed.
- Keep one or two edge needles on both sides of the knitting as plain stitches. This avoids any interruption to the stitch pattern and creates a cleaner finish.

There are few limits to the type of yarn that may be used for miss-stitch textiles, as long as you are careful to use a gauge-appropriate weight in more extreme arrangements. Highly puckered structures can benefit from a strong yarn with good elasticity, such as wool or a similar mix, enabling it to withstand the directional pull. Yarns containing elastic or those that shrink during finishing can further accentuate the relief of shirred and folded fabrics.

Fabrics with gathers and folds can be created when stitches from a previously knitted course are picked up with a transfer tool and placed on the needles of the current one. As the carriage passes the needles, it locks the elevated stitches in place.

Single stitches, groups and whole rows can be picked up. The number of courses knitted between a stitch and the course to which it is lifted will contribute to the fabric's dimension. A stitch that is picked up from a course far below the current one will give a much more voluminous result than if it were picked up from just below.

Ruching is created by elevating single or small groups of stitches. Every time a previously knitted stitch or group of stitches is knitted together with the current stitch or stitches, a pucker or gather occurs. Ruched fabrics form their gathers from the body of the textile, and so the length already knitted is pulled and pinched in patterns dictated by the sequence of lifted stitches.

Ridges, on the other hand, are created by transferring entire rows of previously knitted stitches to the current course. The resulting pleats and pintucks are visible on the knitted face and do not distort the base fabric because extra courses are knitted specifically in preparation for the lifted ridge. As soon as the pleat is formed, the extra courses 'disappear' from the body of the fabric and are contained in the expanse of the ridge itself.

Miss-stitch fabrics (from left to right): highly puckered effect emphasized with stretch yarn, braid-like purl side floats, dimensional folds knit in a graphic two-colour pattern, and subtle linear surface.

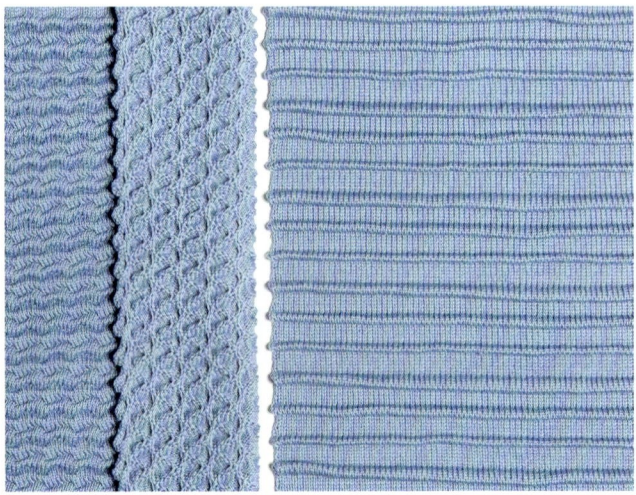

Ruching creates dimension on both sides of the fabric (left), whereas ridges display themselves on the knit side (right).

Method of elevating stitches

Ridges and ruching are both manual methods that can be formed on any type of machine using a transfer tool. To lift a single stitch:

1. Insert a one-prong transfer tool through the stitch on the selected previously knitted course.
2. Raise the tool and held stitch so that it is level with the current course, and place the stitch on the designated needle. The needle on the current course will now hold two stitches.
3. If the method requires more than one stitch to be lifted and placed on the same needle, or if you are working with thicker yarn, it is recommended to place the needle in holding position (with the carriage set to knit it back) before passing the carriage across.

Two- or three-prong transfer tools can be used to elevate groups of two or three stitches at once, as well as to speed up the process of elevating a whole row.

Identifying the stitches to be elevated

One of the trickier elements of ruched and ridged methods, is identifying exactly which stitches are to be picked up. One approach is simply to count the knitted courses below until you reach the desired stitch or stitches. While this may work well with a smooth yarn knitting at a larger stitch size, it can prove more difficult with a textured or very fine yarn. In this case, using markers, whether temporary or permanent, can be helpful.

Two-needle hand-knitting stitch markers can be added and removed easily to highlight individual or small numbers of stitches. Horizontal weaving is also a great way to add a temporary marker (see page 109). Ravel cord or a strong, slippery yarn can be laced under and over a selected number of needles, or the whole course. Once the lifted stitches have been selected, the woven marker is pulled out.

Permanent markers can be created using pattern stitches that contrast with a single-jersey background. A miss stitch, for example, can act as a visual cue directing you to where to insert your transfer tool. Multicoloured stripes or Fair Isle, can also serve as graphic indicators.

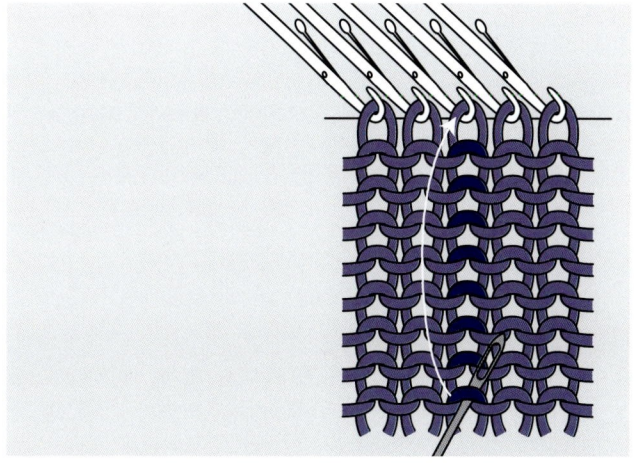

Identifying the stitch to be elevated. The transfer tool is picking up a stitch that is eight rows below the current one on the needle.

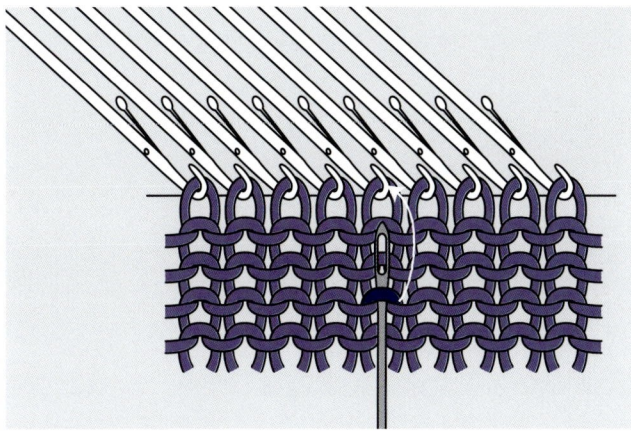

Elevating a single stitch using a one-prong transfer tool.

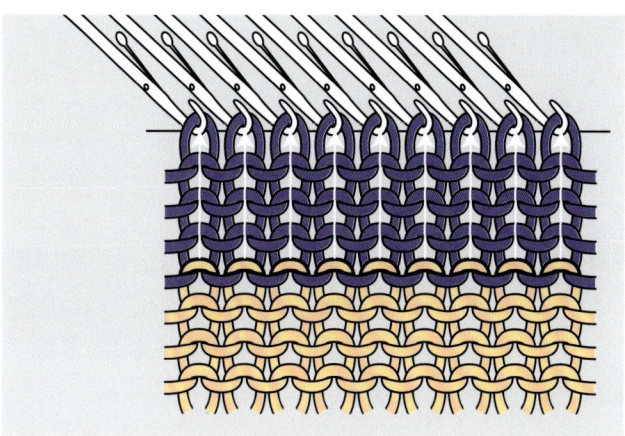

Elevating a whole row of stitches. A contrasting colour helps to highlight the course of stitches to be picked up.

Designing with ridges

The number of extra courses knitted will determine the size of the ridge. The stitches in the course prior to the first extra ridge course are picked up and placed on the current course's needles. The ridge is created as the extra courses fold onto themselves, which in turn requires double the number of courses to be knitted than the required depth of the pleat or pintuck. When a smaller number of extra courses are knitted a pintuck occurs; a pleat stems from a larger number of added rows. Pintucks stay closer to the surface of the fabric than pleats, which can protrude more dramatically.

TIP: *To give the pleat a crisp fold so that it lies flat, a 'turning course' can be knitted. This involves knitting the middle course of the pleat in a much larger stitch.*

Ridges can give form to a fine yarn, and when used in large quantities can mould the fabric into playful designs. Multicoloured and striped effects can be made by changing colours throughout a ridge, and elevating a whole course of an alternative stitch pattern can add to the detail.

Designing with ruching

Hand embroidery, in particular smocking, can provide wonderful inspiration for ruched fabrics. Elevating stitches to needles to the left or right of those directly above creates diagonal lines in the fabric, whereas those that are placed on the needles directly above take on a honeycomb-like cellular appearance.

When ruching occurs in a small section of a fabric, it may not cause much distortion to the edges. If used all over, however, the edges can become heavily warped and it may be difficult to get the textile to adhere to a fixed measurement.

It can be particularly exciting to combine this method with other stitch patterns. Multicoloured or multitextured stripes take on a whole new dynamic once small groups of lifted stitches transform the direction of the lines.

Ridged fabrics: Pleated textile with further manipulation through hand stitching once off the machine (left), and rows of small-scale patterned Fair Isle picked up to create contrasting pintucks in the surface (right).

Ruched fabrics: Cellular patterns formed by lifting stitches to the needles directly above (left), and cable-like braids created by elevating stitches to the needles to the left or right of the ones above (right).

Bobbles

Tactile knitwear adorned with bobbles by Dutch designer Nanna Van Blaaderen.

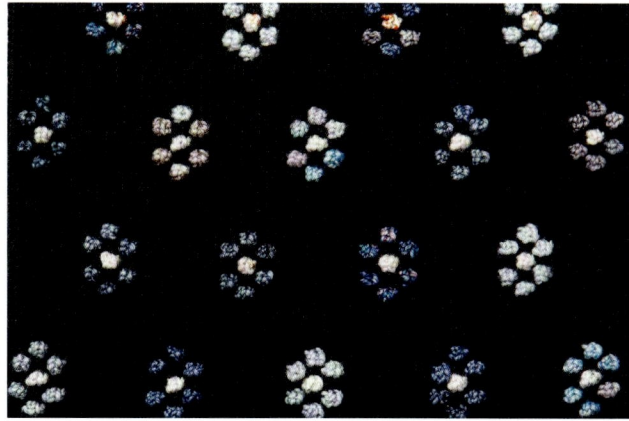

Popcorns can be clustered to form patterned arrangements on the fabric. This floral-inspired outcome used the separate strand method.

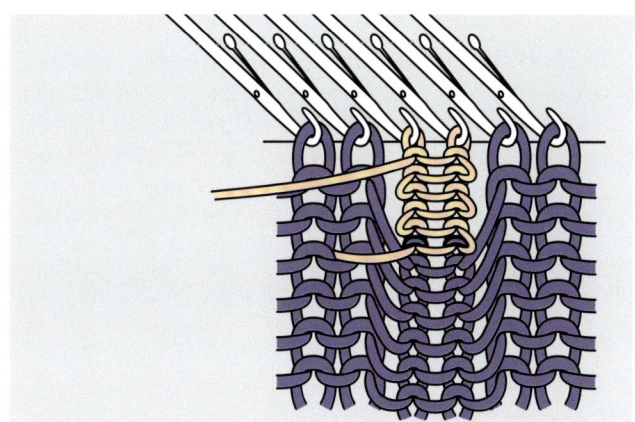

Separate strand method for bobbles. *To lift the bobble, elevate the background stitches (before the first bobble row) to the needles directly above.*

Bobbles or popcorns are small, rounded puffs of texture that pop out of the surface of the fabric. They are used frequently with other decorative stitches, such as cables, and are a whimsical addition to all kinds of knit.

Two approaches, both of which can be performed on any machine model, will create simple bobbles that display on the knit side of the fabric. One involves manually knitting stitches with a separate strand, and the other uses short rows or partial knitting. While the results are similar, the separate strand method can use a contrasting yarn to create the bobbles, whereas the short row method uses the background yarn that is already threaded in the carriage.

Each approach involves elevating stitches to form the popcorn shape. To do so, use a transfer tool to pick up the background yarn stitches that are underneath the first row of bobble stitches and place them on their respective needles directly above. The process of knitting each bobble requires a steadily weighted fabric throughout.

You can play with the ratio of stitches and rows used to knit each bobble, according to the yarn type and thickness. If increased too much, the bobble will lose its roundness.

Separate strand method

This example is worked over two stitches that are hand-knitted for approximately six courses.

1. Cut a length of the main or a contrasting yarn.
2. Once you have reached the row where you want the bobble to appear, use the strand to knit the bobble needles manually for the required number of courses (see page 67), maintaining an even tension that matches the background stitches throughout.
3. Lift the bobble.
4. Knit across to secure the bobble in place.

If several bobbles are situated closely together within a single course, a continuous strand of yarn may be used to form them. Starting at one end, create the first bobble and carry the yarn across the work to the next one.

Partial knitting method

When using short rows to form popcorns, the carriage passes the work several times over isolated stitches. For this reason, before starting, make sure the row counter is stopped before the bobble course and then adjusted accordingly before activating it again.

Knit to the course where you want the bobbles to appear and set the carriage to the hold function.

TIP: *It is easiest to use an odd number of courses to form the length of the bobble, so that the carriage is in the correct place each time.*

This example uses two stitches to form the bobble, with six stitches knitting plain at the edges of the fabric as well as between the popcorns. It uses five knit courses for each popcorn.

1. Starting at the same side of the fabric as the carriage, leave the edge plain stitches and first bobble stitches in working position (six stitches for the edge and two for the bobble) and place everything else in holding position.
2. Knit one course – this is the first course of the bobble. Place the six plain edge stitches in holding position, leaving only the two bobble stitches in working position.
3. Knit all but the final bobble stitch course (three courses); the carriage will end on the same side of the work that it started in Step 1.
4. Before knitting the last bobble course, select needles to set up the next bobble. To do so, place the next set of bobble and plain stitches in upper working position and knit one course.
5. This completes the final course of the first bobble and also makes the first course of the next. Lift the first bobble now.
6. Place all needles except those for the current bobble in holding position.
7. Knit all but the final course (three courses) over the current bobble stitches, ending with the carriage on the same side that it started in Step 1.
8. Place the next set of plain and bobble stitches in upper working position.
9. Knit one course to complete the current bobble and lift it. Place all needles apart from those for the next bobble in holding position.
10. Repeat Steps 7–9 for all bobbles across the course. When knitting the final bobble, place the remaining needles in upper working position, then knit one course to complete it before lifting. The carriage will be on the opposite side to where it started in Step 1.
11. Place all held needles in upper working position and knit across.

Flaps

Flaps or tabs are dimensional additions to the fabric that can take many shapes. They may be created using the short-row method, in which they are constructed while the main fabric also knits, or they can be executed as separate pieces and joined to the main fabric later.

Integrated flaps

If a flap is to be created through partial knitting, it is knitted on its designated working needles while the rest of the needles hold. The flap builds in length and can be knitted either as a straight or shaped tab. Once it has been knitted, the background stitches before the tab are elevated and placed on the current needles. To help identify which stitches are to be elevated, weave a strand of slippery yarn under and over the flap needles before knitting the course prior to the one where the flaps begin.

Playful scarf by Hannah Soukup featuring hundreds of multicoloured loops knit using the short-row technique. The sculptural tabs can link together transforming the accessory into further wearable options.

Unshaped flaps

Decide:

- How many stitches each flap will be (the width of the tab).
- How many courses each flap will be (the length of the tab).
- The number of plain stitches between the flaps and at the fabric selvedges.

The knitting instructions are virtually the same as for bobbles knitted with the partial knitting method (see opposite), but tabs can be any size.

Shaped flaps

Triangular tabs can be constructed by decreasing a group of needles to a single stitch and then increasing back to the original number. Since the triangles decrease to a single stitch, they are formed over an odd number of stitches. The number of stitches will also dictate the protruding depth of the triangle; a larger group requires more courses than a smaller group to decrease to one stitch.

This example uses five stitches for the triangles and three plain stitches between and at the fabric selvedges. To ensure smooth edges to the triangle, wrap the inner held needle on the carriage side.

1. Knit to the course where you want the first triangles to appear and set the carriage to the hold function. Starting on the same side of the fabric as the carriage, leave the first set of plain edge and triangle stitches in working position (three for the plain edge and five for the triangle) and place everything else in holding position.
2. Knit one course and then place the first set of plain needles (three stitches) in holding position, as well as the working triangle needle furthest away from the carriage. One triangle needle is now decreased, and there are now four working triangle stitches.
3. Knit one course and place the next working triangle needle opposite the carriage into holding position. Two triangle needles are decreased, and there are now three working triangle stitches.
4. Knit one course and place the next working triangle needle opposite the carriage into holding position. Three triangle needles are decreased, and there are now two working triangle stitches.
5. Knit one course and place the next working triangle needle opposite the carriage into holding position. Four

triangle needles are decreased, and there is now one working triangle stitch.

6. Knit one course, leaving the middle needle in working position; the decrease is complete and the carriage is on the opposite side of the work from where it started in Step 1.

7. To start increasing the triangle needles again, place one on the opposite side to the carriage in upper working position and knit across (there are now two working triangle stitches).

8. Repeat Step 7 until all but one triangle stitches are active again (there will be four working triangle stitches). The carriage will be on the side it started from in Step 1.

9. Bring the final triangle needle to upper working position, as well as the next set of plain and triangle stitches. Knit across to complete the final course of the current triangle and the first course of the next triangle.

10. Lift the triangle stitches, then place them, the next set of plain stitches and the working triangle needle furthest from the carriage in holding position. One triangle needle is now decreased, and there are four working triangle stitches.

11. Repeat from Step 3 across the course. At the final triangle, place the final triangle needle and selvedge

needles to upper working position, then knit one course. The carriage will end on the opposite side of the work to where it started in Step 1. Lift the final triangle, then place all held needles to upper working position and knit across to secure the elevated stitches.

Separately knitted flaps

As with tabs knitted through short rows, separately knitted flaps can be knitted in many different shapes and sizes. The advantage of this method is that there is less planning involved; while short rows require advance consideration of the knitting sequence, the separate method can be thought of as a fabric collage.

This method results in the flaps displaying on the purl side:

1. Knit the required number of individual flaps, ending each with several courses of waste yarn.

2. Cast on for the background fabric and knit to the course where the first surface additions are to be made.

3. Using a transfer tool, pick up the last course of live stitches knitted in the main yarn on the tab and rehang it on the current working needles (see page 158). Whether you pick up the knit or purl side of the tab will depend

Unshaped (left) and shaped (right) flaps.

Separately knitted flaps created through two-needle hand knitting. The live stitches of each shape were hung on the machine's needles as it knitted the background fabric.

Cable Stitches

on how you want it to be displayed.

4. Once positioned, there will be two stitches on each of the needles holding a tab, and they can be placed in holding position (with the carriage set to knit needles in hold) before knitting.
5. Repeat across the pattern course until all tabs are attached.
6. Remove the waste yarn once the fabric is off the machine.

For knit-side decoration:

1. Stitches must be removed from their needles so that the flap can be hung first. If removing four or more stitches, do so by slipping them onto a stitch holder.
2. Once the flap is hung, the main fabric stitches are replaced.

Cable-stitch fabrics play a leading role in knitwear design. These distinctive designs are born from stitches that travel and twist both physically on the surface of the cloth and figuratively through the history of fashion and textiles. Recognizable in lovingly hand-knitted sweaters from the British Isles, cable stitches are a clan of traditional patterns that were featured in fishermen's garb. The simple square construction of these pullovers provided a vast canvas to be ornamented with elaborate texture.

These cherished patterns were typically not written down, and instead recorded only in the sweaters themselves. The arrangement of stitches was usually unique to the maker's family and where they lived, as can often be gathered from the names of the patterns themselves, such as 'Whitby' or 'Scarborough', and the visual symbolism of certain stitch layouts. In true bespoke form, some sweaters would even have the recipient's name embedded in the fabric, inscribed through the knitting.

Fisherman in Whitstable, England, wearing a traditional gansey sweater recognizable by its simple silhouette and richly textured cable-stitch patterns.

Cable patterns are symphonies of stitches that interlace and cross with one another. Vertical columns of knit stitches are typically used to form the cables. The column is split into two groups of stitches, which are directed to switch places with each other. Depending on how they are crossed over, the pronounced line of the twist will slant to the right or left. Because the cable is created manually, it can be done on any type of machine model.

Purl-stitch effects

These fabrics typically use numerous knit-and-purl stitch combinations to make up a textured framework. Panels of purl stitches appear recessed when placed either side of knit-stitch cable columns. While an elaborate mix of knit and purls may require a lot of time-consuming hand-tooling, integrating a column or two of reconstructed stitches either side of the cable can be formed fairly quickly and still imparts the desired effect. Another approach is to place the cable in between two ladder stitches formed by bordering out-of-work needles. The space provided by the empty needles defines the outline of the twisted stitches, helping the cables to stand out.

Border stitches can help cables to stand out. From left to right the cables are bordered by: both a reconstructed and ladder wale each side, a ladder wale each side, and two reconstructed wales each side.

Method of creating cables

A cable is created with two groups of adjacent stitches and a pair of transfer tools. Each group is removed from its needles and placed on the needles of the neighbouring group. By swapping the groups of stitches, the cable twist is formed.

The number of prongs on the transfer tools depends on the number of stitches that are to be crossed. A two-by-two cable is created over a four-stitch column, for example, and is split into two equal groups of two stitches, so two two-prong transfer tools are needed.

Direction of cable cross

Both groups of stitches are removed from their needles and held temporarily on the transfer tools. The first group to be returned to the needles will be more prominent on the knit side of the fabric, and so that will dictate the direction.

- If the left-hand group of stitches is placed on the right-hand needles first, the cable twist will lean left.
- If the right-hand group of stitches is placed on the left-hand needles first, the cable twist will lean right.

Forming a basic cable

The following instructions detail how to make a right-leaning four-stitch cable. It is useful to number the stitches for reference. Here, Stitches 1 and 2 form the left-hand group and Stitches 3 and 4 the right-hand group. You will need a pair of two-prong transfer tools.

1. Using your dominant hand, transfer Stitches 1 and 2 to the first two-prong tool, then swap the tool to your non-dominant hand.
2. Using your dominant hand, transfer Stitches 3 and 4 to the second two-prong tool, and place them on the empty needles of Stitches 1 and 2. Place the empty two-prong tool to one side.
3. Return the other two-prong tool to your dominant hand and transfer Stitches 1 and 2 to the empty needles of 3 and 4.

TIP: *Place the just worked cable needles in holding position before passing the carriage across (with the carriage set to knit them back). If the needles in holding position appear to be pulled very close to one another, they can be carefully brought back to upper working position instead. This makes the first course of knitting easier for the carriage.*

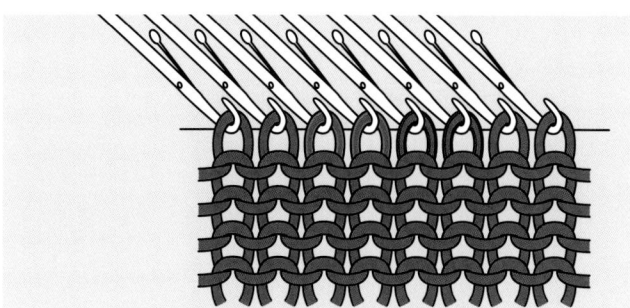

Forming a right-leaning four-stitch cable. *Transfer Stitches 1 and 2 (green) to the first two-prong tool, then Stitches 3 and 4 (red) to the second two-prong tool.*

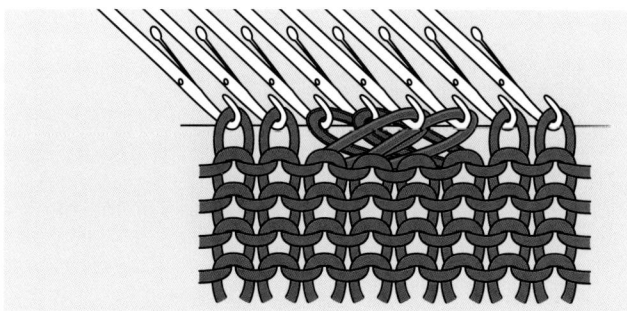

Place Stitches 3 and 4 (red) onto needles 1 and 2, then Stitches 1 and 2 (green) onto needles 3 and 4.

Once the first cable cross is complete, the carriage knits the designated number of courses before the next twist. Fewer courses knitted between crosses result in a more tightly coiled rope, whereas larger numbers of courses spread out the cable twists and create a wider-looking cord.

Creating different cable arrangements

Other common stitch groupings are one-by-one and three-by-three, as well as odd-numbered arrangements such as two-by-one cable. These involve crossing one stitch over one stitch, three stitches over three stitches and two stitches over one stitch respectively.

Working a four-by-four cable or larger, or creating fabrics with numerous crosses in one course, can present difficulties. Large groups of stitches simply cannot stretch far enough over each other to create wide cables. Several repeats of cable crossings close to one another can put a strain on the fabric, causing the stitches to become very tight and difficult to manipulate.

Easing strain on the machine

There are several ways of making the cable crossings easier. Yarn choice and stitch size are very important; the natural resilience of wool or wool blends will result in easier crosses than fibres with little stretch. The stitch size should be set looser than for single jersey, from one to several whole numbers higher depending on the yarn and pattern. Ladder border stitches used for decorative effect will also lend ease to the fabric.

Isolating the cable stitches and enlarging them while the background stitches remain the same size can be the perfect solution for larger cables. By using a separate strand of yarn, the same as the one knitting, you can form the stitches within the cable group manually (see page 67) so that they expand just before they are crossed. These additional strands can later be tidied, for a flawless finish.

Designing cable-stitch fabrics

Cable's rich history provides a wealth of inspiration for designers today. The meaning and symbolism behind each stitch arrangement are unique; each bears its own name and characteristics, signifying the daily sightings and experiences of the fishermen.

The sprinkling of knits and purls that create 'moss stitch' is symbolic of green landscapes, and 'zigzag' speaks to winding cliff paths. The up-and-down direction of 'marriage lines' needs no further explanation, while the laced diamonds and twists of cables themselves depict the fishermen's prized tools: net and ropes.

When designing your own fabrics, this symbolism is worth exploring: you could interpret your habitual observations and environment through stitches. The layouts of various types of regional sweater – Guernsey, Jersey and Aran – can be also examined.

Hand-knitting stitch books are an excellent resource, and many of these patterns can be adapted for the single-bed knitting machine. Cable designs for hand-knitters are often displayed in charts that communicate the number of stitches, the direction of the twist and the number of rows between crosses.

- The number of squares in a horizontal line dictates the total number of stitches used to form the cable column.
- The cable symbol consists of two diagonal shapes, which cross one another. The shape at the back represents the stitches that are placed on their needles first, and the shape at the front depicts the stitches that are returned to their needles second.

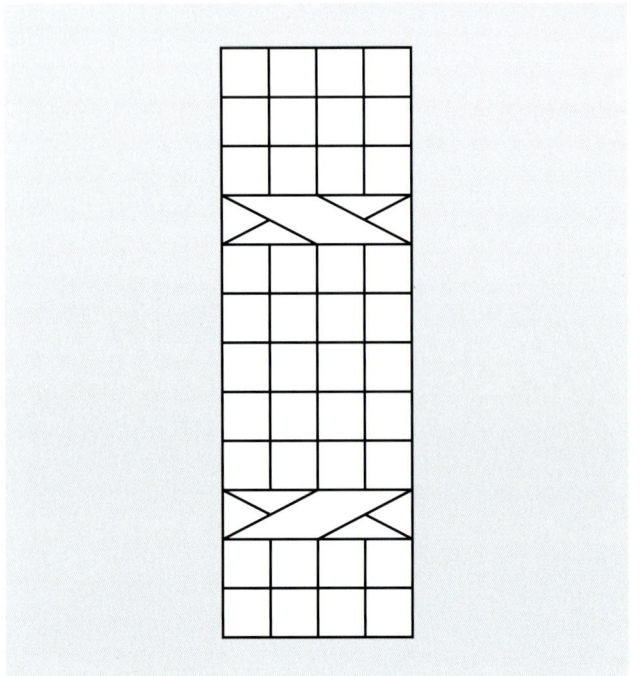

Hand-knitting charts are drawn to represent how your knitting will appear from the right side of the fabric. This chart is for a four-stitch cable alternating with a right-leaning (bottom) and left-leaning (top) cross. There are twelve rows in each pattern repeat

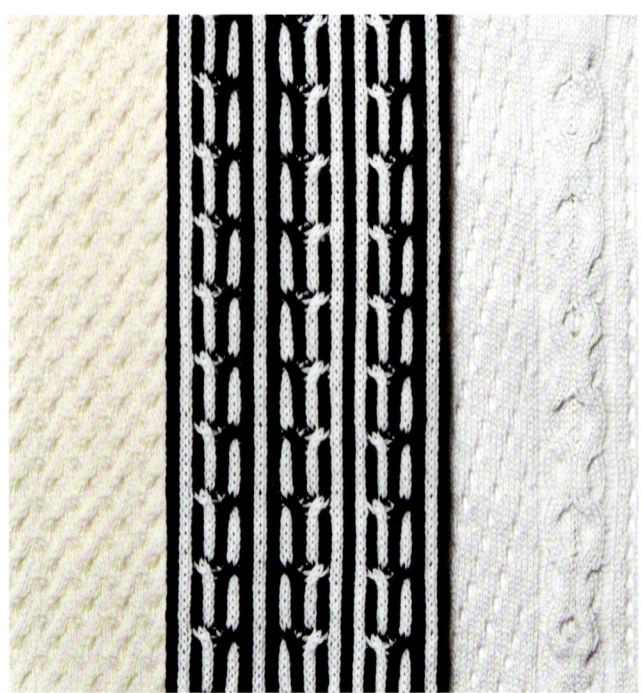

Cable-stitch fabrics (from left to right): four-stitch cables create an all-over basketweave texture, an optical effect created through Fair Isle stripes and cable crosses, and two four-stitch cables with alternating twists form honeycomb columns.

- The number of squares in a vertical line equates to the number of rows used to form the pattern repeat.

As with any contemporary interpretation of a trusted method, experimentation is key. Taking risks, mixing techniques and going against the status quo will all yield fresh results.

Exploring visual effects

Although very large cables may not be replicated like for like, several smaller cables can be placed next to one another to achieve a similar effect. A few methods can also be implemented to make a cable appear wider than it truly is. One way is to create a cable over an odd number of stitches – for example a two-by-three arrangement. The larger group should be placed on their designated needles first, so that they will be more visible from the knit side than the smaller group that will cross behind it. From the face of the fabric, this cable will appear as a three-by-three construction, but fewer needles make it easier to construct.

The number of courses knitted between crossings will also have an impact on the perceived width. Less frequent crossings allow the stitches to spread out before being pulled in again for their next twist, producing a much wider-looking cable than one built from the same stitches but with more closely repeated crossings.

Numerous other stitches may be combined with cabled ropes. Lace and openwork provide a dimensional balance, while tuck, bobbles and partial knitting can be integrated to add volume. Colour can also be incorporated in unique ways, and intarsia in particular can yield eye-catching results.

Pattern layout

As well as their usual vertical orientation, cable columns can:

- shift and travel along the fabric, appearing as linear diagonal formations;
- be combined in precise patchworks of all-over repeated patterns;
- lie horizontally or asymmetrically in the fabric as inserts
- be placed to follow the contours of the body;
- work as decorative details on hems, cuffs, neckbands, seams and openings.

Faux cables

As the name suggests, faux or mock cables are not true cable-knit structures, but are used to imitate their qualities. They may be incorporated into a design for aesthetic or practical reasons; for example, they may require less hand-tooling and put less strain on the fabric. Faux cables can also push the boundaries of this perennial favourite. They can be formed using various techniques:

- Tactile tuck- and miss-stitch patterns can emulate the woven effect of cable fabrics.
- Braids and cords can combine to form cable-like proportions.
- Ruching can suggest the diagonal twists of cable cords.
- Hand-sewing methods such as smocking can be explored to pull the fabric together at selected points so that it mimics the movement of a cable.

Knitwear designer Norah Gaughan is known for her innovative approach to reinterpreting cable stitches, arranging them into contemporary garments. Blocks of cables fit together like puzzle pieces in her aptly named 'Intersect' cardigan for Brookyn Tweed.

In this mixed technique fabric, the 'seam as you knit' method (page 186) is used to join two-needle hand knit cables to machine-knit sections. I-cords are threaded through machine-knit eyelet holes, to emulate the movement of cables.

Woven Patterns

Also known as knit-weave, this technique is formed with a background yarn that knits and a contrasting or weaving yarn that lies on the purl side of the fabric. The weaving yarn is never knitted, and therefore does not form stitches itself. There are several variations and approaches:

- Weaving yarns can be incorporated in a horizontal configuration across the width of the knitting, or lead vertically through the length of the fabric. In both cases, the resulting pattern is illustrated through a sequence of floats of varying length.
- Additional surface effects can be created by wrapping needles with the highlight yarn, resulting in puffed or bobble-like details.
- Further manipulation can lead to fringe, loops and pile-like surfaces.

Fabric type

Woven-effect fabrics can be stiffer and firmer than other methods, with less stretch. This inherent stability makes them especially suitable for interior uses such as furnishing and upholstery, as well as structured garments and accessories such as bags.

To bring more give to the fabric, certain amendments can be made during knitting:

- casting on with every other needle;
- using a weaving yarn that is finer than the background yarn;
- spacing the weaving pattern out;
- knitting at a much looser stitch size;
- incorporating stretch yarns.

When introducing the highlight yarn in weaving and wrapped methods, it is necessary to adjust the stitch size to a slightly higher number.

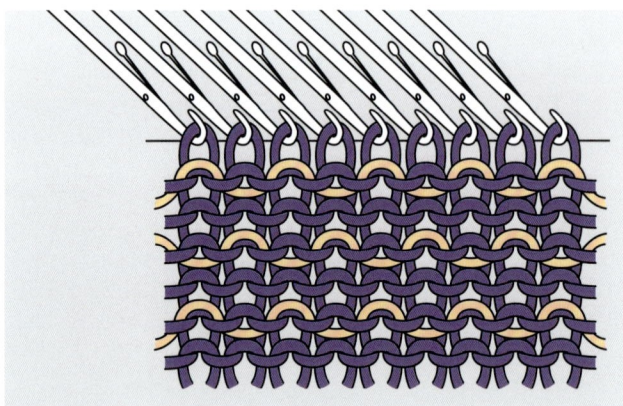

Horizontal weaving. The effect yarn interlaces through the purl surface of the fabric.

Kitty Pennybacker creates timeless knitted designs for the home using 100% Geelong wool. Her blanket displays inviting textural interest that is achieved through the horizontal knit-weave method using custom knitted cords.

Regardless of the type of woven effect, the resulting pattern will always dominate on the purl side of the knitting, so this is usually selected as the fabric's right side.

The lighter the weight of the background yarn, the more visible the woven effects will appear from the knit side. In addition, casting on with alternate needle set-ups, or incorporating areas of lace holes or ladders in the background structure, will create windows in which the woven areas can be viewed from the knitted face.

Yarn

Since the weaving yarn need not fit into the hooks of the needles to form stitches, a wider range of materials can be incorporated, including those that are too thick or textured to knit with ease on the chosen machine gauge. Unconventional knitting materials, such as trimmings, ribbons, fabric strips, cord and leather, can also be used.

Horizontal weaving

This can be carried out automatically with patterning machines, or by hand on manual machines.

For punchcard machines, the weaving yarn is threaded through the auto tension unit, in a separate pathway to that of the background yarn. If working manually, the weaving yarn can be kept on the floor in front of the machine.

Automatic patterning method

These machines have carriages that carry the weaving yarn across the needle bed. It is placed in the yarn holders either side of the carriage, according to the direction in which the carriage is leading. With every successive course of horizontal weaving, as you pass the carriage, the weaving yarn is swapped into the alternate holder, ensuring that it is always kept ahead of the carriage. This means the yarn should be placed in the right side holder in preparation for the carriage to knit to the right side of the bed, then swapped to the left side holder for the carriage to

knit back to the left side of the bed. The carriage also contains weaving brushes that are lowered before introducing the weaving yarn.

The weaving yarn laces over or under needles that are knitting with the background yarn, according to the desired pattern. The punched holes in a punchcard direct the weaving yarn to pass over the background yarn stitches, and the unpunched areas tell the weaving yarn to pass under the background yarn stitches. When two or more punched holes are next to each other, the weaving yarn floats across the fabric until it reaches an unpunched hole, where it continues to be woven into the surface.

Usually the weaving yarn does not pass over more than five adjacent needles, so that the ensuing float does not become too long.

Check-inspired horizontal knit-weave fabrics. A mix of yarn types are used to create dimension and depth to the surfaces, laid in using the manual method.

Manual method

This method entails bringing all needles to holding position and configuring the carriage so that it is set to knit the needles back to working position.

1. With the weaving yarn on the floor in front of the machine, bring it over and under the needles according to your design.
2. Make sure the laced yarn is pushed firmly against the sinker posts before passing the carriage across.
3. If using a continuous end of yarn from a cone that you wish to weave over several successive courses, there is no need to cut it. Instead, it will travel up the work and alternate the side of the fabric from which it begins weaving after every woven pattern course.

Even for more complex machines, laying yarn in by hand may be preferable when the woven pattern is only a few courses. You may also choose to weave manually when working with unconventional yarn or materials. Adding the material in this way gives you more control, particularly if you are using something thick and of unusual texture. Furthermore, short fabric strips or trimmings may not be long enough to be threaded through the auto tension unit, and so must be integrated by hand. Adding the woven-effect yarn manually allows an artistic approach, and often the most exciting fabrications are the result of mixing automatic patterning and manual methods.

Long float effects

Manipulating the floats of yarn formed by horizontal woven patterns can add even more possibilities. Beautiful fabrications can be constructed by using longer floats that are gathered together, picked up and secured in a woven composition.

Single or groups of floats may be lifted with a one-prong transfer tool and placed on a needle either directly above or off-centre. To help the floats stay in their lifted position, the needle holding them can be brought into holding position before you pass the carriage across (with the carriage set to knit it back).

TIP: *Be careful the yarn is not too thick when lifting large groups of floats. It may be better to lift smaller groups of floats over fewer courses.*

Long woven floats can also be cut, transforming them into fringing and revealing windows of the plain knitted background. The type of fibre and yarn you use will have a strong impact on how the fringe will appear and behave once the floats are sliced. It is important that long floats are integrated securely into the knitted background before they are cut. This will be determined predominantly by the weaving pattern in which the floats are created; long floats must be anchored on either side by other sections of denser knit-weave.

TIP: *It is generally easier to cut floats when the fabric is taut, either while it is attached to the knitting machine or by pinning it to a surface once it is off the machine. Small, sharp scissors are the best tool; just take extra care that you cut only the woven yarn forming the floats.*

Long float effects: openwork structure with areas of cut floats create a tactile pile-effect (left), and lifted floats within a simple knit-weave pattern leading to a graphic outcome (right).

Vertical weaving

When highlight yarns are laced through the knitting vertically, they contribute to a surface effect that resembles embroidery. The effect yarn is laid over the needle shafts or in their hooks and secured to the surface of the fabric once the carriage passes across. As this method is carried out manually, any machine can be used.

Each vertical line of pattern requires its own strand of yarn for weaving, and yarn may be used directly from the cone or ball or prepared as cut strands. Keep the weaving yarn on the floor in front of the machine. Cut strands of yarn are best for when the pattern is formed from several columns of vertical weaving. As a general rule, these should be cut to at least three times the length of the desired line of pattern, and even more if the vertical weaving yarn is being laid to create a column with shifting diagonal floats. To introduce the yarn:

1. Leave a tail long enough to finish once the piece is off the machine. Alternatively, a cut strand double the required length can be folded over itself and joined into the fabric at the middle point of the strand. Doubling the yarn in this way removes the need to finish the tail at the start of the vertical weaving, and the resulting pattern will have more dimension than a single strand.
2. The yarn can be laid into the hook or across the shaft of a needle. If you are laying into the hook, keep the needles in working position and push them slightly forward to help them catch the highlight yarn (and return them afterwards). If you are laying across the shaft, the needles should be placed in upper working position or holding position (with the carriage set to knit them back).
3. As the carriage passes across, the laid yarn is secured against the background fabric.

Method

The body of the pattern is formed by bringing the weaving yarn up vertically and laying it across the next designated needle. If it is laid over the same needle as on the previous pattern course, the woven column is fashioned from straight floating strands. If laid over a needle to the left or right of the one previously used, the floating strands create a zigzagging diagonal route.

Typically, two plain courses are knitted between woven courses, but this can of course be experimented with, depending on the type and thickness of the yarn as well as the desired appearance.

As well as simply laying the yarn across the top of the needle or in the hook, you can wrap it around the needle shaft in the same motion used as when forming the e-wrap cast-on (see pages 54–55), resulting in a slightly different appearance.

New vertical weaving yarns can be added throughout the body of the knitting in the same way that the beginning pattern strands are integrated.

The shifting lines achieved through vertical weaving work beautifully to display unusual or novelty yarns.

Using a yarn end holder

Vertical weaving designs with numerous ends of yarn can become difficult to navigate. For this reason, yarn ends can be threaded through the holes in a handmade cardboard guide, fashioned for the particular gauge of machine you are working on. Not only does this increase the rate at which the yarns are arranged on their needles, but it also keeps them tensioned and ensures they are kept separate. To make your own yarn guide:

1. Cut a piece of lightweight cardboard about 10cm (4in) in length, with a width that is dependent on the number of ends you intend on threading through it.
2. Using a pencil, draw two lines 0.5cm (¼in) from the top and bottom edges.
3. Place a blank punchcard (in the correct gauge for your machine) on the cardboard so that a horizontal row sits on top of the pencil line. Using the small hole in each square along the punchcard pattern row as a guide, mark dots along the pencil lines.
4. When you remove the punchcard guide, the cardboard will have a series of dots along the top and bottom that are spaced to correspond exactly with the machine gauge. Use a sewing pin to carefully pierce each dot marked in the cardboard. This helps the punching tool grasp the cardboard in the next step.
5. Using a punchcard punching tool, make holes at every marked dot.

Cardboard yarn guide before the marked dots are punched (left), and after they are punched with weaving yarns threaded through (right).

To thread the weaving yarns into the guide:

1. Bring them up through the holes at the bottom of the card and back down through the holes at the top.
2. Once the weaving yarns are introduced into the knitting, slide the holder down the strands so that it is 10–15cm (4–6in) away from the fabric.
3. Maintain this distance as the vertical weaving pattern progresses. Allowing space for the carriage to pass the needle bed helps to stop it from colliding with the holder.

Wrapping

When a highlight yarn is wrapped manually around a needle or stitch, or a group of needles or stitches, in a motion that mirrors that of the e-wrap cast-on, it creates an intriguing texture.

You may need to be sensitive to the number of wraps if you are using a thick yarn, but this method invites you to explore different compositions, sequences and types of wrapping freely.

Wrapping needles

1. Place the designated needles in holding position (with the carriage set to knit them back) and, working from one side of the fabric to the other, e-wrap single or groups of needles in the desired pattern.
2. The yarn may be wrapped once or several times around the needle or needles; the more it is wrapped, the more dimensional the resulting texture will be.

Wrapping stitches

1. A stitch or group of stitches is removed from the needle or needles using a transfer tool.
2. While they are held, the highlight yarn may be wrapped around them once or several times before they are replaced on their respective needles.

The yarn used for wrapped stitches will appear on both sides of the textile.

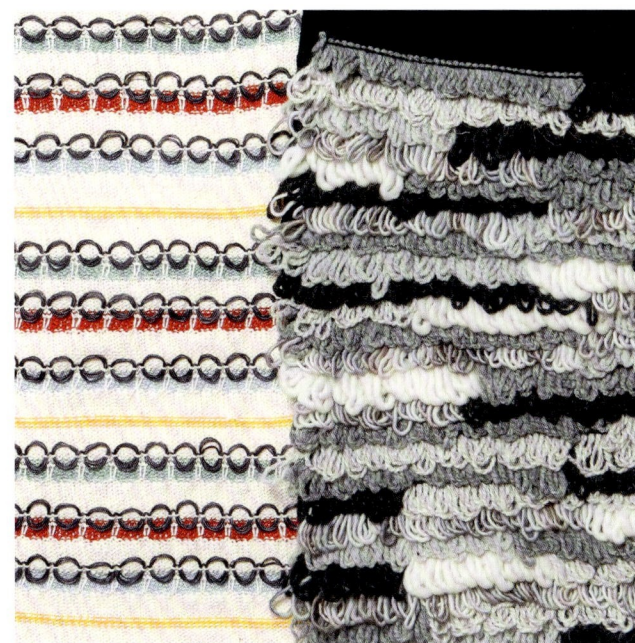

Wrapped fabrics: courses of wrapped needles integrated into a tuck-and stripe-pattern fabric (left), and long loops of heavier-weight yarn are repeated to emulate fur-like fringe (right).

Wrapping to create loops

Long loops or fringing can be created by modifying the wrapping method. Wrap only one needle at a time, and elongate the bottom of the e-wrap so that instead of hugging the needle, it stretches and forms loops that hang down. As one hand makes the yarn loops, use a finger from the other hand to hold the loops against the sinker posts. Loops can be continued across the whole course or only on certain groups of needles throughout a course. Hold the loops as close as possible to the sinker posts as the carriage passes the needles. For a neater finish, use a ruler or large hand knitting needle as a tool to pass the yarn around. Repeating this for numerous courses, with a few plain rows between, can result in a fur-like fabric. Ends of yarn can be plied up to increase the thickness of this surface interest.

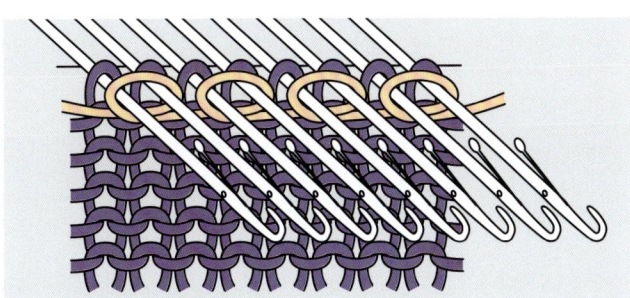

Wrapping needles. The effect yarn laces or 'e-wraps' around the needles to create puffs of texture.

Chapter 6

Decoration

The presence of holes in knitted fabric can elicit very different reactions. New knitters are familiar with that feeling of dismay identifying unwelcome openings that have embedded themselves firmly into the foundations of the cloth. Yet when those same holes are made on purpose, they can create beautifully intricate patterns. There is an impressive assortment of lace and openwork knitting techniques, all producing fabrics formed from a harmonious combination of open areas, solid areas and lines. Clean, crisp yarns or those with special dyeing effects lend themselves particularly well to these stitches.

Embellishments can contribute to the creation of couture-level fabrications, add personality or whimsy to a textile, or simply bring an additional layer of depth. While arguably all knitted fabrics are decorative in their own way, certain aesthetic approaches can transform a simple textile canvas into a captivating work of art. Beads and embroidery can travel through the twists or fill the openings of cables, turn a two-colour Fair Isle into a Technicolour rainbow or add opulence to the openings of floral lace grounds.

Lace and Openwork

At their most extreme, such knits can be as lacy as cobwebs, with stitches interlocking and netting at spaced-out points. The lattice structure of these mesh-like fabrics makes solid areas of stitches appear to float in the trellised surface.

Naturally, integrating windows of light into the fabric creates a more airy and agile outcome, suiting it to warm-weather designs. The delicacy of open-space knitwear and the featherweight yarns used to knit it are also an obvious choice for evening garments and accessories. But contemporary lace need not adhere to rules. Fabrics that are bold in their execution with sharp, linear openings can be well-defined and made from substantial yarns.

TIP: *The stitch size settings in lace and openwork fabrics can be explored thoroughly; a much looser tension complements the relaxed feel of these knits, adding to the lacework's webbed characteristics, and a tighter gauge can represent the crisp contrast of orchestrated open and closed outlines.*

Transferred lace

Transferred lace fabrics, also known as pointelle or eyelet knits, are recognizable by their mix of decorative holes and prominent lines. This method is the closest relation to traditional two-needle hand-knitted, or 'true' lace. Whether hand- or machine-knitted, these fabrications are comprised of a sequence of open lace stitches and decrease stitches. Lace of this type made on the machine can be constructed manually using transfer tools, or by using a lace carriage suitable for automated pattern machines. Owing to the breadth of creative options and technical possibilities with hand-tooled lace, this method is the one detailed here.

Machine-knitted eyelets are created by moving stitches from one needle to another. The newly empty needle remains in working position and receives a new stitch once the carriage passes it. The direction in which the stitch has been transferred (whether to the needle to the left or right) contributes to the subtly raised lines. After the transfer, this needle holds two stitches (sometimes more, with advanced patterns), and is called the decrease needle. Depending on the position of these simple components, the resulting openwork can bear numerous outcomes ranging from geometric to organic.

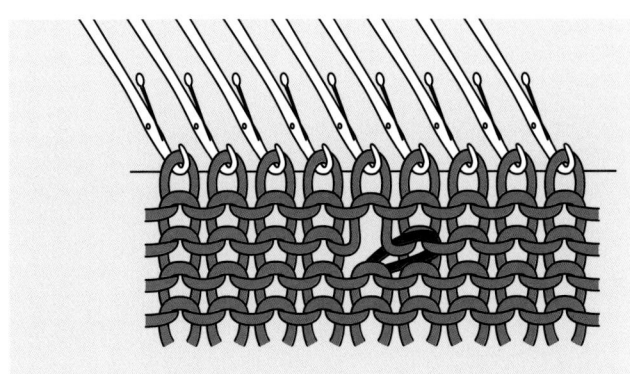

Single-transfer lace hole in the fabric formed by moving one stitch to an adjacent needle.

TIP: *Realign the empty needle if it has shifted out of place after transferring its stitch, so that it is not accidentally pushed into nonworking position when the carriage passes, potentially causing a ladder instead of a lace hole.*

Single- and multiple-transfer lace

According to the desired complexity of pattern, one stitch (single transfer) or several stitches (multiple transfer) can be transferred to neighbouring needles. Multiple-transfer patterns generally take longer, as they entail moving several stitches in a group to form one eyelet. However, the resulting slanted stitches are extremely decorative.

Single-transfer lace fabric: motifs and free-form open patterns may be knitted easily with this method.

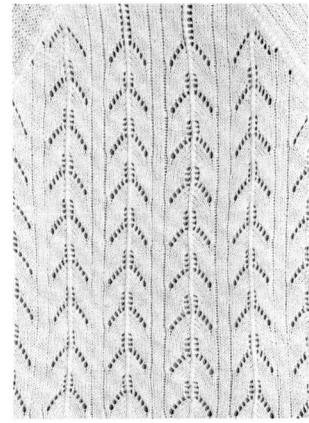

Multiple-transfer lace fabric: these structures are recognizable by their directional stitches which lend depth and movement.

To form an eyelet by moving one stitch:

1. Determine where you want the eyelet to appear, and use a one-prong transfer tool to transfer this stitch to the adjacent needle to the left or right.
2. The eyelet needle will now be empty, and the adjacent needle will hold two loops in its hook.
3. Ensure the empty needle is left in working position (realigning it if necessary).
4. Knit one course. The empty needle gains a new loop and will continue to knit as normal.

Multiple-transfer fabrics require a little more planning. The stitch to be transferred first is the one furthest from the eyelet needle, and the eyelet needle has its stitch transferred last. Use multi-prong transfer tools to shift stitches in groups to minimize the amount of hand-tooling. To create an eyelet by moving five stitches:

1. Determine where you want the eyelet to appear. This stitch, plus four adjacent stitches (to the left or right), will be moved in order to create the hole.
2. Skipping the eyelet needle (needle 1) and its adjacent needle (needle 2), use a three-prong transfer tool to transfer the next three stitches (needles 3, 4 and 5) one place over (moving away from the eyelet needle), to the adjacent needles. The third needle is now empty.
3. Use a two-prong tool to transfer the eyelet stitch (needle 1) and its adjacent stitch (needle 2) one place over, to the adjacent needles. The eyelet needle is now empty.

It often takes a few repeats of multiple stitch transfers to see the raised line and moving stitch pattern develop.

TIP: *Forming a lace pattern of this type at the bottom of a fabric can create an attractive scalloped edging.*

Creating larger eyelets
A double eyelet is formed when two adjacent needles are emptied:

1. Choose the two needles that you wish to form the double eyelet over. Use a one-prong transfer tool to transfer the left stitch to the next needle to the left, then the right stitch to the next needle to the right.
2. Ensure the empty needles are in working position (realigning them if necessary), and knit one course.
3. The newly cast-on strand produced by the carriage forms across both empty needles, and if left would continue to knit in this way, with two needles sharing one stitch. To give each needle its own stitch, remove the new loop of yarn from one needle. This needle will now be empty, with the cast-on strand only on the other needle.
4. Knit one course. The empty needle will now have its own loop.
5. A diagonal strand of yarn will be visible crossing in the eyelet space. Use a transfer tool to place this strand on the adjacent non-eyelet needle for a clean finish.

For lace holes larger than this, it is best to use the cast-off openings method described on page 128.

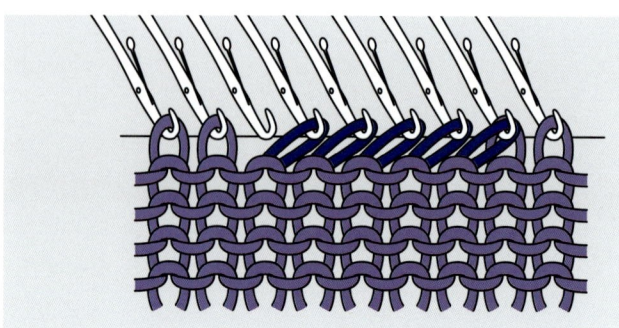

Forming a lace hole through multiple-transfer. Five stitches are transferred to the right, resulting in an empty needle.

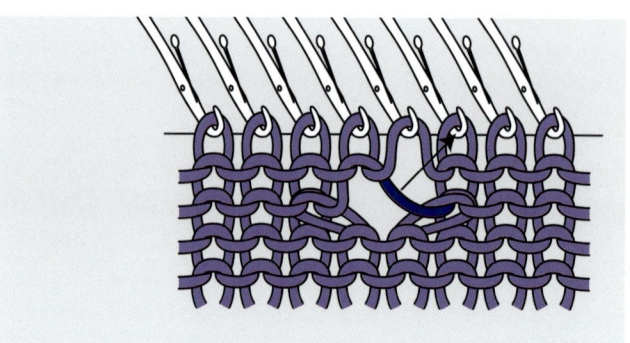

Creating a two-stitch eyelet. *Step 5: For the final step and to create a crisp appearance, place the strand of yarn in the eyelet space onto the adjacent needle.*

Designing transferred lace fabrics

There is no doubt that translating elaborate traditional lace motifs and patterns onto the machine can give stunning results – the fabrics in question can be works of art – but those with technically uncomplicated open-space arrangements can make just as strong an impact.

Hand-knitting stitch books containing lace patterns are an excellent place to start inspiring your own designs. Some patterns may not be directly convertible, but you can always invent your own interpretation. If a particular stitch pattern is detailed only as written instructions, use graph paper to adapt it into a chart before trying it on the machine. This layout allows you to visualize and organize the lace-hole and decrease patterns in relation to the machine's needles.

A freer approach is to develop ideas directly on the machine, using references from inspiration and research or simply your own curiosity. For example, you could create a series of swatches that show a progression in openness, or explore interrupting traditional lace compositions with courses of single jersey or contrasting stitches. Aim to include transfers in various directions, since if eyelets are formed by moving stitches in only one direction, the fabric will bias or slant.

Simple silhouettes provide creative opportunities for engineered lace placements. By Nanette Lepore, Spring/Summer 2013.

Placement of pattern

As well as an all-over pattern, transferred lace works particularly well as an inset detail. Not only does it provide a contrasting surface, but also lines and the arrangement of eyelets can form contours within a garment. Customizing lace patterns to an exact silhouette is also an excellent way to control precisely which parts of the garment should be closed and solidly knitted for practical reasons.

Leaving two or three edge stitches without openings in a lace fabrication is recommended. For single-stitch transfer patterns, simply eliminating any transfers in the edge stitches will automatically create a border. For multiple-transfer fabrics, however, the directional movement of the patterned stitches may be interrupted and so closed eyelets can be created. To close an eyelet and thus make it invisible, use a transfer tool to pick up the purl bump from the stitch to the left or right of the empty needle (see page 147).

Decorative transferred-lace fabrics: single-transfer lace ground adorned with crochet appliqués and ribbon embroidery (left), and multiple-transfer lace with colourful bobbles (right).

Yarn and material exploration

Even the simplest use of colour and yarn mixes can transport transferred stitch designs into fresh domains. The movement that multiple-transfer eyelets bring can be accentuated with colour changes. The choice of yarn will also define the clarity of the lace structure; cut-outs will be clean and crisp with a smooth and tightly spun plain yarn, but may be obscured with a fluffy, textural fibre.

Transferred lace fabrics can also serve as a ground for cords, embroidery and other decorative elements. Eyelets can be the perfect markers to follow like a grid when planning a base knitted ground that you wish to build on. In some cases, once additional materials have been laced through the pointelle holes, the openness of the fabric may be obscured completely.

Ladders

Ladders are linear openings in the fabric that can be present throughout the knitting or just in carefully selected areas. These vertical runs give the cloth lightness, adding fluidity and a gossamer touch. Laddering can work with many design sensibilities, from ethereal to graphic, and can highlight the beauty of a special yarn.

When the carriage passes a needle arrangement that contains one or more nonworking needles between two working needles, the yarn floats across the empty space. If the needles remain in this position, with each consecutive pass of the carriage the yarn floats form a vertical column. A ladder can be integrated in the following ways:

- by casting on with the designated ladder needles left in nonworking position;
- by transferring a stitch within the body of the knitting, then placing the empty ladder needle in nonworking position;
- by dropping a stitch off the ladder needle and letting it run down the length of the fabric.

TIP: *Always leave several selvedge needles knitting plain, and take note of how very open areas might affect the strength and finish of a fabric that is to be seamed. Joining small swatches together can help you practise and solve problems as you develop your design.*

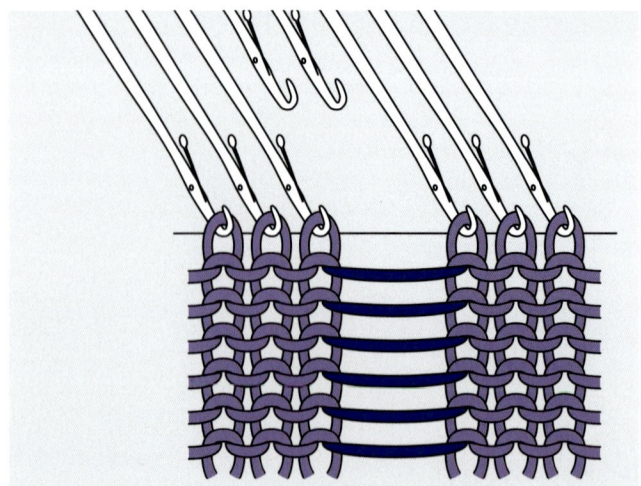

A ladder formed over two empty needles. Each float of the ladder represents a knitted row.

Incorporating ladders for added ease in the fabric

As well as being decorative, ladders can loosen tight stitch patterns created from a lot of hand-tooling, such as cables. The open space created by these vertical runs eases the framework of the textile. Whether these ladders are later reconstructed as purl or knit stitches or left as they are is a matter of preference.

Instructing ladders to knit again

The machine can be instructed to knit the empty needle again by placing it back in working position. When the carriage passes the empty needle, it forms a newly cast-on stitch.

When a ladder begins knitting again, a pointelle hole occurs between the top of the float column and the first newly formed stitch. This may be seen as a decorative feature, but it can also be hidden by closing the space with the purl bump of an adjacent needle (see page 147).

When a ladder spans two needles, use the same method as described for larger eyelets (see page 116), to help the stitches begin knitting again. For a ladder made over three or more needles, bring them back to work in stages, over several rows.

Instructing ladders to knit again (from left to right): one-stitch ladder with pointelle hole, one-stitch ladder with closed space, two-stitch, and three-stitch ladders brought back to work in steps.

After treating with fabric stiffener, this textile by knitwear designer Drew McKevitt appears both architectural and fragile. Laddering lines are accentuated by the crispness of cotton and origami-inspired folds.

Ladders created through alternative needle set-ups

The basis for this approach is using arrangements built from a mix of needles in working and nonworking position. An every-other-needle method is the simplest example, and wider ladders can be formed by leaving more needles out between groups that are knitting. Experimentation is required to find the balance between floating and closed areas of the netted fabric.

TIP: *It's important to compare the knitted fabrics both on and off the machine throughout the design development stage. While on the machine, the fabric is taut and the ladders appear defined, but once it is no longer stretched across the needle bed, the crispness of the ladders can decline.*

Ladders created through stitch transfers

Here, floating lines are created by transferring a stitch and placing the empty needle out of work at the point in the fabric where you wish the ladder to begin. The ladder continues to grow with every pass of the carriage until the needle is instructed to return to work.

Integrating irregular ladders into an otherwise orderly knit pattern can give a sense of anarchy, while engineered placements can grow to create skeletal-looking stitches. Detailed designs benefit from planning; use knitter's graph paper to plot the relationship of one ladder to another.

Ladders created through dropped stitches

Knitting a fabric to its required length and subsequently dropping a selection of needles to form ladders is essentially a reverse-engineered approach to what can also be achieved through the alternative needle set-up method. Although the results appear very similar, a dropped stitch forms a looser, more open ladder than one initiated from the cast-on. This is because knitted stitches require more yarn than floats do, so the unravelled stitch spreads out further when forming the ladder.

Dropped stitches take on new creative realms when they run down only to a certain point in the fabric. A dropped stitch will stop running only when it reaches the most recent cast-on stitch in its vertical column. The cast-on stitch is not necessarily the bottom of the fabric. If a simple stitch transfer is made in the body of the fabric and the empty stitch is left in working position, the next pass of the carriage brings a newly cast-on stitch to the needle (the same method by which a single-transfer lace hole is created). After knitting several courses, the same needle

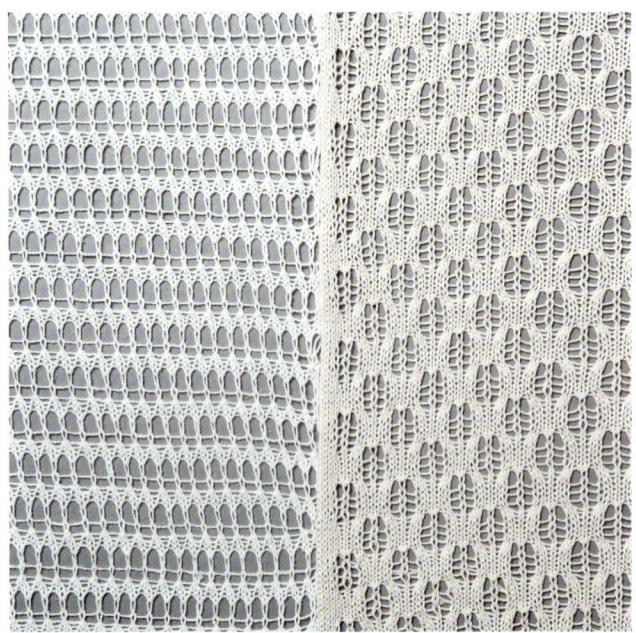

All-over drop lace creates gauzy delicate knits with an heirloom quality.

Intricately webbed design by Julien Macdonald, Spring/Summer 2016. Macdonald's signature laddered structures transport his knitwear into glamorous realms.

can have its stitch dropped. The stitch will unravel down the knitted column, until it reaches the course where the single transfer (and cast-on stitch) was made. This transfer essentially acts as a stopper or anchor for the ladder, enabling you to control the start and finish.

Keep notes when orchestrating patterns in this way. Dropping the stitch from the correct needle is crucial to the success of the fabrication, and, since the needles always remain in working position, selecting the right one may become confusing.

Designing ladder fabrics

Ladders are simple to execute, which allows them to be combined with almost any other machine-knitting technique. Because the open structures can look different when taut on the machine and relaxed off the machine, you might find that the greatest challenge is the translation of idea to physical result.

Ladders and drop stitches can add delicacy and lightness to heavier fabrics or shapely stitches, providing a contrast of grounds. Floating openings also bring a rawness that celebrates the beautifully imperfect. The process of decay and erosion in nature might inspire gauzy thread-worn knits with a vintage feel.

When openwork is uniform and repetitive, it creates organized grids within the fabric. Research for this type of ordered pattern could be derived from detailed anatomical or architectural layouts. Ladders can also be shaped throughout the body of fabric using transfer tools to increase and decrease their outer stitches.

TIP: *Experiment with gradually creating positive or negative space in the cloth. For example, you could begin knitting with an open, lacy needle set-up that slowly closes by bringing needles back into action. Alternatively, a built up textile could become increasingly fragile and transparent.*

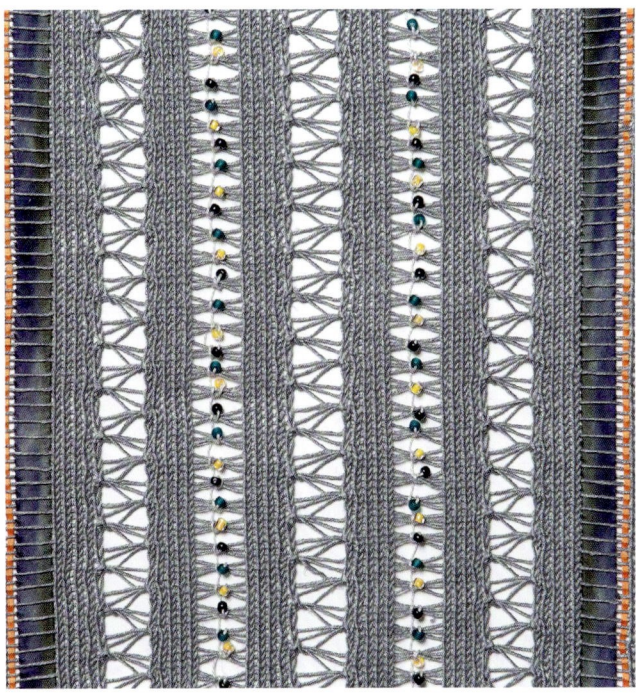

Using ladders as a canvas to add decoration to the textile.

Machine-knit fabrics inspired by crochet stitches. Isolating stitches through short-rows (top), laddering tuck layouts (middle), and double eyelets (bottom) are used to give a similar feel to crochet-stitch outcomes.

Manipulating ladder floats

Ladder floats respond particularly well to manipulation and decoration:

- If wide vertical ladders are created through alternative needle set-ups, the horizontal floats can be elevated onto working needles either side of the run. Lifting the floating strands in this way can create a beautiful trellis effect.
- Bands of floats, created by leaving many needles out of work and only a few working needles either side, can be used as fringe trimming (see page 136).
- Conventional and unconventional materials alike can be threaded or woven through the floating bars of linear ladders, which can also be added once the fabric is off the machine for more control.
- Finer threads used to fill ladders or drop stitches by needle-weaving can bring a homespun feel to the fabric, akin to an ornamental take on repair.

Crochet effects

While true crochet can be achieved only by hand, certain characteristics can be emulated through considered knitted stitches. Crochet methods can yield textiles that are just as patterned, dimensional or textural as their knitted counterparts. It is, however, for their openwork and lace structures that crocheted fabrics are particularly revered. These mesh and filigree patterns are very ornamental and are valued for warm-weather and high-end fashions that showcase detail and craftsmanship.

When interpreting another category of textiles in this way, it is useful to identify the key characteristics of its visual and compositional make-up. Crochet lace fabrics often boast large open spaces, with tall, pillar-like stitches and organic motifs. While a knitted adaptation will not be a carbon copy of this traditional craft, it can certainly have a similar feel and aesthetic.

Material choice can accentuate the desired aesthetic of crochet-inspired knits. The shimmering tape yarn used here in Jo Bee's openwork fabric would translate beautifully into an eveningwear design.

Creating open spaces

Eyelets spanning two stitches or more will create greater openings. Empty needles can be instructed to knit again straight away, or can be placed in nonworking position and systematically brought back into work to incorporate laddering.

The contrast of dense and light stitches can also form crochet-like fabrics. For instance, a few courses of small tucked or lifted stitch patterns can be sandwiched between courses of open eyelets or very loosely knitted single jersey.

Creating tall stitches with horizontal drop stitch

Very large knitted stitches can also be created to emulate the greater height of those recognizable from crochet, using a horizontal drop-stitch process. This stitch can be manipulated to resemble the broomstick lace crochet technique, as well as alternative needlework forms such as drawn-thread embroidery.

A course of horizontal drop stitch is formed by wrapping the main yarn around a ruler (or similar object) to form very long stitches, while manually knitting all the needles in the row. The larger the device, the longer the stitches will be.

1. Unthread the main yarn from the carriage, but leave it connected to the fabric on the machine.
2. Since the course will be knitted manually, the carriage should be placed to the other side of the needle bed using a free pass (see page 66).
3. Hold the ruler underneath the needles and bring the working yarn around it from back to front.
4. Place the edge needle closest to the working yarn into holding position and lay the yarn in the hook to form the stitch manually.
5. Continue in this way, bringing the yarn around the ruler from back to front and hand-knitting each stitch.
6. Once you have made the final stitch, the yarn can be threaded back into the carriage.
7. To keep the elongated stitches secure, place all needles to holding position (with the carriage set to knit them back), then carefully slide out the ruler.
8. Gently tug on the fabric to stretch the stitches to their full length.
9. Pass the carriage across to knit one course.

TIP: *Don't pass the yarn too tightly around the ruler, or it will be difficult to slide it out at the end.*

Creating tall stitches with horizontal drop stitch. *Step 3: Place the working yarn around the ruler to create the first long loop.*

Step 5: Manually knit each long loop across the course.

Many variations of this method can be explored, yielding decorative results if the elongated loops are manipulated before passing the carriage across. Begin by working Steps 1–8, but leave the needles in working position in Step 7.

The elongated stitches can be rearranged in several ways. For example:

1. Transfer the first and third stitches from their needles one at a time to the second needle. The first and third needles are now empty and the second needle holds three stitches.
2. Skip the fourth stitch, then transfer the fifth and seventh stitches to the sixth needle. Skip the eighth stitch, then continue the transfer pattern in this way.
3. Knit one course: needles with three stitches are knitted together as one, and empty needles gain a new loop.

If the stitches are rearranged in a pattern that results in two or more adjacent empty needles, it will be problematic to knit the next course. Manually knitting the course of stitches after they are transferred helps them form.

As two rows are hand knitted in the following two examples, the carriage can stay on the same side of the bed before making the elongated stitches.

1. After the transfer pattern is complete, place all needles to holding position.
2. Using the working yarn, e-wrap cast on every empty needle, and manually form the stitch on every needle holding one or more stitches.

Alternatively, to transfer stitches for a broomstick lace effect:

1. Remove the first stitch from its needle using a one-prong transfer tool, then remove the second and third stitches in the same way so that all three are on the tool.
2. Transfer the stitches as a group back to the three empty needles by spreading them open together and slipping them onto the needles as if they were one. To help with this, place another one-prong transfer tool into the group of stitches to hold them taut, and bring the empty needles to upper working position before sliding them on. Repeat throughout the course.
3. Place all needles to holding position, ready to form the next course of stitches manually.
4. To manually knit the needles sharing a group of stitches, lay the working yarn in the hook of the first stitch and bring the needle back to working position. Then place the same needle back to holding position and manually form the stitch again. Repeat.

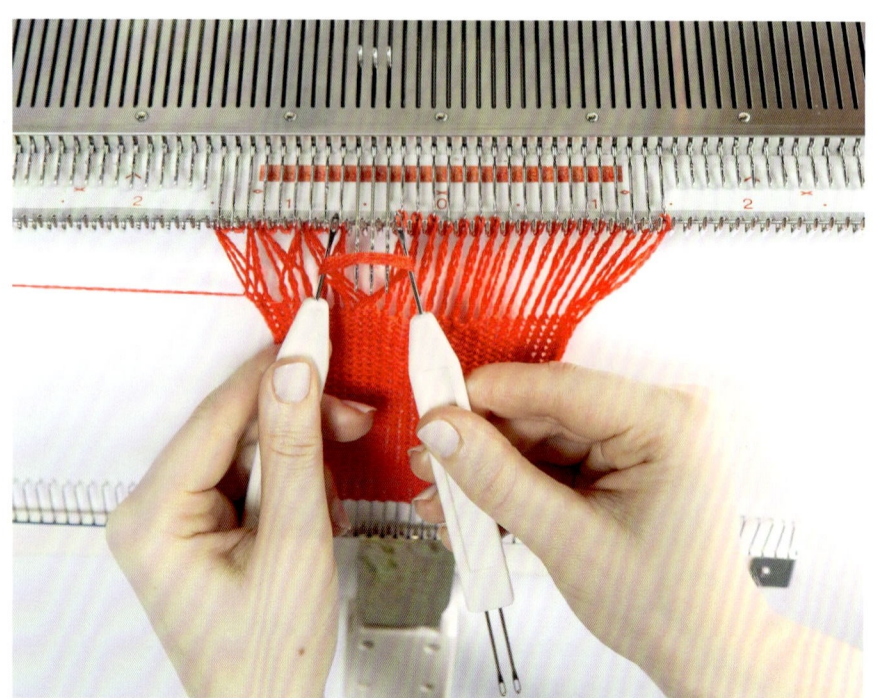

Creating a broomstick lace effect. *Step 2: Use two transfer tools to hold open the group of elongated stitches as they are transferred back to their needles.*

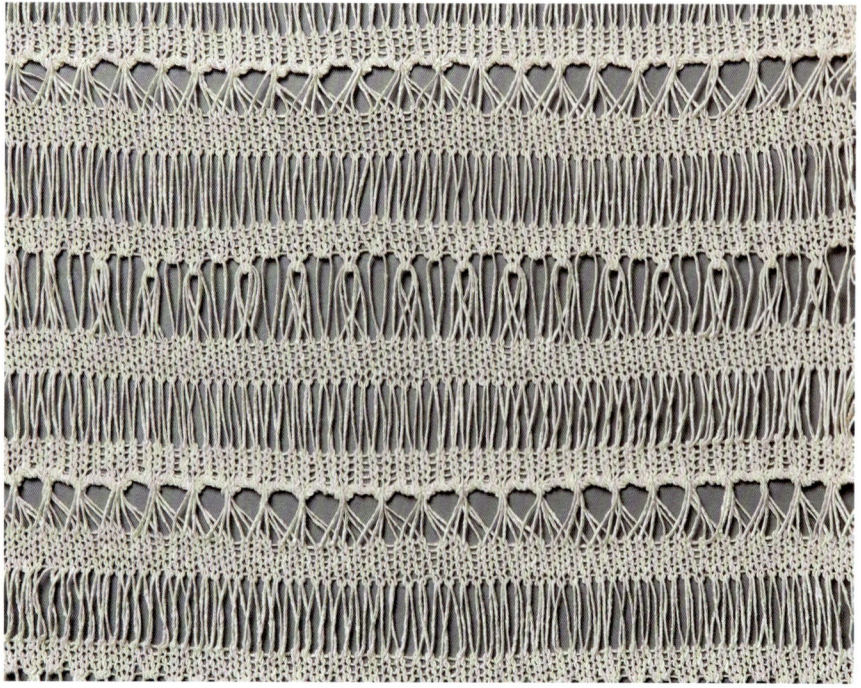

Bands of horizontal drop stitch left plain and with transferred stitch effects.

Tuck lace

By simply having a mix of needles in working and nonworking position, tuck-stitch fabrics can be transported into a new category.

The only difference between this version of tuck stitch and others is the open needle set-up. Therefore, this type of fabric must adhere to the same set of requirements as standard tuck stitch (see pages 93–94).

Creating the needle set-up

To create the lace effect, certain stitches are transferred to their neighbouring needles, and the newly empty needles placed in nonworking position. Depending on the pattern that is being set up, the stitches can be moved to the needle to the left or right. In some very open structures there may be several nonworking needles surrounding those that tuck. In that case, you can decide to transfer all the stitches at the same time within the same course, or in stages over several courses. Alternatively, it can be easier to establish this structure by leaving ladder needles out of work when casting on.

Once the needle set-up is complete, start knitting the tuck design according to the manual or automated machine instructions.

Adapting tuck-stitch patterns for tuck lace

Many of the stitch patterns used for regular tuck stitch can be easily adapted to create these lace fabrics. There is no need to physically change the written chart (for manual machines) or the punchcard. Instead, make a note or mark where the transferred stitch ladders will be added to the existing pattern. Any needles knitting as plain background stitches can be transferred to form the open ladders, while the tucking stitches should remain as they are. It is possible to create several variations of tuck lace from the same initial pattern; increasing the number of needles out of work will result in lacier versions.

Repeats formed by tucking the same stitch throughout the fabric are often the simplest to work with. Once the stitches have been transferred at the start of the pattern to create the ladders, the needles are left out of action until the end of the sequence. If the pattern contains tuck stitches that are staggered throughout the repeat, however, the empty ladder needles might also need to be shifted around in order to follow. This will entail placing the first repeat of ladder needles back in action, and transferring the next set so that they are out of work.

Tuck-lace fabrics can be suitable for a wide range of applications depending on the openness of the laddering needle set-up.

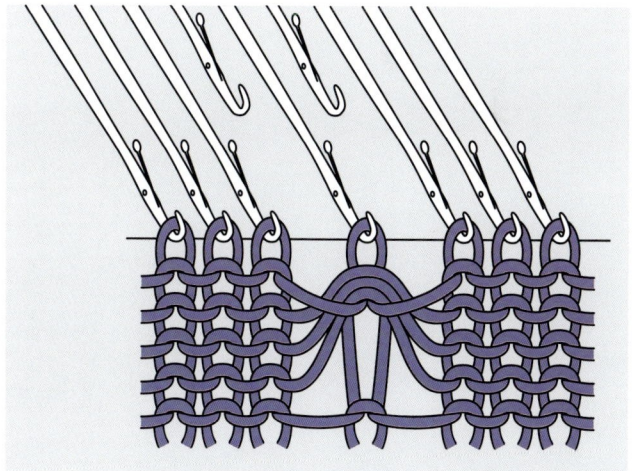

Tuck lace is created by combining tuck and ladder stitch structures.

Thread lace

Also described as punch lace, this technique is worked on machines that can knit automated patterns. The clever visual outcome results from the juxtaposition of two contrasting yarn weights. While there are no true openings in the fabric, stitches knitted in a very fine yarn give the appearance of a lattice when patterned with those in a thicker yarn.

Yarn

Using sewing thread or a very fine yarn that is transparent or of the same colour as the thicker main material gives the appearance of real cut-outs. A contrasting colour will create a striking lace effect too, but will be more obvious. The main yarn will be the most visible, and it must be a suitable weight for the machine gauge.

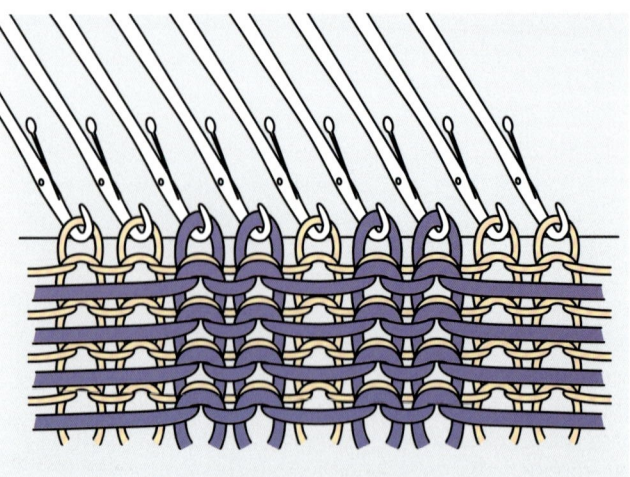

Two contrasting weight yarns give the appearance of openings in thread lace patterns. Both yarns knit the 'closed' areas, but only the finer one knits the 'open' areas.

Knitting method

To knit thread lace:

1. Cast on with the thicker yarn and complete the punchcard pattern preparation row.
2. Add the finer yarn into the carriage feeder so that they are threaded in the same way as for Fair Isle: the background (thicker) yarn in the main feeder and the contrast (finer) yarn in the second feeder.
3. Set the punchcard to the feed position and the cam to knit punch lace.
4. As the carriage brings both yarns across the bed, they knit according to the pattern card.
5. The punched areas in the pattern card represent the lace openings in the fabric. The unpunched signify the textile's solid ground.
6. Both the lace and the main yarn knit as one throughout the solid stitches (in a similar way to plating). The lace stitches, however, are formed by the lace yarn only, and as it knits, the thicker main yarn floats across the purl side of the work (as in Fair Isle).

Experimental thread lace outcome using a floral motif punchcard pattern. After knitting, the organic shapes within the solid ground were highlighted through thicker wool embroidery.

Designing thread-lace patterns

Most patterns designed for Fair Isle will also produce exciting thread-lace fabrics. Small-scale arrangements with closely formed repeats of open and closed areas will produce mesh-like textiles. Alternatively, the design can be based on larger solid motifs on a mesh background, which can emulate more classic pictorial lace effects.

By ensuring that the thread-lace stitches are implemented in small clusters, you can prevent the resulting reverse-side floats from becoming too long. Since no floats occur when both yarns knit together, there is no restriction in the size of these closed areas. If the fine yarn knits two vertical repeats of the same stitch, the resulting area will look like a larger opening or 'lace hole', more pronounced and contrasting against the thicker main yarn.

While a typical or traditional lace appearance is best achieved with a transparent lace yarn and minimal floats, you can create other very creative effects when you go against this. Yarns of contrasting colour and texture, as well as different lengths of float, can impart an air of fragility to the fabric, making it perfect for sensual garments or evening styles.

TIP: *If feeding fine yarn evenly from its source proves difficult, add a yarn sock to help control it (see page 36). Dropped stitches in a fine, slippery yarn can become tricky to fix, so knit more slowly than normal. Bringing a few selvedge needles into holding position (with the carriage set to knit them back) can prevent accidents from occurring on the edge stitches.*

Cast-off openings

In this method, it is possible to create openings of any size. It uses a strand of yarn to cast stitches off and cast them back on, and it can match or contrast with the one threaded into the carriage.

If the stitches are cast off and cast on again straight away – without the carriage knitting a course in between – the openings will appear more like horizontal slits with cleanly finished edges. However, if the carriage knits one or more courses between casting off and casting on, horizontal floats or ladders will occur. Both types will yield equally exciting outcomes.

Cast-off openings can create very different fabrics depending on their size, shape and arrangement. Small, organized versions can resemble cut-work embroidery, while several slits formed close together can emulate open nets. The more stitches that are cast off, the larger the resulting hole. There are also opportunities to work into the outlines of these openings manually, using a crochet hook to chain around the hole, or adding embroidery or beading. You can create a single slit or several slits in the same course.

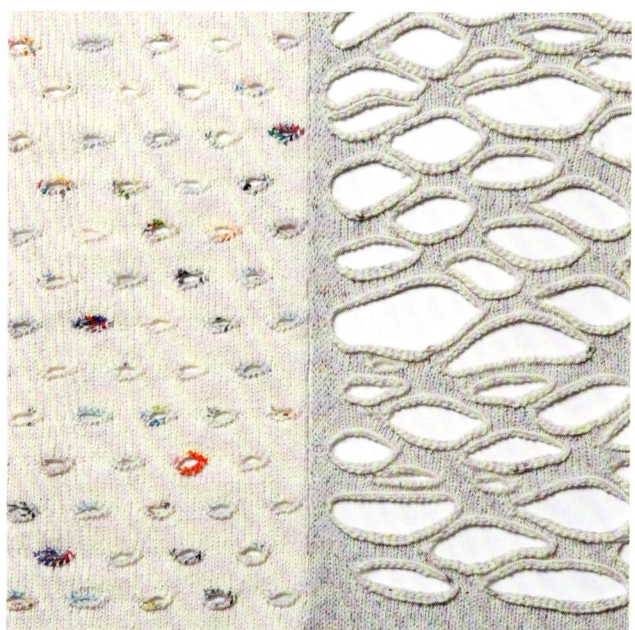

Openings that are cast off and cast on in one sequence: small openings provide an opportunity to introduce new yarns as a subtle embellishment (left), and large cut-outs slash into the structure, transforming it into netting (right).

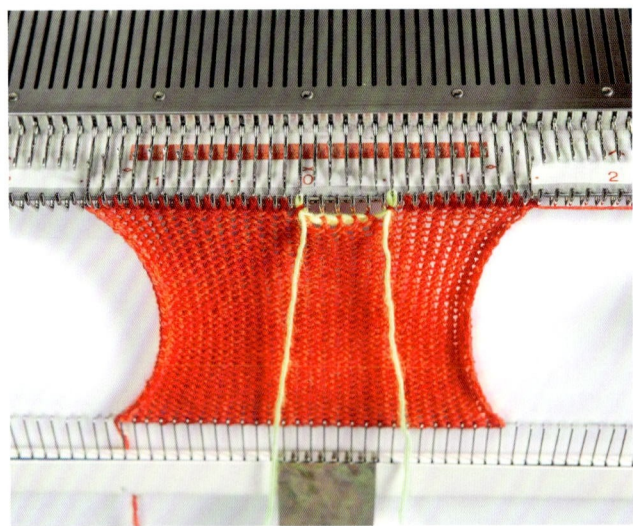

Openings that are cast off and cast on in one sequence. *Step 5: Cast off all the stitches in the opening.*

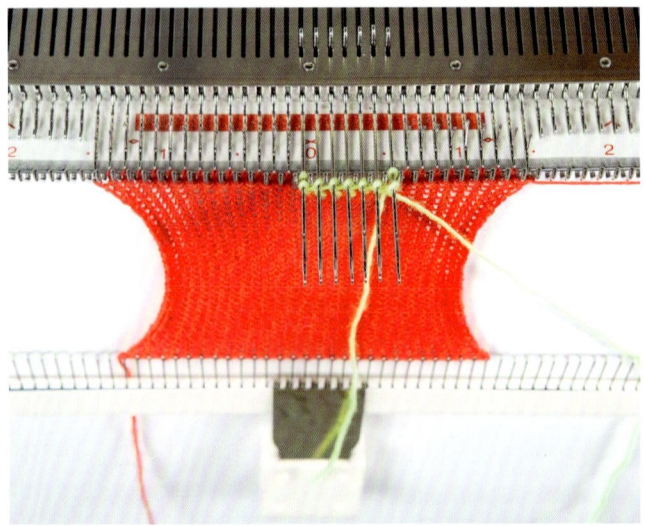

Step 6: Cast on the stitches by placing the anchor and opening needles to holding position and e-wrapping them.

Openings that are cast off and cast on in one sequence

Two edge needles, one either side of the opening needles, are used in this method to anchor the yarn strand and create an even-looking hole. For this example, the slit is worked over seven needles, five of which will become the opening and two the edge anchor stitches:

1. Cut a length of the main or a contrasting yarn.
2. Place the right edge (anchor) needle of the opening to holding position.
3. Leaving a 15–20cm (6–8in) tail (to be woven in later), lay the yarn in the right edge (anchor) needle hook and bring it back to working position so that it knits manually.
4. Place the next needle to the left to holding position – this is the first needle from the group forming the opening. Lay the yarn in the needle hook and manually knit this stitch too.
5. Use the transfer-tool method (see pages 58–59) to cast off all stitches in the opening. For the final opening stitch, transfer it to the left edge (anchor) needle, then manually knit the two stitches together. Each edge (anchor) needle now contains one stitch, and the opening needles are empty. If you are wrapping the yarn around the sinker posts to help even the tension, make sure you remove the loops after the last stitch is cast off.

6. Place the two anchor needles and the newly empty opening needles to holding position. E-wrap the left edge (anchor) needle, followed by each of the empty needles and the right edge (anchor) needle. Each anchor edge needle will now contain a stitch and an e-wrap loop, and the opening needles will each have one e-wrap loop.
7. Cut the yarn, leaving a tail to finish off later. If you are creating more openings across the same course, do so now. Pass the carriage across. Place the newly cast-on stitches to holding position for the first few courses (with the carriage set to knit them) to ensure that they form stitches properly.

Openings with knitted courses in between

This is created in a similar way, with a few modifications:

1–5. Work these steps as before, but when introducing the yarn strand into the hook of the right edge (anchor) needle, leave a tail at least double the length (more for taller openings). This tail will be used to manually knit stitches up the right side of the opening, so that the yarn is carried up the edge of the slit. If you want additional openings starting on the same row, cast the stitches off now.

6. Place the empty needles to nonworking position and set the carriage to the hold function. Place the edge (anchor) needles to holding position.

7. Knit one course. The background yarn floats over the edge (anchor) needles.

8. Lay the yarn tail closest to the right edge (anchor) needle in the right edge needle hook and knit it manually. Repeat for the left edge needle, using the end of the yarn closest to this needle.

9. Place the edge (anchor) needles to holding position. As you do so, make sure the background yarn float is now under the edge (anchor) needles, rather than floating over them. Knit one course.

10. Repeat Steps 8 and 9 for the required number of courses. Manually knit the edge (anchor) needles once more.

11. Disengage the hold function on the carriage and place the two anchor needles and empty needles to holding position. Using the left edge yarn tail, e-wrap the left edge (anchor) needle, each empty needle and the right edge (anchor) needle. Each anchor edge needle will now contain a stitch and an e-wrap loop, and each opening needle will have one e-wrap loop.

12. Cut the yarn, leaving a tail to finish off later. Pass the carriage across to knit one course. Be mindful of the newly cast-on stitches; bring them to holding position for the first few courses to ensure they form stitches properly.

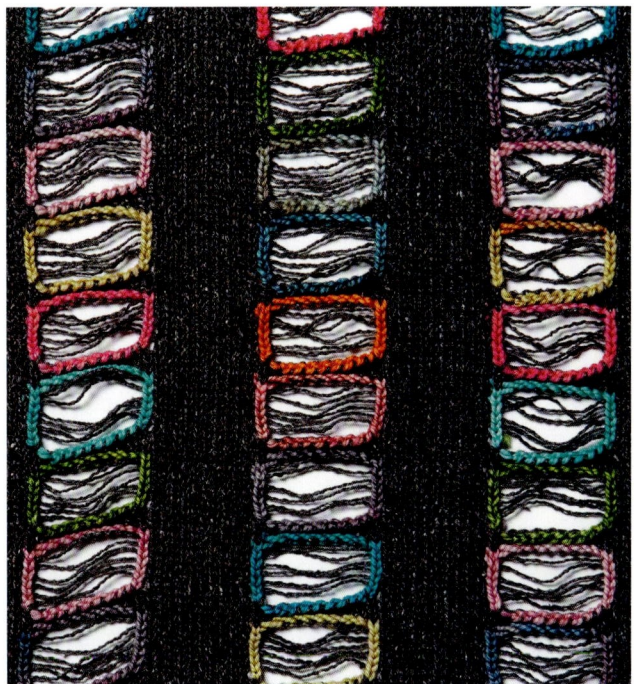

When courses are knitted in between casting off and on for an opening, the outcome appears more geometric. This is further emphasized by the regularity of the opening's pattern placement.

Embellishment

The anatomy of knitted fabric lends itself particularly well to embellishment and adornment, and the composition of knitted stitches can indicate which areas might be highlighted through decoration.

The methods detailed here are only a small sample of the possibilities. There is no reason why textile treatments not typically associated with knitwear cannot be explored.

TIP: *Testing smaller swatches that are finished and blocked allows you to analyze the weight and visibility of the embellishment in relation to the knitted ground, test the colourfastness of embroidery threads, and ensure that any additions are secure and practical for the wearer or user.*

Beading

Beads and sequins add intricacy to knitted fabrics and they can be introduced in a range of aesthetics and styles. They can give a subtle sparkle to an already multifaceted fabric, complement and add another layer to colour work, accentuate directional and pronounched stitches, and even transform the simplest of knitted structures into a shimmering second skin. Bejewelled knits can be created in two ways: by adding adornments while the fabric is knitting on the machine; or by sewing them onto a finished piece. Aside from the preference of the maker, the approach depends on the materials, and the desired design.

Selecting beads

The abundant finish, size, shape and composition of commercial embellishments can provide a wealth of inspiration for designers. Hardware outlets, sewing notion stores and resellers of vintage clothing are all places where you can obtain less conventional trimmings.

Any item with a hole of the appropriate size can be affixed to knitted fabric, although it is important to consider the relationship of the embellishment to the yarn. If a very large bead is applied to a textile knitted from a fine yarn, it may cause strain, hang awkwardly and overpower the surface. On the other hand, small embellishments may become hidden in a fabric created from a more substantial yarn, or one that is highly textured. Paying attention to this balance also helps to prevent the textile from becoming too heavy, since adornments add weight that may pull or distort a delicate knit. Heavier beads should be used sparingly and paired with a yarn that is strong enough to support them.

Striking hooded knit top adorned with feather-like embellishments. By Delpozo, Autumn/Winter 2017.

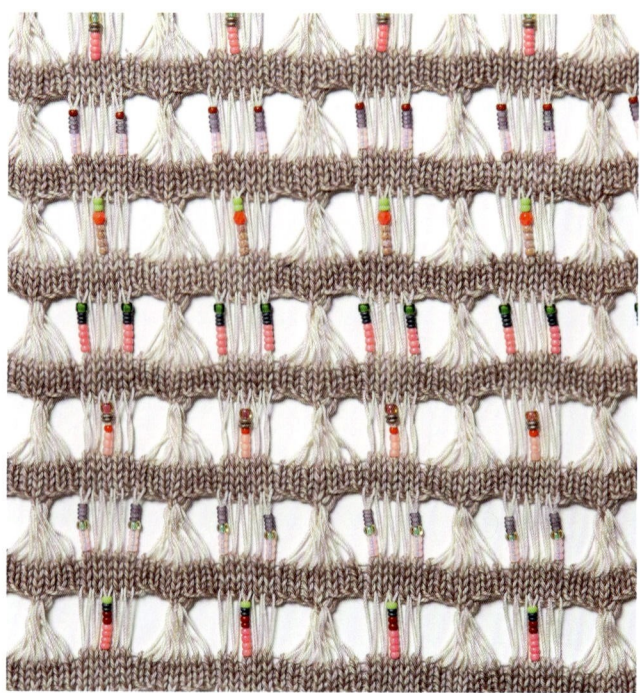

Seeds beads stacked onto long loops created with horizontal drop stitch.

Beading during knitting

Adding beads while you knit is the most secure way to attach them, as they are firmly embedded in the makeup of the fabric and there is less risk of them becoming loose with wear and laundering. This approach can yield a uniform look, allowing you to count needles easily for pattern placement while the knitting is held taut on the machine. The other main advantage to synchronizing knitting and embellishing is that the fabric is essentially complete once it is cast off (albeit with some simple finishing).

The most common way of adding beads while knitting produces fabrics with visible embellishments on both knit and purl side. Beads are added one at a time, suspended on the stitches themselves. The bead's hole must be large enough for the knitted stitch to be pulled through. To check this, thread your chosen bead onto a double strand of the yarn (which represents both 'legs' of the knitted stitch). A thread crochet hook fine enough to fit through the bead is also used to help. To add a bead in this way:

1. Slide the bead onto the crochet hook.
2. Use the hook to remove the selected stitch from its needle. Once the stitch is on the hook, pull it through the bead.
3. Use a one-prong transfer tool to return the now beaded stitch to its needle.
4. Before passing the carriage across, make sure the bead is positioned securely under the needle so that it doesn't get caught.

Beads are sprinkled in to this Fair Isle pattern, adding pops of colour.

Adding larger beads during knitting

Larger beads risk becoming too close to the carriage as it passes to knit. To create more space for the bead and a clearer path for the carriage, additional courses must be knit. To add a larger embellishment:

1. Knit to the course where you want it to appear, then knit at least one more course.
2. Slide the embellishment onto the crochet hook.
3. Place the hook into the stitch where you want to place the embellishment, and drop the above stitch from its needle so that it unravels to this point.
4. Pull the stitch through the embellishment, then reconstruct the dropped stitch using a latch tool. Reconstructing as purl stitches will give an invisible finish, whereas latching up as knit stitches can contribute to an additional design feature. Return the stitch to its needle.

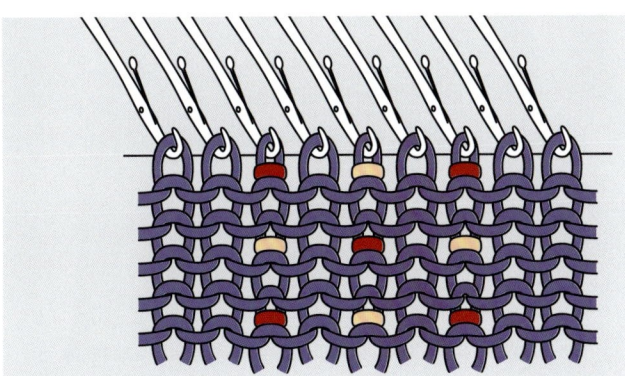

Adding beads during knitting ensures they are locked securely into the construction of the fabric.

Adding beads through weaving

An alternative way of adding beads while you knit is by incorporating them through weaving or wrapping. As with all knit-weave outcomes, the surface detail will be displayed on the purl side of the fabric. The embellishments must be pre-strung onto the highlight yarn before weaving. Large, unusually shaped adornments or those that dangle or drop from the surface may benefit from being added in this way. For bead weaving:

1. String the required number of embellishments onto the yarn. For vertical weaving, tie a knot or add a clip or stopper to the yarn tail to prevent the beads from falling off.
2. Place the desired number of needles to holding position and set the carriage to knit them back.
3. Weave or wrap the beaded yarn loosely over and under or around the needles by hand, making sure the beads stay below them. Keeping the interlacing a little slack ensures that there is room for the carriage to pass above the bead.
4. Pass the carriage across. Pull the woven yarn gently to remove any slack. This neatens the yarn and leaves the bead in the correct place.

Beading after knitting

Attaching adornments after the fabric has been knitted and is off the machine can yield a more creative and free-form result, since it allows the designer to view the textile or garment as a whole. This is useful when mapping out a complex, organic or large-scale design, and also permits changes to be made at will.

Through sewing, a more diverse range of beads, sequins and other materials can be applied with fewer restrictions. Sewing thread and a fine embroidery needle have the advantage of being able to travel easily through the smallest of bead holes, opening up a multitude of dainty and delicate jewelled options. Large or unusually shaped embellishments benefit, as they can be secured to the surface of the cloth without becoming entangled in the carriage's path.

Particularly beguiling fabrics can be created when embellishments applied in this way follow the knitted stitch pathway. This gives you the opportunity to highlight an aspect of the textile in a way that would be difficult while it is still on the machine.

Mixed yarn knit-weave fabric featuring larger beads and wrapped beaded loops.

Burberry's Spring/Summer 2012 reinterpretation of a handcrafted pullover utilizes graphic wooden beading to give the appearance of a traditional Fair Isle patterned yoke.

Embroidery

Knitted fabric is the perfect canvas to stitch into. Such decoration allows the designer to integrate numerous colours that could become unwieldy to knit. Embroidery can also give fresh tactile interest to the cloth, enhancing stitches or garment details in eclectic ways. The frame of knitting lends itself particularly well to embroidery, with its horizontal stitches and vertical rows acting as a grid to guide the composition.

Embroidering differing fabric types

A plain knit fabric allows the embroidery to take centre stage, and may be best for large intarsia-like designs, detailed motifs or graphics. The potential for customization can be exemplified even further if a garment has a very simple shape, such as a drop-sleeve sweater.

When a largely single-jersey ground is scattered with other stitches (such as eyelets, tuck or reconstructed ones), they can provide subtle visual markings for embroidery, ensuring that the layout of the applied stitches appears uniform. These stitch guides may be barely noticeable once the surface is worked into.

Another approach is to use embroidery in such a way that it does not hide but in fact emphasizes a knitted stitch or method. In this case, the build of the textile leads the way, and once it is off the machine it can be analyzed to suggest how and where the embroidery might go. As a result, the surface decoration appears integral to the stitch arrangement of the cloth, bringing with it a unique design interpretation.

Whether you are embroidering a plain fabric or one comprised of complex stitches, consider the relationship between the two design elements. To stop them jarring with each other, parallels can be made through colour, texture, line and scale. Depending on your approach, the yarn and stitch for the knitted ground might dictate the embroidery design, or you might use an embroidery layout as a starting point and determine the stitch pattern that it suggests.

Scattered lace holes were integrated into this knitted ground to guide the positioning of its surface embroidery.

Detail of a garment that is heavily decorated with bead embroidery. The tuck-stitch fabric provides a grid-like base to inform the needlework style and placement.

Selecting embroidery materials

Knitting yarns, specialist threads and novelty materials such as ribbons and cords can all be used in surface embroidery. The process causes the material to twist and turn as it moves through the fabric, and some threads and yarns will respond better to this than others. If the yarn struggles to lie flat, it may not be suitable for longer embroidery stitches, for example. To test how your chosen materials react, complete a small area in the selected stitch or design.

It may take some exploration to settle on a yarn or thread weight that works with the knitted ground. If the embroidery stitches are too fine in relation to the knitted ones, they may lack dimension and be visually lost. Designs completed in thicker yarn may contribute to a certain aesthetic statement, but they can also stretch or overpower the knitted fabric. Finding a balance is key to a successful visual outcome that does not compromise the textile form.

Inspiration and approach

There are countless stunning examples of decorative cloths that span historical and cultural horizons and display mixes of intriguing colour, pattern and artistic arrangement. Embroidery can elevate a knitted textile to a couture creation or draw attention to a stylistic line in an otherwise minimal garment.

A multitude of traditional embroidery stitches can be developed and explored in a knitwear context. Knitted stitches can be imitated through cross stitch or duplicate stitch (see page 85), while satin stitch can emulate sketchy lines akin to graffiti, and bullion knots add a coiled dimension.

TIP: *It can be helpful to begin an embroidered design by drawing it on paper, including as much detail as possible. With the help of a book of embroidery stitches, translate the sketched lines, matching their movement and character. Existing stitches can be altered and manipulated for a fresh interpretation.*

Cords, braids and fringe

These are narrow strips of fabric that can be constructed using a range of techniques. Since only small groups of needles are selected for each trimming, they can feature elaborate hand-crafted methods that might not be considered for a larger knitted area. They can be used in a garment as an interesting edging, inset, lacing or surface appliqué, or can be used in multiples to form a textile. Woven braids such as passementerie, which boast tassels, fringing and exquisite detailing, can be inspirational starting points for decorative knitting of this type.

Cords, braids and fringe can be utilized as trimmings or as fabrications in their own right.

Braids

Knitted braids can be formed over more stitches than cords. If methods such as cables, tucking or partial knitting are worked over the group of stitches, they bring body and shape, and interesting contours can be produced, with edges that curve and wave. Very ornate braids may be created from weaving methods, as thicker, decorative yarns as well as machine-knitted cords can be laced into the fabric as it knits. Several cords or woven strands can be introduced, crossed and intertwined with one another at different points on the knitted braid.

Some designs may be better suited to being knitted horizontally, with the cast-on stitches forming the length of the braid rather than the width. While this is fine for small trimmings, be aware that longer lengths will be limited to the width of the machine. Assess whether several smaller pieces can be joined to form a larger one, or if the design should be adjusted so that it is knitted in the other direction.

London based brand WLE by Egle Vaituleviciute combines knit and woven methods in her bespoke pieces for the home. After constructing lengths of knitted cord, Vaituleviciute interlaces her handmade materials into sophisticated patterns.

Cords

Simple cords can be created by knitting over a very small group of stitches. The most straightforward method is to knit a single-jersey strip of fabric no more than five stitches wide. Since the natural inclination of plain knitting is to roll at the edges, the result is a tightly curled cord rather than a flat ribbon. Wider strips of fabric knitted in this way will still have rolled edges but will look more like a flap than a cord.

For a more rounded effect mirroring that of a two-needle hand-knitted I-cord, the machine must be configured so that it knits the needles in one direction and misses them in the other. On every miss-stitch course a float is formed, which, when repeated several times, pulls the edges of the strip together. Machine-knitted I-cords are most successful when knitted over no more than six needles. For both approaches, a tighter stitch size will yield a more compact cord.

Cords can be laced and threaded through many fabric structures. They may also be used to build the fabric itself, by weaving, knotting or tying several together in various configurations.

Fringe

Knitted fringe is created using alternate needle arrangements, by casting on the left- and right-edge stitches of the trim with the yarn floating over the empty needles in between. With every pass of the carriage, the edges knit as normal while floating strands build between them. There is little limit to the size of fringe that can be created; the needle set-up can be altered in various ways to construct differently sized edges and floats.

Once it is knitted, fringe made in this way may be used exactly as is, or with an edge cut to release the knitted strands into a tasselled effect. To cut it, use sharp scissors to trim away one of the knitted edges. If you are cutting, it is not necessary to knit more than two stitches over the edge that is to be trimmed.

TIP: *Fringe generally looks most effective when the strands appear full and plush. Tightening the stitch size and combining several finer ends of yarn can achieve this.*

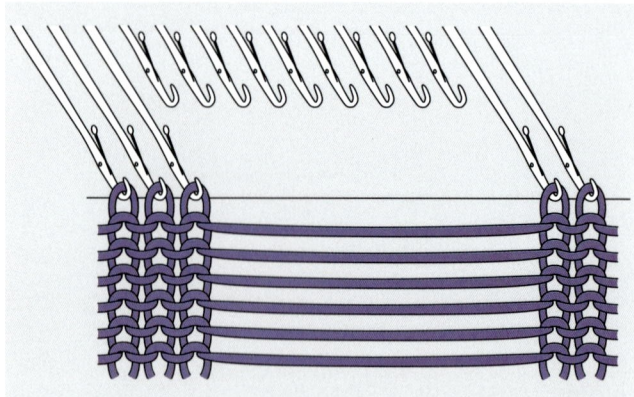

Fringe requires several needles to be in nonworking position, with edge stitches knitting either side.

For cut fringe, trim carefully along one of the knitted edges.

Felting

Most people have experienced the effect of washing a beloved item of knitwear at too high a temperature. What was once a perfectly fitting garment can turn into a dense and minute shadow of its former self. But when it is done as a controlled surface treatment, felting or fulling can transform the appearance and handle of a knitted textile for the better.

This type of finish is created by washing the fabric in soapy water, either by hand or in a washing machine. As the knitting is washed, the hot water penetrates the fibres, causing them to open up and swell. At this point, friction is applied to the fabric, agitating the malleable fibres and causing them to entangle permanently with one another. Exposing these fibres to cold water locks them together further, changing the cloth.

Detail of a knitted cushion by Emily Watts, the designer behind The Good Shepherd, who creates richly textured home products using 100% British wool. After knitting, Emily boil washes the fabric to achieve a felted finish.

Yarn

The type of yarn is the most important factor in the success (or otherwise) of a felted finish, and animal fibres, such as wool, mohair, alpaca and cashmere, all respond very well. Blended yarns will still felt to some degree, as long as there is enough of the animal fibre present. Manufactured fibres will not felt at all, but they can be combined with those that do to create fabrics with contrasting surfaces. Avoid yarns that have been treated with a finish to help prevent them from shrinking in the wash.

Approach and applications

Exploring felting can be similar to a science experiment, in that the intended effect is often achieved only through repeated testing and recording of results. This is because of the difficulty of predicting how the yarn will respond when washed, the rate at which the fabric will shrink, and the time or method it takes to make it do so.

The fabric should be knitted at a much looser stitch size than normal, to leave space for the fibres to contract. This may also need to be altered through experimentation; if the resulting felted textile is too dense, select an even looser stitch size next time. Keep detailed notes so that it becomes clear what needs to be adjusted.

For a gentle and controlled effect, wash and agitate the textile by hand. This can be done in a very subtle way, to yield a knit that appears lightly brushed. Felting a range of different stitches can be an inspiring way to start this process. Textural techniques such as pleats, tucks and ruching respond particularly well to felting, as the denseness of the cloth emphasizes their traits.

While there may be limits to the types of garment these firmer fabrications can be used for, they become excellent choices for accessories or interior applications. Densely felted fabric can be cut without the risk of unravelling, and so shapes or pattern pieces may be sliced and sewn from it. In addition, smaller shapes may be used for surface decorations such as appliqués and embellishments.

Part 3

Construction

Uniquely structured knit-weave
fabrication utilizing different coloured
I-cords, by Anna Husemann.

Chapter 7

Tension and Shaping

Tension or 'gauge' refers to the number of stitches and rows per centimetre or inch in a knitted fabric. Determining the tension of a textile is the first step in creating a garment or other outcome to a particular set of measurements. To do so, a large piece of fabric known as a tension or gauge swatch is knitted, blocked and measured.

Using information gathered from the swatch, you can determine the knitting instructions that will enable the intended design to be created to the precise size. These include how many stitches to cast on; how many courses to knit; and, if it requires shaping, the frequency in which increases or decreases are to be made. Accuracy in this phase of the design process is imperative if the result is to match your intention.

Tension

A knitted course, or horizontal line of loops within a fabric, is used to determine the stitch tension, and a knitted wale, or vertical line of loops, determines the row tension. For example, the stitch tension of my fabric may read as 2 stitches per centimetre (5 stitches per inch) and the row tension as 2.8 rows per centimetre (7 rows per inch). A fabric's tension will change according to a broad range of variables such as the type of yarn, the stitch size, the pattern and the knitting machine.

The tension swatch

No matter your experience or skill, it is impossible to knit a fabric to exact measurements correctly by eye or using guesswork. Measuring the knitting while it is still on the machine, or not following the correct procedure for a tension sample, will result in inaccuracy. You may be tempted to save time (and yarn) by measuring a small swatch created during design development, rather than

knitting a new one, but be assured that the larger sample is well worth the effort; it will give a much more accurate reading than a small piece of fabric.

Before you knit a tension sample, complete all the necessary design development work. If there are further iterations to explore, such as alternative yarn mixes, adjustments to stitch size or different placement of pattern repeats, keep doing so until you are happy with the result. The swatch must exactly match the fabric of the end product. The following factors should be kept consistent throughout:

Yarn Even if alternate yarns appear to be a similar weight or texture, it is essential that the yarn for the end project is used. It is even important to use the same colour, since dyeing can affect the quality of the yarn and its behaviour as it is knitted.

Stitch and pattern Each stitch type can affect the tension of a fabric differently. Single jersey will yield a unique reading from tuck stitch in the same yarn, for example. Do not adapt a stitch or pattern to fit the scale of the swatch. Keep to the exact proportion of the pattern repeat, selecting the same number of needles and knitting the same number of courses in between, as you intend to do for the final outcome.

Stitch size Even the slightest alteration in stitch size will affect the outcome. If the knitted textile design contains several stitch sizes (because of a mix of yarns or stitches, for example), this must be reflected.

Machine Knitting on a machine that isn't the one you will use for the final product can lead to irregularities. Even if the machines are an identical brand and gauge, their unique calibration can be subtly different.

Blocking and finishing The textile should be treated exactly as you intend to treat the final piece – for instance when washing, blocking, embellishing or carrying out surface manipulations such as felting.

TIP: *Keeping detailed notes will ensure that the swatch and the final design are knitted identically, leading to a well-executed outcome.*

Knitting a tension swatch ensures the garment design will fit as intended. This is particularly important for close-fitting silhouettes such as this, constructed with set-in sleeves and travelling cable stitches. By Norah Gaughan for Brooklyn Tweed.

Working with different fabrics

It is sometimes necessary to knit more than one tension sample for a project. A sweater with different fabric designs on the front and back, for example, will require a separate swatch for each piece, and a scarf featuring a patchwork of patterns will require a swatch to reflect each stitch type. To establish the number needed, determine how many individual fabrics make up the design. You will need a sample for each one.

If, after measuring, you discover a significant discrepancy between the tension reading of the fabrics, you will need to assess if they are suited to be used with one another. A difference in row tension between two fabric types can be addressed relatively easily; one fabric may require more or fewer courses than the other to achieve the same knitted measurement. A vastly contrasting stitch tension is more difficult to deal with, however, without physically changing the needle set-up on the machine. If two stitch readings are too different, you may need to make so many alterations while knitting that the piece will be very awkward to knit.

TIP: *For simplicity, when working with two fabrics with only slightly different stitch tensions you may choose to use the average number throughout. But do remember that this adjustment will affect the end measurements.*

Knitting the tension swatch

Before beginning the sample, select a waste yarn in a contrasting colour but similar weight to your main material.

Always take notes during the process. If you are testing several stitch sizes in the same design, or creating similar-looking outcomes, use markers to identify the different fabrics. For example, create eyelet holes at the bottom of the knitting to indicate the stitch-size number or to assign the sample a number that corresponds to your written notes. You can also weave or sew a small strand of contrastingly coloured thread or yarn into the surface as a visual indication of the specifications of the piece.

Although the concept and formula of knitting a tension swatch are the same regardless of the machine gauge, the numbers in the knitting instructions can be customized to keep the fabric in proportion as best suits the machine.

Several tension samples are needed to calculate the measurements and knitting instructions for designs constructed from a mix of stitch patterns. Patchwork pullover by Missoni, Autumn/Winter 2020.

Markers help to classify similar looking tension swatches. These two fabrics use lace holes (left), and a contrasting colour yarn woven into the surface (right) as distinguishing details.

These directions give instructions for the four different machine gauges: fine, standard, mid and bulky. As long as you knit a large enough piece to obtain an accurate tension reading, any combination of cast-on stitches, knitted courses and needles between the yarn markers can be used.

1. Cut two strands of waste yarn approximately 15cm (6in) long. These will be placed into the fabric in Step 6 to serve as stitch markers.
2. Using the main yarn, cast on:
    *   Fine gauge – 90 stitches in the centre of the needle bed (45 needles both sides of the centre mark '0')
    *   Standard gauge – 70 stitches in the centre of the needle bed (35 needles both sides of the centre mark '0')
    *   Mid-gauge – 60 stitches in the centre of the needle bed (30 needles both sides of the centre mark '0')
    *   Bulky gauge – 40 stitches in the centre of the needle bed (20 needles both sides of the centre mark '0')
3. Using the main yarn, knit in the fabric design pattern for:
    *   Fine gauge – 30 courses
    *   Standard gauge – 20 courses
    *   Mid-gauge – 15 courses
    *   Bulky gauge – 10 courses
4. Change to the waste yarn and knit two courses in single jersey.
5. Change to the main yarn and knit in the fabric design pattern for:
    *   Fine gauge – 40 courses
    *   Standard gauge – 30 courses
    *   Mid-gauge – 20 courses
    *   Bulky gauge – 15 courses
6. Using the waste yarn markers, mark:
    *   Fine gauge – the 26th needle on both sides of the centre mark '0'
    *   Standard gauge – the 21st needle on both sides of the centre mark '0'
    *   Mid-gauge – the 16th needle on both sides of the centre mark '0'
    *   Bulky gauge – the 11th needle on both sides of the centre mark '0'
    Push the two needles into holding position, and lay each yarn marker in the needle hook. Place the two needles back to working position – the yarn markers are now in place.

Tension swatch knitted on a standard gauge machine.

7. Using the main yarn, knit in the fabric design pattern for:
    *   Fine gauge – 40 courses
    *   Standard gauge – 30 courses
    *   Mid-gauge – 20 courses
    *   Bulky gauge – 15 courses
8. Change to the waste yarn and knit two courses in single jersey.
9. Change to the main yarn and knit in the fabric design pattern for:
    *   Fine gauge – 30 courses
    *   Standard gauge – 20 courses
    *   Mid-gauge – 15 courses
    *   Bulky gauge – 10 courses
10. Cast off.

Measuring the tension swatch

While the knitting is stretched widthways across the needle bed, it is being pulled taut. After it is removed from the machine, it must be allowed to relax so that the stitches can assume their natural shape. To aid this process, let the length of the fabric roll onto itself and, holding the top and bottom edges, pull it gently.

TIP: *It is recommended to leave the sample for as long as possible before blocking it, ideally several hours or overnight.*

The sample should be blocked in the same way as you intend to do for the final outcome (see page 175).

Place the knitting on a flat tabletop and have a ruler, notebook and pencil to hand. The width of the main fabric between the yarn markers indicates the stitch tension, and the length of the main fabric between the waste yarn is the row tension. Decide whether you are working in metric (centimetres) or imperial (inches), and record the measurements to the nearest one decimal point or ⅛in for accuracy.

Determining the stitch tension

1. Write down the total number of stitches between the inside edges of the yarn markers. For example, if you marked the 21st needles both sides of the needle-bed centre '0', there are 40 stitches between.
2. Measure and write down the width of the fabric in centimetres or inches between the inside edges of the yarn markers. This number is referred to as 'S'.
3. To calculate the number of stitches per centimetre or inch of fabric, divide the number from Step 1 by the number from Step 2.

stitches/S = stitch tension

Example
When there are 40 stitches between the yarn markers and the width of the fabric is 12cm (4¾in):

40/12cm (4¾in) = 3.3 stitches per cm (8.4 stitches per in).

Measuring between the separate strand yarn markers to determine the stitch tension of the fabric.

Measuring between the courses of waste yarn to determine the row tension of the fabric.

Determining the row tension

1. Write down the total number of courses knitted in the main fabric in the centre of the swatch, between the courses of waste yarn. For example, if you knitted 30 courses, placed yarn markers and then knitted 30 more courses, there are 60 courses in total.
2. Measure and write down the length of the fabric between the courses of waste yarn in centimetres or inches. This number is referred to as 'R'.
3. To calculate the number of rows per centimetre or inch of the fabric, divide the number from Step 1 by the number from Step 2.

\# courses/R = row tension

Example
When there are 60 courses knitted between the courses of waste yarn and the fabric is 12.7cm (5in) long:

60/12.7cm (5in) = 4.7 rows per cm (12 rows per in).

Applying the fabric's tension to the design

Once you have worked out the tension of the fabric, you can combine it with the intended measurements of the design to determine the knitting instructions.

Schematic

A schematic is a drawing (done by hand or digitally) of a garment or other outcome that illustrates the scale and measurements of the design and the construction of the piece, such as the direction in which it is knitted. Every differently shaped or sized piece of the outcome should have its own sketch. For example, for a simple sweater there should be drawings of the front piece, the back piece and one sleeve (assuming the sleeves are identical). The measurements displayed in the diagram are used in combination with the fabric's tension to calculate the knitting instructions.

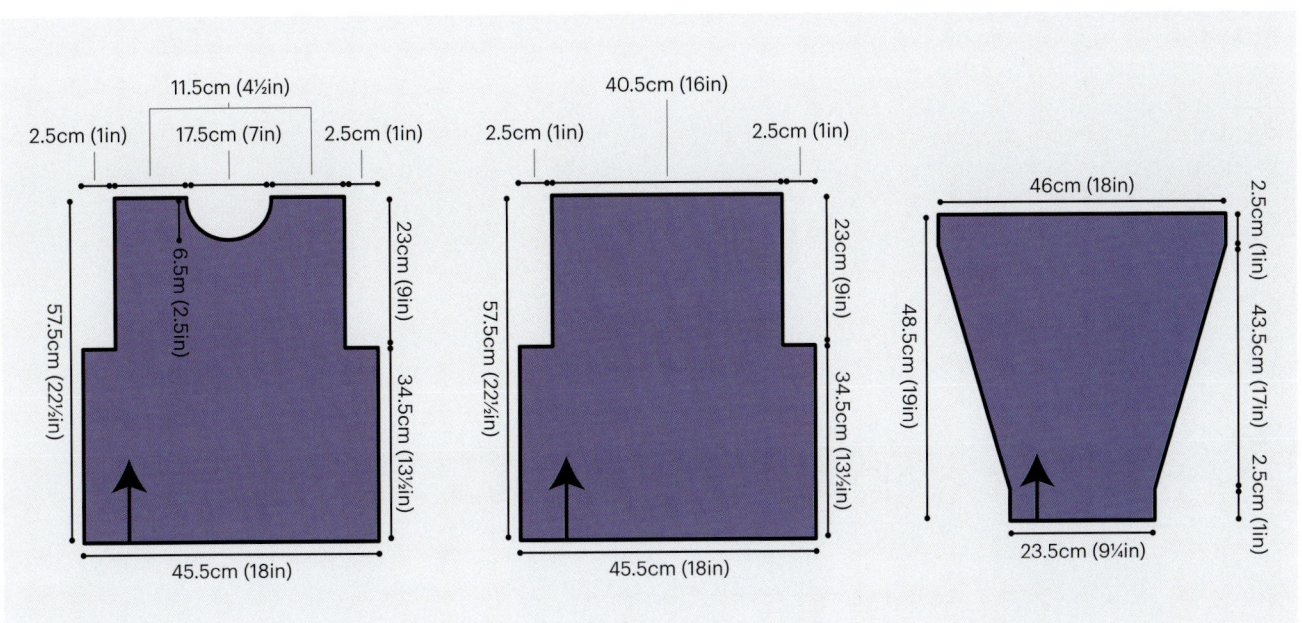

Schematic for a simple sweater illustrating the front, back and sleeve. Measurements display the intended size of the design and the arrows communicate the knitting direction of each piece.

Shaping

Translating measurements into stitches and rows

The horizontal or crosswise measurements in the schematic represent stitches. The vertical or lengthwise measurements in the schematic represent rows.

When translating measurements into stitches and rows, you must round up or down to reflect the nearest whole stitch or row number. Stitch and row numbers may also need to be adjusted to fit into the pattern repeat.

1. Write the fabric tension on the schematic so that you can refer to it easily.
2. Multiply each horizontal measurement on the schematic by the stitch tension. Write these down next to the measurements.
3. Multiply each vertical measurement on the schematic by the row tension. Write these down next to the measurements.

Example: Rectangular scarf
The fabric tension is 3.3 stitches per centimetre (8.4 stitches per inch), and 4.7 rows per centimetre (12 rows per inch). The intended size of the scarf is 25.5cm (10in) wide and 170cm (66⅞in) long.

To calculate the knitting instructions:

1. Stitches to cast on: Scarf width of 25.5cm (10in) × fabric tension of 3.3 stitches per cm (8.4 stitches per in) = 84.2 stitches (84 stitches) rounded to 84 stitches.
2. Courses to knit: Scarf length of 170cm (66⅞in) × fabric tension of 4.7 rows per cm (12 rows per in) = 799 rows (802.5 rounded to 803 rows).
3. Stitches to cast off: 84 stitches.

Therefore, to knit the scarf, you would cast on 84 stitches, knit for 799 rows (803 rows) and cast off 84 stitches.

Fabrics are often shaped to create the pieces that make up a knitted garment such as a skirt or sweater, or to create accessories such as triangular shawls, hats and socks. Shaping is also used for other outcomes that are beyond a simple square or rectangle. It can be split into three categories:

• Increasing and decreasing at the edges of the fabric
• Increasing and decreasing evenly across a row
• Increasing and decreasing with short rows

Increasing and decreasing at the edges

The number of stitches that are being added to or subtracted from the fabric is the main factor in determining which of the following methods should be used, but quality of finish is also a consideration.

• **Simple increases and decreases:** This is quick and easy but can produce irregular edges, because only a single stitch is moved. Each time the edge stitch is shifted, the column of stitches at the edge of the fabric is interrupted. As uneven edges can make seaming more difficult, simple shaping methods are best reserved for fabrics constructed from intricate stitch patterns (where the fully fashioned method would just add another layer of complexity) or for textiles that do not need to be seamed.
• **Fully fashioned increases and decreases:** This involves moving two or more stitches simultaneously using a multi-prong transfer tool. Because a group of stitches is moved, the needle holding two stitches (for a decrease) or no stitches (for an increase) is further from the edge of the fabric. As a result, the selvedge stays smooth and straight, resulting in a clean finish that is perfect for seaming. Fully fashioned shaping creates decorative lines, and will add interest to a simple single-jersey garment, for example. While it is most common to move two or three stitches, larger groups can be transferred for a more pronounced effect.

TIP: *When shaping textiles that are created from repeating stitches or patterns, it is better to complete the fully fashioned increase or decrease first, then form the stitch pattern. The newly increased or decreased and edge stitches should be left free of any stitch patterns or manipulations so that the selvedge remains clean and undisturbed.*

- **Multiple increases and decreases:** When shaping involves adding or subtracting two or more stitches at the fabric edges, that is done by casting on additional needles, or casting off existing needles.

Increasing

Increasing the edges of the knitting makes the fabric wider. Making an increase by transferring edge stitches out will leave an empty needle one or several needles in from the edge of the work. If left, a lace hole or eyelet will occur as the carriage knits across. This may be decorative, particularly if increases are created at the same rate with the same number of courses between. But if the lace holes are not desired, the empty needle can be filled using a one-prong transfer tool.

TIP: *When picking up the purl bump, it can be helpful to bring the needle back slightly (towards nonworking position). This stretches the stitch on the needle hook, allowing you more room to place the transfer tool.*

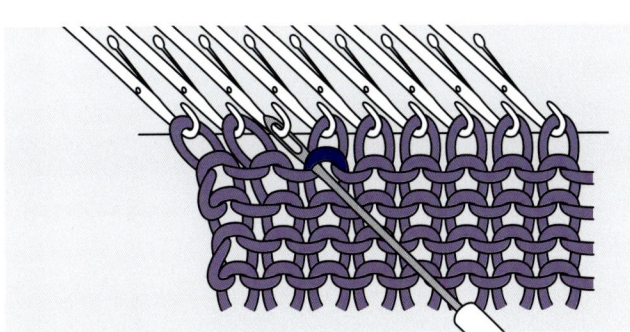

To prevent a lace hole from occurring when increasing, fill the empty needle with the adjacent needle's purl bump.

Simple transfer increase

This method uses a one-prong transfer tool. It can be worked on both edges of the knitting at the same time.

1. Bring one adjacent nonworking edge needle to working position.
2. Transfer the edge stitch of the knitting one needle out (away from the centre). The second needle from the edge is now empty.
3. To fill the empty needle, use the transfer tool to pick up the purl bump from the adjacent stitch (third needle from the edge) and place it on the empty needle.

Fully fashioned increase: Increasing by one stitch

A three-prong tool is used in this example. When moving a larger group of stitches, transfer the outside stitches first. This method can be worked on both edges of the knitting at the same time.

1. Bring one adjacent nonworking edge needle to working position.
2. Transfer the three edge stitches one needle out (away from the centre). This leaves the fourth needle from the edge empty.
3. To fill the empty needle, use a one-prong transfer tool to pick up the purl bump from the adjacent stitch (fifth needle from the edge) and place it on the empty needle.

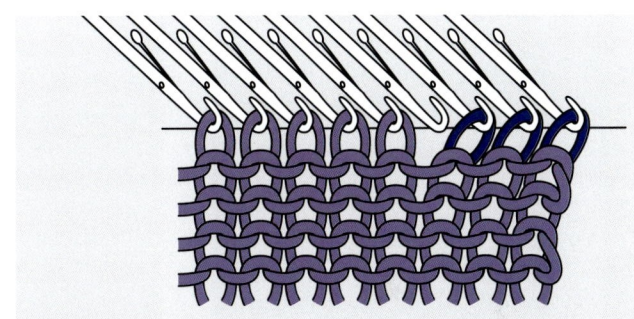

Fully fashioned increase.

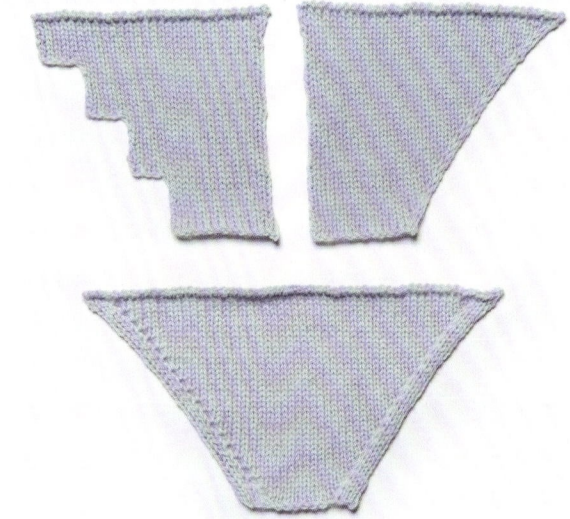

Multiple stitch increase (top left), simple transfer increase (top right), and fully fashioned increase (bottom). The left side of the fully fashioned fabric displays eyelets from empty needles and the right shows closed stitches from filled needles.

Increasing by two or more stitches

This requires new stitches to be cast on using the e-wrap method (see pages 54–55). It can be worked on only one edge of the knitting at a time – the same side as the carriage.

1. Place the required number of additional needles from nonworking position into holding position. Make sure the carriage is set to knit needles in holding position.
2. Using the main yarn from the carriage, e-wrap the additional needles, keeping an even tension.
3. Ensure the cast-on stitches are flush with the sinker posts. If the yarn between the needles and the carriage has become slack from the cast-on, pull it back through the tension unit to tighten it.
4. For the initial knit courses, manually push the newly cast-on needles to holding position using one hand, and keep the stitches held against the sinker posts with the other hand. This helps the new stitches form. Once there is enough fabric hanging from the additional needles, add a claw weight.

Decreasing

Decreasing the edges of the knitting makes the fabric narrower. After completing several repeats of decreases, you may find that the shaped edge of the knitting becomes tight, leading to unevenness or distortion. To prevent this, make sure the decreasing edges are weighted properly by hanging claw weights and frequently moving them up the knitting.

Simple transfer decrease

This method of decreasing by one stitch uses a one-prong transfer tool. It can be worked on both edges of the knitting at the same time.

1. Transfer the edge stitch of the knitting one needle in (towards the centre).
2. Place the now empty needle to nonworking position.
3. The new edge needle now contains two stitches that will knit together on the next course.

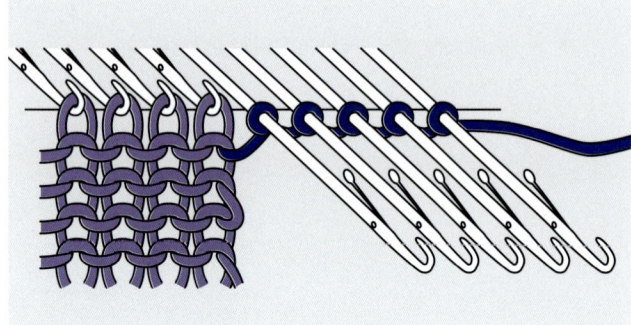

Multiple stitch (two or more) increase.

Fully fashioned decrease (top), simple transfer decrease (bottom left), and multiple stitch decrease (bottom right).

Fully fashioned decrease: Decreasing by one stitch

A three-prong tool is used in this example. When moving a larger group of stitches, transfer the inside stitches first. This method can be worked on both edges of the knitting at the same time.

1. Transfer the three edge stitches one needle in (towards the centre). This leaves the edge needle empty.
2. Place the empty edge needle to nonworking position.
3. The third needle from the edge now contains two stitches that will knit together on the next course.

Decreasing by two or more stitches

This requires stitches to be cast off using the transfer-tool method (see pages 58–59). It can be worked on only one edge of the knitting at a time – the same side as the carriage – unless a separate strand of yarn is used for the non-carriage side.

1. Cast off the required number of needles using the main yarn coming from the carriage.
2. Place the last decreased stitch on the adjacent working needle. This needle now contains two stitches.
3. Place the now empty needles to nonworking position.
4. If you used the sinker posts to create an evenly tensioned edge, make sure to lift it off.
5. Before knitting across, add a weight to the cast-off section and ensure it is out of the carriage's pathway.

Using a separate strand of yarn

If you want to decrease multiple stitches at both ends of the knitting, you can use the yarn coming from the carriage for one side, and a separate strand of main yarn for the other side. To cast off with a separate strand:

1. After transferring the edge stitch to the adjacent needle on the non-carriage side of the work, lay the separate strand in the hook to manually knit the two stitches together.
2. Use the introduced strand to complete the multiple stitch decrease.

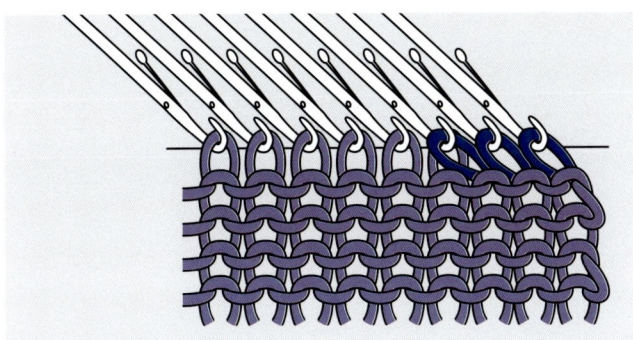

Fully fashioned decrease.

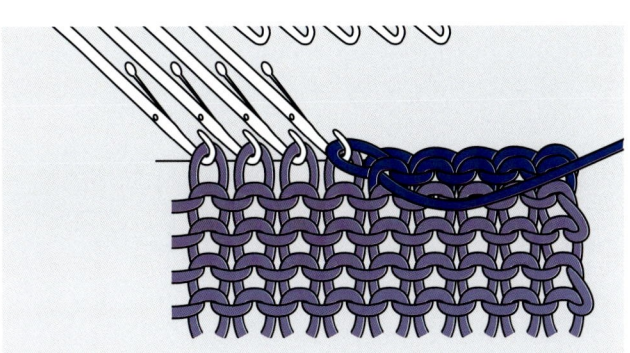

Multiple stitch (two or more) decrease.

Increasing and decreasing evenly across a row

Adding or subtracting a number of stitches in a single row of knitting will shape the overall body of the fabric. You may be required, for example, to increase by a number of stitches after knitting a trim and transitioning into the body of a sweater, to give the garment more ease. Alternatively, you may need to decrease by several stitches after knitting a skirt that must be gathered in to a waistband.

Both increasing and decreasing across a row involve temporarily removing the knitting from the machine using waste yarn. Once the required number of needles have been added or taken away, the knitting is rehung so that the increased or decreased live stitches are dispersed evenly (see page 158). Remove the waste yarn once the fabric is completed and off of the machine.

TIP: *It may be problematic to try to increase by too many stitches across the same course, as there is a limit to how much the knitting can stretch. If the increase involves a significant number of stitches, split the shaping over two or more courses.*

Increasing across a row
1. Knit to the course in which you wish to increase stitches.
2. Knit one course of ravel cord and several courses of waste yarn, then remove the knitting from the machine.
3. Place the required additional needles to working position.
4. Use a transfer tool to replace the last course of main yarn stitches on the machine. Rehang the work evenly over the new set of needles, skipping each needle that represents an increase. There should be approximately the same number of stitches between the empty needles.
5. Fill each empty needle by using a one-prong transfer tool to pick up the purl bump of the stitch next to it.

Decreasing across a row
1. Knit to the course in which you wish to decrease stitches.
2. Knit one course of ravel cord and several courses of waste yarn, then remove the knitting from the machine.
3. Place the required number of needles from working position to nonworking position.
4. Use a transfer tool to replace the last course of main yarn stitches on the machine. Rehang the work evenly over the new set of needles, placing two stitches on each needle that represents a decrease. There should be approximately the same number of stitches between the doubled-up needles.

Increasing and decreasing with short rows

Shaping with short rows or partial knitting involves placing needles in holding position in order to decrease, and out of holding position in order to increase. The same number of stitches remain on the knitting machine throughout the shaping process; some are working and others are held.

This method works well for gradual shaping and creating gentle slopes, particularly when making garments. It is very effective at achieving a smoothly finished edge when shaping shoulder slopes, necklines and curved hemlines. When used to shape the body of the fabric, it can create forms such as darts and sock heels.

Shaping through short rows eliminates the 'stepped' effect that can come from frequently increasing or decreasing several stitches at the edges of the fabric. This creates edges that are easier to seam or otherwise finish.

It is possible to shape only one side of the knitting at a time when using short rows. Needles can be placed in holding position (to decrease) and out of holding position

Increasing (left) and decreasing (right) evenly across a row.

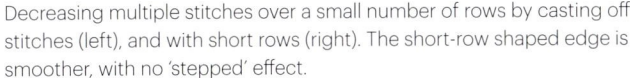

Decreasing multiple stitches over a small number of rows by casting off stitches (left), and with short rows (right). The short-row shaped edge is smoother, with no 'stepped' effect.

The heel and toe of this knitted sock are shaped with short rows.

(to increase) only on the opposite side of the work to the carriage. Therefore, to shape both sides of the knitting simultaneously, they must take turns, one course after another. It is important to remember to wrap the inner held needle on the carriage side to prevent a hole from occurring (see page 65).

Short-row shaping works best when there are no more than two knitted courses between decreases or increases. If more courses are knitted between shaping, the fabric may gather.

Increasing with short rows

For short-row increasing at only one side of the fabric, follow the steps without the instructions in bold. For short-row increasing at both sides of the fabric, follow the steps with the instructions in bold. The carriage should be set to the hold function throughout.

1. At the opposite side of the work from the carriage, place the required number of needles to be increased out of holding position and into upper working position.
2. Knit one course.
3. To avoid a hole forming in the fabric, wrap the inner held needle at the carriage side by bringing the working yarn underneath it and over the remaining needles. **At the opposite side of the work from the carriage, place the required number of needles to be increased out of holding position and into upper working position.**

4. Knit one course. **To avoid a hole forming in the fabric, wrap the inner held needle at the carriage side by bringing the working yarn underneath it and over the remaining needles.**
5. Repeat Steps 1–4.

Decreasing with short rows

For short-row decreasing at only one side of the fabric, follow the steps without the instructions in bold. For short-row decreasing at both sides of the fabric, follow the steps with the instructions in bold. The carriage should be set to the hold function throughout.

1. At the opposite side of the work from the carriage, place the required number of needles to be decreased in holding position.
2. Knit one course.
3. To avoid a hole forming in the fabric, wrap the inner held needle at the carriage side by bringing the working yarn underneath it and over the remaining needles. **At the opposite side of the work from the carriage, place the required number of needles to be decreased in holding position.**
4. Knit one course. **To avoid a hole forming in the fabric, wrap the inner held needle at the carriage side by bringing the working yarn underneath it and over the remaining needles.**
5. Repeat Steps 1–4.

Using the fabric tension to calculate shaping

The tension of the fabric is used to determine how a fabric is to be shaped – i.e. how many stitches are to be increased or decreased over how many rows. Alternative frequencies of shaping create differently angled lines. It is important to have the pattern piece drawn to scale so that you can measure it accurately. When calculating shaping:

- the stitches represent the number of *times* an increase or decrease must take place.
- the rows represent the number of *opportunities* for the increase or decrease to take place.

To determine the frequency of shaping, the widths and lengths of the pattern piece are measured at the beginning and end of the shaped area. The shaped area might encompass the entire pattern piece, or just a section of the pattern piece. The following steps explain how to determine the rate of shaping when you have a greater number of rows than stitches.

1. Measure the width of the pattern piece at the start of the shaped area. Multiply this by the stitch tension. This is the number of stitches to begin shaping with.
2. Measure the width of the pattern piece at the end of the shaped section. Multiply this by the stitch tension. This is the number of stitches to end shaping with.
3. Subtract the smaller number of stitches from the larger number. That will give you the number of stitches that must be increased or decreased. If shaping is taking place on both sides, as for a symmetrical piece such as a sleeve, this number must be divided by two.
4. Measure the length of the shaped area in the pattern piece. Multiply this by the row tension. This is the number of courses to knit in which the shaping can take place.
5. For practical reasons, it is not recommended to create an increase or decrease on the first or last course. If you account for an additional section of shaping within the knitting while keeping the actual number of stitches to be increased or decreased the same, you can spread out the frequency of shaping, leaving the first and last courses clear. To provide this extra space, add 1 to the total number of stitches to be increased or decreased.
6. Divide the number of rows to knit by the number of stitches to be increased or decreased. The result will tell you how many courses are to be knitted between increases or decreases.

For example, if 19 stitches are to be increased both sides of the knitting over 120 rows, 20 sections must be accounted for so that shaping does not occur on the first or the last course. 120 rows/20 sections = 6 rows per section. This means that we must increase by one stitch both sides of the knitting every sixth row. After making 19 increases every 6 rows, the total number of rows is 114. Therefore, there are 6 additional buffer courses taking the total rows to the required number of 120. The additional courses can be knitted before the first shaping course takes place or after the last shaping course takes place, or split between the two.

If the number of rows to knit divided by the number of stitches to be increased or decreased does not result in a whole number, **the increases or decreases must be distributed at different rates**. This can be fairly easy to calculate, but for more complex situations a formula will help you to determine the exact spacing.

The Magic Formula

The Magic Formula is used to determine the number of courses to knit between increases or decreases when the number of stitches to be shaped is not evenly divisible into the number of rows to knit.

Step 1

For shaping on one side:
A = the number of stitches that must be increased or decreased within the shaped area +1.

For shaping on both sides (symmetrical piece):
A = the number of stitches that must be increased or decreased divided by two +1.

(The +1 accounts for the extra section needed to avoid an increase or decrease taking place on the first or last course of knitting.)

B = the number of rows to knit within the shaped area.

C = the whole number before the decimal when B/A.

D = A × C

E = B – D

Step 2

F = A – E

G = C + 1

H = E – 1

Step 3

Draw a line matching C to F and G to H
This completes the formula calculations.

Increase or decrease 1 stitch every C courses for a total of F times.

Increase or decrease 1 stitch every G courses for a total of H times.

To check the calculation:
Add the number of stitches, F + H.
Add the number of courses, (C × F) + (G × H).

Mix or alternate the two rates of shaping so that it is dispersed evenly within the knitting.

Example: Sleeve for a drop-sleeve sweater

In this example, the fabric tension is 3.1 stitches per cm (7.8 stitches per in) and 4.3 rows per cm (10.9 rows per in). To determine the frequency of shaping:

1. **Initial number of stitches:** Width of 23cm (9–9⅛in) × fabric tension of 3.1 stitches per cm (7.8 stitches per in) = 71.3 (70.2-71.2), rounded to 71 stitches.
2. **Ending number of stitches:** Width of 45.5cm (17⅞–18⅛in) × fabric tension of 3.1 stitches per cm (7.8 stitches per in) = 141 (139.4-141.4 rounded to 141) stitches.
3. **Stitches to shape:** 141 stitches – 71 stitches = 70 stitches to increase. Since the sleeve is symmetrical, divide this by two, resulting in 35 stitches to increase on both sides.
4. **Rows to knit:** Length of 48.5cm (19⅛in) × fabric tension of 4.3 rows per cm (10.9 rows per in) = 208.6 (208.5), rounded to 209 rows. That means 209 opportunities to increase by 35 stitches on both sides.
5. **Add an extra section to avoid shaping on first or last row:** 35 shaped sections + 1 = 36 shaped sections.
6. **Ratio of shaping:** 209 rows/36 sections = 5.8 rows between increases.

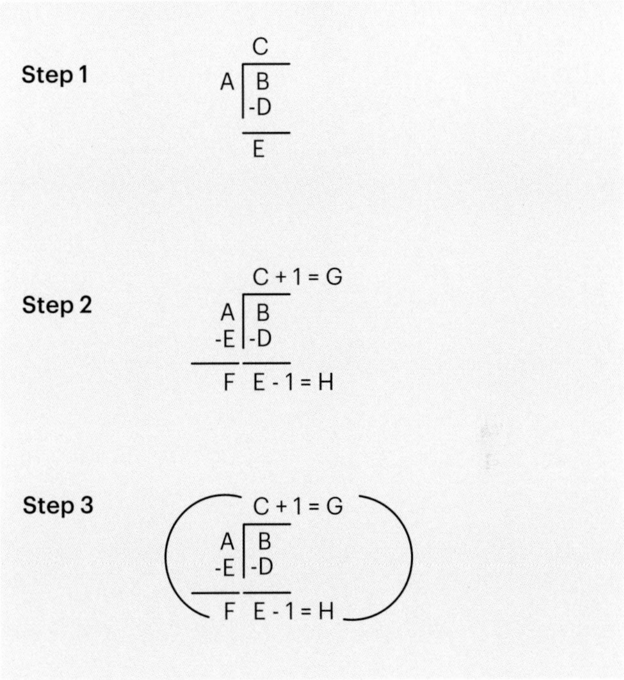

The magic formula.

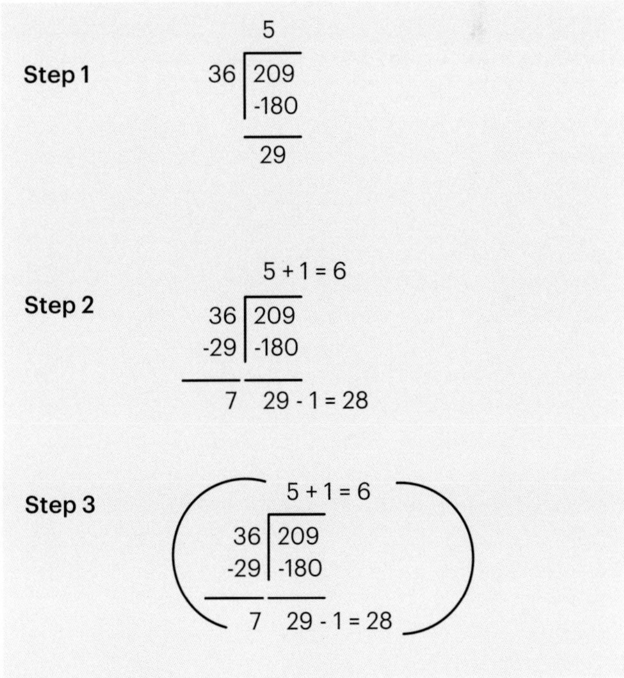

Using the magic formula to calculate the rate of shaping for a drop-sleeve sweater example.

Since the number of stitches to increase divided into the number of courses to knit is not a whole number, **two different frequencies of shaping must take place.** The numbers are inserted into the Magic Formula to determine this.

From the Magic Formula calculation there must be:
- 1 stitch increased (both sides) every 5 courses a total of 7 times, and
- 1 stitch increased (both sides) every 6 courses a total of 28 times.

Alternate the two increase intervals evenly throughout the knitting.

To check the calculation:
Add the number of stitches: 7 + 28 = 35 stitches increased (both sides).
Add the number of courses: (5 × 7) + (6 × 28) = 203 courses.

This leaves 6 buffer courses, taking the total rows to the required number of 209. The buffer courses can be knitted before the first shaping course or after the last shaping course, or split between the two.

Calculating curves

Curved lines are used to create round necklines, armholes and sleeve caps. Large curved areas are often most easily calculated in sections, each with its own ratio of shaping. Before you can calculate each section, you must translate the curves into horizontal, vertical and diagonal lines. The three types are approached in the following way:

- Horizontal – stitches are cast on (increased) or cast off (decreased) within the same course.
- Vertical – courses are knit with no shaping.
- Diagonal – stitches are increased or decreased over a set number of courses.

Calculating the ratio of shaping for diagonal sections
Turning each diagonal section of shaping into a triangle is a simple way of calculating the ratio of shaping, because stitches and rows are always at right angles to one another. To create a triangle:

1. Use a ruler to extend the horizontal line.
2. Use a ruler to extend the vertical line.
3. The point where both these lines meet creates a right angle. This right angle is the shaping calculation point.

Calculating the rate of shaping:
1. Measure the horizontal line and multiply it by the stitch tension. This is the number of stitches to increase or decrease.
2. Measure the vertical line and multiply it by the row tension. This is the number of courses to knit.
3. Divide the larger number by the smaller number to determine the rate of shaping.

The resulting numbers may need to be shifted when you convert to knitting instructions. For example, with shallow angles it is often necessary to increase or decrease several stitches every course. Increasing or decreasing two or more

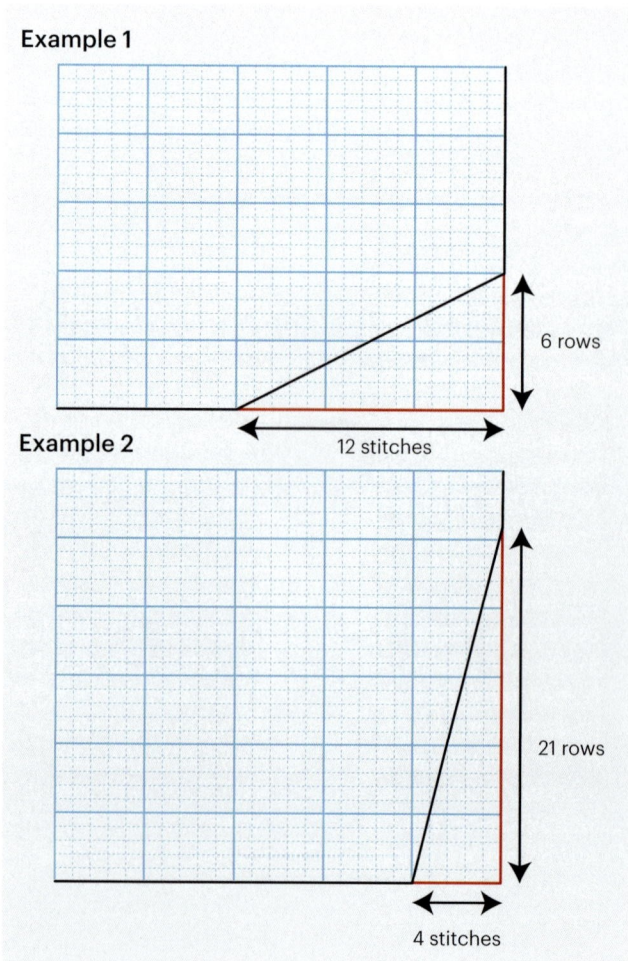

Example 1

6 rows

12 stitches

Example 2

21 rows

4 stitches

Turning diagonal lines into triangles is a simple way to calculate the ratio of shaping needed to achieve the angle.

stitches at a time requires the carriage to be on the correct side, which happens only every other course. Therefore, more stitches must be knitted over one course, with a non-shaped course in between.

Example 1
- When converted to stitches and rows, the horizontal line of this triangle equals 12 stitches, and the vertical line equals 6 rows.
- There are more stitches than rows.
- 12 stitches/6 rows = 2 stitches to decrease every row.
- Therefore, to create this angle of shaping, two stitches must be decreased every row for a total of six rows.

Example 2
- When converted to stitches and rows, the horizontal line of this triangle equals 4 stitches, and the vertical line equals 21 rows.
- There are more rows than stitches.
- 21 rows/4 stitches = 5.3 rows between decreases.
- If you round this down to 5 rows, you would increase by 1 stitch every 5 rows, four times. This could be on the third, eighth, fourteenth and nineteenth rows, for instance.

Example: Shaping a round neckline
Necklines are usually worked in two halves, starting with one half (while the other is held in holding position or with waste yarn) and knitting it to completion before starting the other half. This is how you might break down the steps of calculating the shape of a round or crew neckline:

1. Use a ruler to translate the curved lines into horizontal, vertical and diagonal lines.
2. Use a ruler to draw a centre line to divide the neckline into two equal halves. You need to calculate the shaping for only one half, since the second half is knitted in the same way, with mirrored shaping instructions.

To calculate one half of the neckline:
1. Measure the horizontal line in the centre of the neckline. This is the number of stitches to cast off.
2. Turn the first diagonal line into a triangle to calculate the rate of shaping for this angle.
3. Turn the second diagonal line into a triangle to calculate the rate of shaping for this angle.
4. Measure the vertical line that ends at the shoulder point. This is the number of courses to knit with no shaping, and completes this half of the neckline.

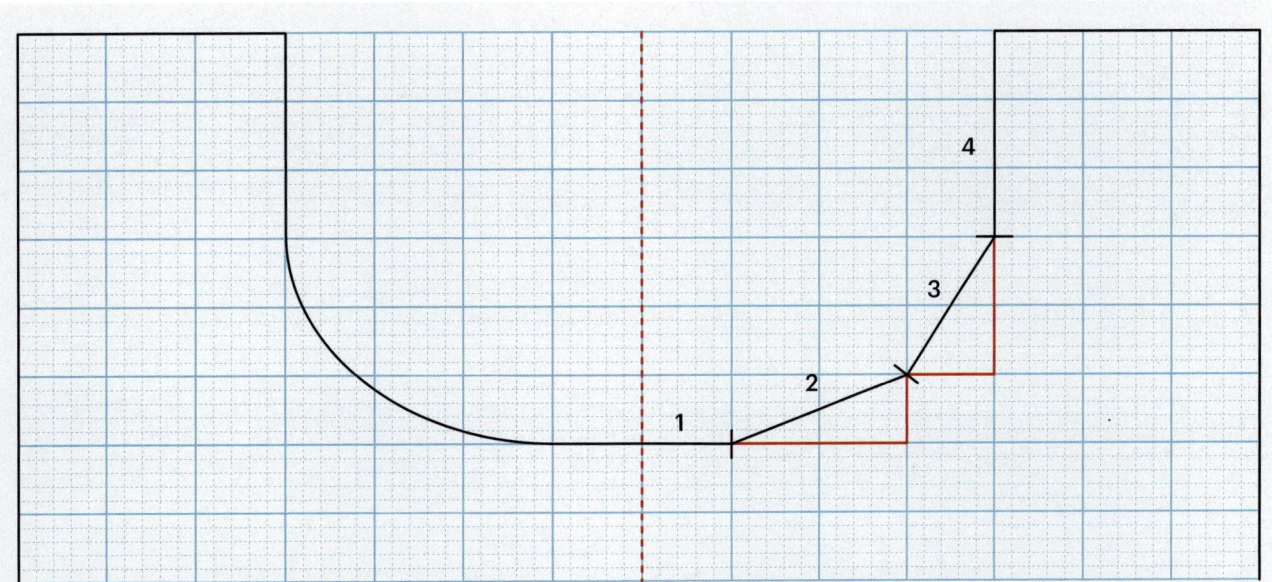

Calculating the ratio of shaping for a round neckline.

Chapter 8

Trims and Details

Trims, such as hems, edgings, bands and borders, often form the final details of a knitted garment or accessory, visually framing and finishing the design. They are an important part of the design process and should be considered just as carefully as colour, yarn, stitch and silhouette. Executing trims well will ensure that the knitted outcome looks thought-out, complete and professional.

In this chapter, we focus on hems (that is, trims used on the bottom and top edges of the fabric) and edgings (trims used on the selvedges of the fabric).

Trims

Knitted fabric often requires a trim because of its natural inclination to curl or roll at the edges. It may curl a little or a lot, depending on the yarn, stitch size, stitch pattern and fabric size. Blocking can eliminate most of the curl, but for any raw edges (those left plain and not in a seam) it is recommended to integrate a trim for structure and stability.

Trims are often used on the shaped edges of a garment, such as a neckline or the armhole of a sleeveless top. Curved edges like these can appear irregular after they have been shaped, and so a trim will smooth them out visually. Trims do not need to be solely functional; decorative stitches such as lace may be integrated to add another layer of interest to the design.

Decorative trims by label Alice Lee, featuring alternative materials.

Preparing for Trims

Finishing methods such as seaming or adding a trim often require the fabric's stitches to be picked up and rehung on the machine's needles. Stitches at the edge of the fabric may be live, closed or along the selvedge. To work with live stitches, several courses of waste yarn and ravel cord must also be knitted, to act as a stitch-holder and keep the main yarn stitches from unravelling before the edge is finished. Picking up stitches along the bottom or selvedges of the fabric also allows the orientation to be switched, resulting in a piece that is knitted in different directions. Instead of being rehung on the machine's needles, stitches may also be picked up and continued with a hand technique, such as two-needle knitting or crochet.

TIP: *It is easier to rehang picked-up stitches on machine needles in working position. After rehanging the stitches, placing the needles in holding position (with the carriage set to knit them) ensures the stitches are safely positioned before the carriage passes across.*

Picking up live stitches
To pick up and rehang live stitches:

1. If the knitting ends with waste yarn, the live stitches from the last course of main yarn are picked up. If the knitting starts with waste yarn, the live stitches from the first course of main yarn are picked up.
2. To help you see the course of live stitches to pick up, fold the waste yarn out of the way. Fold it towards you when picking up stitches from the knit side of the fabric, and away from you when picking up stitches from the purl side.
3. Use a transfer tool to pick up the course of main yarn stitches and rehang them on the machine needles. Use a finger to stretch the fabric gently widthways in order to see the stitches more clearly, particularly at the edge. Check that all live stitches have been accounted for.
4. Remove the waste yarn and ravel cord once the knitting is off the machine.

TIP: *When picking up live stitches from the first course of main yarn, there will be one stitch fewer than the original number. To rectify this, pick up an edge stitch.*

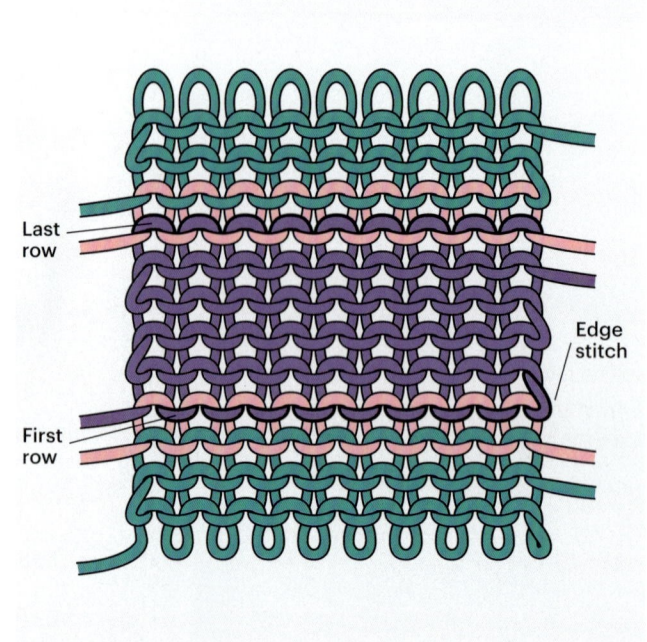

Picking up live stitches from the purl side (above) and knit side (below) of the fabric. The first and last row of main yarn stitches are highlighted, as well as the edge stitch to also be picked up on the first row.

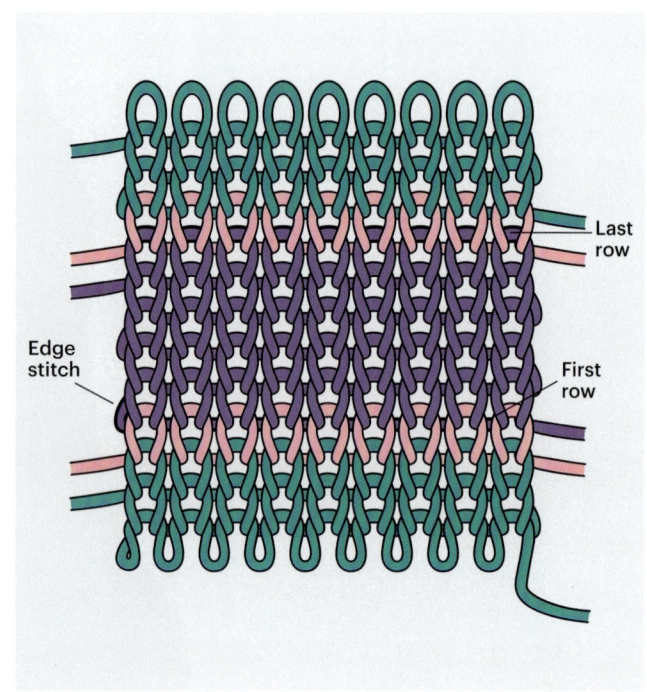

Picking up selvedge stitches

Selvedge stitches appear as a sideways V or chain with two sides or legs. When picking up, place the transfer tool under both sides of the V. If the yarn is particularly thick or the finish appears bulky, it may be better to pick up just one side of the V.

It is important that selvedge stitches are picked up and rehung according to the correct ratio. This is because the vertical length of the fabric, along which the edge stitches run, is rarely the same tension as the horizontal width. If every edge stitch were picked up and rehung (as live stitches are), the fabric could become stretched. Picking up too few stitches, however, can cause the edge to appear gathered.

To calculate how many stitches to pick up, multiply the stitch tension by the intended width of the outcome. For example, to knit a trim that measures 46cm (18⅛in) on the front opening of a cardigan when the fabric tension is 3 stitches per cm (7.6 stitches per in): 46cm (18⅛in) x 3 (7.6) = 138 (137.8 rounded to 138) stitches. Therefore, 138 stitches along the edge of the cardigan must be picked up and rehung on 138 needles (69 needles either side of the centre '0').

To calculate how many stitches *not* to pick up, subtract the number of stitches to be picked up from the total number of stitches along the edge of the cardigan. For example, if there are 150 stitches along the edge: 150 – 138 = 12. Therefore, 12 stitches along the edge would not be picked up and rehung for the cardigan trim.

To pick up and rehang edge stitches:

1. Bring the required number of needles to working position.
2. Make sure the fabric is orientated the chosen way, with either the right or the wrong side facing you (depending on the intended outcome).
3. Use a one-prong transfer tool to pick up the edge stitch at the right-hand end and rehang it on the machine. Repeat with the edge stitch at the left-hand end.
4. Pick up the middle stitch, then place the remaining stitches evenly on the needles.

TIP: *Stitches within the body of the fabric can be picked up to create decorative dimensional and appliqué effects. This can be done in any direction: a horizontal course of stitches, a vertical column of stitches or diagonal or staggered arrangements. This is a free-form method that invites experimentation.*

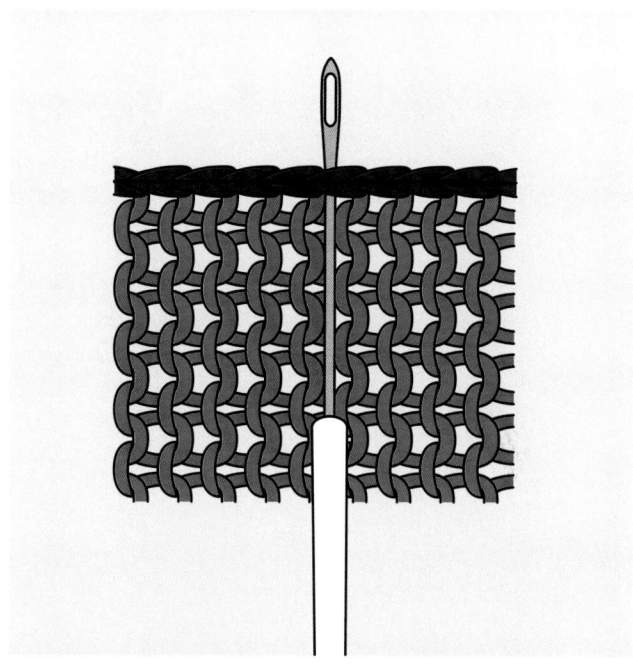

Picking up a selvedge stitch by placing a transfer tool under both sides of the knitted V.

Hems

Hems are trims that can be used at the bottom, top or both ends of a knitted fabric. Since garments are usually knitted from the bottom up, it is most common to knit the hem after casting on. If a garment is knitted from the top down, the hem is knitted before casting off. Hems may be mirrored at both ends if you are knitting a garment with a waistband, or an accessory such as a scarf.

Adding a lifeline

When knitting a hem at the end of the fabric, a separate strand of yarn (known as a 'lifeline') can be used. Since it can be difficult to identify where the main fabric ends and the hem begins, the lifeline thread works as a marker. As well as highlighting a course of stitches, it also holds them in place so that if the knitting unravels it will not run further than this point.

For the lifeline, choose a yarn that is finer than the main yarn. It should be smooth, so that it can be removed easily, and in a contrasting colour so that it stands out. The strand should be at least twice as long as the knitting is wide.

1. Thread the lifeline strand through a tapestry needle and, starting at the left edge, bring the tapestry needle through the front of the first stitch on the machine needle.
2. Repeat across the course, bringing the lifeline through the front of each stitch you wish to mark. If the machine needles are in working position, it may be helpful to bring them slightly forward before inserting the tapestry needle. (Just remember to readjust them before knitting the next course.) If the machine needles are in holding position, it can be helpful to lift them slightly to allow more space for the tapestry needle.
3. Be careful that the lifeline thread stays in front and out of the way of the sinker posts. Let it hang down out of the carriage's pathway before knitting across.
4. The lifeline can be removed once the knitting is finished and the piece is off the machine.

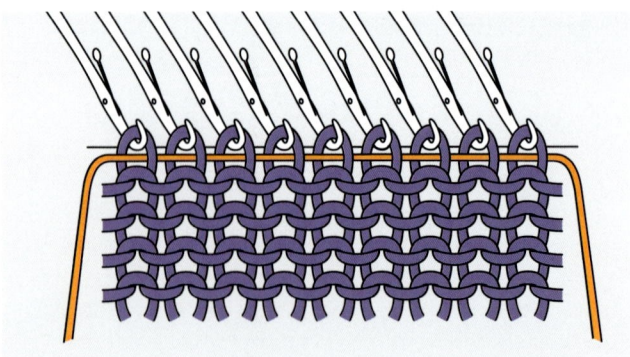

A lifeline strand of yarn threaded through the fronts of each stitch on the needles.

Ribbing

Ribbing is commonly used for knitted hems because of its elasticity and flexibility. Both are caused by the structure of the rib fabric, which consists of columns of knit stitches next to columns of purl stitches; the fabric appears the same on both sides. There are many variations of ribbing, ranging from simple ribs such as single (1 × 1) and double (2 × 2) to types that incorporate tuck stitches and lace.

To create ribbing on a single-bed machine, the hem must be created using the latch tool so that it can reconstruct columns of purl stitches into columns of knit stitches. When casting on, make sure the stitch repeat of the rib is divisible by the total number of needles.

It can be helpful to add extra selvedge stitches to the fabric so that the stitch pattern can be mirrored on the left and right edges of the ribbing. For example, a single rib has a stitch repeat of two stitches: one knit and one purl repeated across the fabric. If an extra stitch is added, the stitch arrangement becomes symmetrical. Incorporating additional selvedge stitches also saves you from having to latch up a column of stitches on the very edge of the fabric, which can be difficult.

Knitting the length of the rib hem in a tighter stitch size will ensure that it pulls in the rest of the knitted fabric.

Ribbing at the start of the fabric

For single rib/1 × 1 rib:

1. Cast on a multiple of two stitches + one edge stitch using a closed cast-on method.
2. Knit the required number of courses for the length of the rib.

3. Starting with the second needle from the left edge, follow the stitches down until you locate the bottom stitch. Place the latch tool into this stitch from the front.

4. Bring the second needle from the left edge into holding position and then back to working position, so that the stitch drops. Unravel the column of stitches until it reaches the bottom stitch that is being held on the tool.

5. Make sure this stitch stays behind the latch of the tool, then catch the float above in the hook. Bring the tool towards you to reconstruct the stitch. Continue to latch up this wale of stitches and then return the final loop to its needle.

6. Reconstruct every other column of stitches in this way to complete the rib.

TIP: *If the wale of stitches unravels without the bottom stitch being secured in the latch tool, the result is a column of floats with no visible loop to place the tool in. To create one, hold the latch tool upside down and place it behind the bottom float from top to bottom. Turn the tool the right way up; the float will twist around the tool and create a loop.*

Different rib formations can be created by adjusting the number of stitches that are cast on. In general, it is much simpler to achieve a neat result when only one column of stitches is latched up, as in a 2 × 1 rib, than when more are, as in a 2 × 2 rib, for example.

A 2 × 1 rib is created by casting on a multiple of three stitches + two edge stitches. The stitches from the third needle on the left edge are latched up, and that is repeated for every third needle. A 3 × 1 rib is formed by casting on a multiple of four stitches + three edge stitches. The stitches from the fourth needle on the left edge are latched up, and that is repeated for every fourth needle.

Ribbing at the end of the fabric
When creating a rib at the end of the knitting, a lifeline thread highlights and secures the selected stitches, holding them safely so that they are unable to unravel past that point and disrupt the fabric design below. If you prefer, you can count down the knitted wale from the current course's stitch to determine into which stitch the tool should be inserted in the fabric below. These instructions assume a lifeline is being used.

1. Knit one row (this is the first course of the trim), then place the needles that will have their stitches latched up in holding position. Set the carriage so that it knits needles in hold.

2. Thread the lifeline yarn through a tapestry needle.

3. Starting at the left, bring the tapestry needle through the front of the stitch on the held needle. Repeat through the front of all held needles.

4. Knit the remaining courses required for the rib trim.

5. Place the same needles as in Step 1 in holding position and then back to working position, so that the stitches drop. The stitches will stop dropping when they reach the lifeline thread.

6. Starting at the left, place the latch tool in the stitch held by the lifeline. If this is difficult, first place a one-prong transfer tool in the stitch to stretch it, then slide the latch tool in. Make sure this stitch stays behind the latch of the tool, then catch the float above in the hook. Bring the tool towards you to reconstruct the stitch. Continue to latch up this wale, then return the final loop to its needle.

7. Continue to latch up stitches in this way, then cast off.

Ribbing at the start and end of the fabric (clockwise from top left): 1 × 1 plain, 1 × 1 tucked, 3 × 1, and 2 × 1.

Folded hems

A folded, hung or turned hem is a simple yet professional-looking trim for single-bed fabrics. Since this trim is doubled on itself, the number of rows knitted is twice the length of the finished hem. After knitting, the stitches from the first course of the hem are picked up and rehung on the needles directly above. These instructions call for folded hems at the start of the fabric to be cast on with waste yarn, followed by several courses knitted and one row of ravel cord, before you start with the trim yarn. This helps the first course of main yarn stitches to be more visible, for when they are picked up and rehung later.

While folded trims can be knitted at the same stitch size as the main fabric, a tighter stitch can help them lie flat and appear structurally firm against the rest of the fabric. To create a crisp fold in the centre of the hem, the middle course is knitted in a looser stitch size than the main tension.

For example, if the ideal stitch size for the body of the garment is 5, the first half of the hem could be knitted in size 3, with a looser middle course at size 7 and the second half in size 3. The adjustments that are given in the hems included here should be used as guide; it is good practice to tweak them and analyze the results.

TIP: *If the hem is not lying as flat as it should, try knitting the inside facing slightly tighter or with one less course than the outside facing. For a crisper fold, knit the middle row at the loosest stitch size possible.*

Basic folded hem at the start of the fabric

1. After knitting with waste yarn and ravel cord, thread the main yarn into the carriage and tighten the stitch size by two numbers (main tension -2). Knit the required number of courses for the inside facing of the hem.
2. For the middle course, loosen the stitch size by four numbers (main tension +2).
3. Tighten the stitch size by four numbers (main tension -2). Knit the required number of courses for the outside facing of the hem.
4. To fold the hem, use a transfer tool to pick up the first course of main yarn stitches, placing them on the needles directly above.
5. Bring the needles out to holding position, with the carriage set to knit them back. Adjust the stitch size to the appropriate main yarn tension and continue to knit.

Basic folded hem at the end of the fabric

1. Tighten the stitch size by two numbers (main tension -2). Knit the first course of the outside facing of the hem.
2. Thread the lifeline yarn through a tapestry needle. Starting at the left, bring the tapestry needle through the front of the first stitch on the machine needle. Repeat through the front of all stitches on this course.
3. Knit the remaining number of courses for the outside facing of the hem.
4. For the middle course, loosen the stitch size by four numbers (main tension +2).
5. Tighten the stitch size by four numbers (main tension -2). Knit the required number of courses for the inside facing of the hem.
6. To fold the hem, use a transfer tool to pick up the course of stitches highlighted by the lifeline thread running through, placing them on the needles directly above.
7. Cast off.

Basic folded hem at the start and end of the fabric.

Mock-rib hem

Also known as a false or continental rib, this folded hem looks similar to a true rib, but it is much quicker. It is important to note that it lacks the elasticity of a true rib and may not be suitable for outcomes that require the hem to have a lot of give.

Mock-rib hem at the start of the fabric

For 1 × 1 or single mock-rib hem (worked over an odd number of needles):

1. Cast on alternate needles with waste yarn and knit several rows. Knit one course with ravel cord. Tighten the stitch size by two numbers (main tension -2), then with the main yarn knit the required number of courses for the inside facing of the hem.
2. For the middle course, loosen the stitch size by four numbers (main tension +2).
3. Tighten the stitch size by four numbers (main tension -2). Knit the required number of courses for the outside facing of the hem.
4. To fold the hem, bring the empty alternate needles into working position. Use a one-prong transfer tool to pick up the first course of main yarn stitches, placing them on the empty needles directly above.
5. Bring all needles out to holding position, with the carriage set to knit them back. Adjust the stitch size to the main yarn tension and continue to knit.

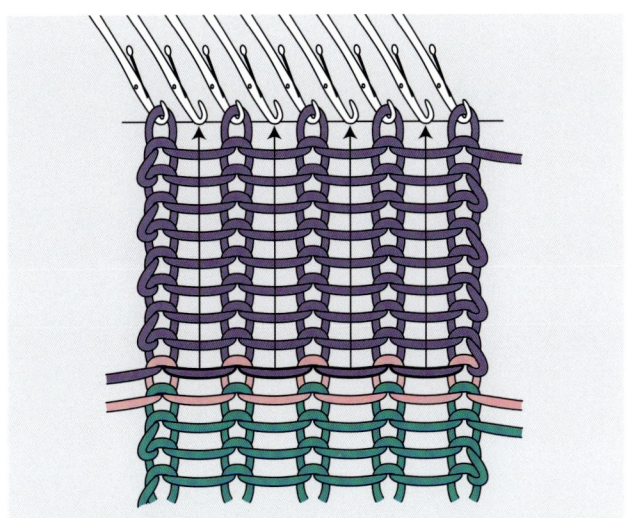

Step 4: To fold the 1 × 1 mock-rib hem at the start of the fabric, place the first course of main yarn stitches onto the empty needles directly above.

Alternative mock-rib arrangements

Variations of mock rib can be created by alternating the needle arrangement. They are then knitted in the same manner as the 1 × 1 mock rib. Because there are more needles knitting for other arrangements than for the 1 × 1 set-up, there are also more main yarn loops to be picked up and rehung when folding the hem in Step 4. Do this evenly, always placing a loop on each empty needle, as well as on some of the needles that already hold stitches.

For a 2 × 1 or double mock-rib hem at the start of the fabric (worked over a multiple of three needles + two):

- Cast on the following arrangement with waste yarn: two needles cast on, one needle in nonworking position, repeated across. End with two needles cast on.
- Knit the inside facing, middle course and outside facing as for the 1 × 1 set-up.
- To fold the hem, bring the empty needles into working position. Use a one-prong transfer tool to pick up the main yarn stitches, placing them on the empty needles directly above as for the 1 × 1 mock-rib. Then, pick up the remaining main yarn stitches and place them on some of the needles above that already hold a stitch.
- Follow Step 5 as for the 1 × 1 set-up.

For a 3 × 1 or triple mock-rib hem at the start of the fabric (worked over a multiple of four needles + three):

- Cast on the following arrangement with waste yarn: three needles cast on, one needle in nonworking position, repeated across. End with three needles cast on.
- Knit the inside facing, middle course and outside facing as for the 1 × 1 set-up.
- To fold the hem, bring the empty needles into working position. Use a one-prong transfer tool to pick up the main yarn stitches, placing them on the empty needles directly above as for the 1 × 1 mock-rib. Then, pick up the remaining main yarn stitches and place them on some of the needles above that already hold a stitch.
- Follow Step 5 as for the 1 × 1 set-up.

Mock-rib hem at the end of the fabric

For a 1 × 1 or single mock-rib hem (worked over an odd number of needles):

1. Tighten the stitch size by two numbers (main tension -2). Knit the first course of the outside facing of the hem. Place the second needle from the left edge and every alternate needle in holding position.
2. Thread the lifeline yarn through a tapestry needle.
3. Starting at the left, bring the tapestry needle through the front of the stitch on the held needle, then bring the held needle back to working position so that the stitch slides off. The live stitch is held securely with the lifeline strand. Repeat for all held needles, then place these empty needles in nonworking position.
4. Knit the remaining number of courses for the outside facing of the hem.
5. For the middle course, loosen the stitch size by four numbers (main tension +2).
6. Tighten the stitch size by four numbers (main tension -2). Knit the required number of courses for the inside facing of the hem.
7. To fold the hem, bring the empty alternate needles back into working position. Use a transfer tool to pick up the stitches held on the lifeline thread, placing them on the empty needles directly above.
8. Cast off.

To end with a 2 × 1 (worked over a multiple of two needles + one) or 3 × 1 (worked over a multiple of three needles + one) mock-rib hem, follow the 1 × 1 instructions with these amendments:

- In Step 1: For a 2 × 1, place the third needle and then every third in holding position; for a 3 × 1, place the fourth needle and then every fourth in holding position.
- In Step 7: To create a firm fold, it is necessary to pick up and rehang more stitches in the course than just those held in the lifeline thread. The more stitches that are picked up, the sturdier the fold.

Mock-rib hem at the start and end of the fabric: 1 × 1 (top), 2 × 1 (bottom left), and 3 × 1 (bottom right).

Picot hem

Picots are created by making eyelets at the middle point of the hem. As the hem is turned, the lace holes form the dips between the picot's recognizable points. The hem requires an odd number of needles.

Picot hem at the start of the fabric

See instructions for the basic folded hem (page 162), except work Steps 2 and 3 as follows:

2. Use a one-prong transfer tool to transfer the second stitch from the edge to the adjacent needle to the right or left. Repeat across the course, transferring every other stitch to its neighbouring needle. Make sure the empty needles remain in working position.
3. Knit the required number of courses for the outside facing of the hem.

Picot hem at the end of the fabric

See instructions for the basic folded hem (page 162), except work Steps 4 and 5 as follows:

4. Use a one-prong transfer tool to transfer the second stitch from the edge to the adjacent needle to the right or left. Repeat across the course, transferring every other stitch to its neighbouring needle. Make sure the empty needles remain in working position.
5. Knit the required number of courses for the inside facing of the hem.

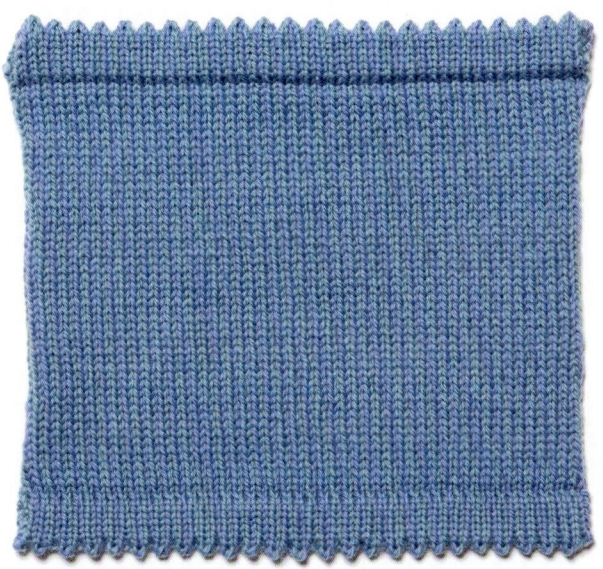

Picot hem at the start and end of the fabric.

Tucked scallop hem
This hem is formed with a pattern repeat that involves one stitch that tucks over several courses, with a group of stitches knitting plain in between. The needles that tuck pull the fabric up, forming the decorative curves. The stitch repeat of this hem can be altered and explored depending on the gauge of the machine and the type of yarn.

Scallop hem at the start of the fabric
(Worked over a multiple of six needles + five):

1. After knitting with waste yarn and ravel cord, cast on again with the main yarn over the ravel-cord stitches. Leave the stitch size as it is or tighten it by one number (main tension -1). Knit one or two courses.

2. Place the sixth needle from the left edge in holding position, then repeat for every sixth needle across the course. Set the carriage to the hold function.
3. Knit 4–8 courses, depending on the yarn and stitch size. Set the carriage to plain knitting.
4. If necessary, adjust the stitch size to the main yarn tension, then continue to knit.

Scallop hem at the end of the fabric
Follow the instructions for a scallop hem at the start of the fabric, in reverse. When you reach the course where you want the hem to start, adjust the stitch size if desired, then place the selected needles in holding position. Knit the desired number of courses with the carriage set to hold. At the end, set the carriage to plain knitting, knit one or two courses, then cast off.

Tucked scallop hem at the start and end of the fabric.

Hand-made trims
One of the advantages of knitted textiles is the flexibility and ease with which the various techniques can be combined. Interchanging machine-knitting, hand-knitting and crochet is a clever way to combine unique design with efficiency and a professional appearance. Hand-knitted or crocheted trims can be integrated seamlessly into a machine-knitted garment or accessory, and can open up a new realm of creativity for the designer.

Rib, moss and garter stitch are all commonly used in two-needle hand-knitting to form trims. These simple stitch patterns can be knitted quickly and easily by hand, and, most importantly, they lie beautifully flat with no roll at the edges.

Decorative trims such as detailed lace or crochet compositions can also be integrated. Here, the trim may provide the primary aesthetic focus and detail. If the yarn used to knit the trim is not the same as the one that will be used later on the machine, ensure that it is the same weight.

This is also a great opportunity to explore non-traditional knitwear trims – for example by combining woven fabrics, lace and commercial trimmings with a machine-knitted fabric. When sourcing such alternative materials, choose those with open structures, such as mesh or eyelets, so that the edge may be picked up easily.

Hand-knitted trim at the start of the fabric

1. Hand-knit the trim using the desired number of stitches and courses. After the final course, leave the stitches on the needle.
2. Hold the hand-knitting needle horizontally so that it lines up with the edge of the machine bed. If the trim has a right and wrong side, make sure it is held up to reflect this.
3. Insert a one-prong transfer tool into the first stitch, sliding it off the hand-knitting needle and rehanging it on the machine needle. Repeat with all live stitches on the knitting needle.
4. To ensure the first machine-knit course is smooth, place all needles in holding position (with the carriage set to knit them back) before passing the carriage across.

Hand-knitted trim at the end of the fabric

1. Machine-knit to the course where you want the hand-knitted trim to begin, then knit one course of ravel cord and several courses of waste yarn.
2. Remove the knitting from the machine.
3. Place the live main yarn stitches on the hand-knitting needle by inserting the needle into each stitch from back to front. This can be with either the right or the wrong side of the fabric facing, depending on whether the trim begins with a right- or wrong-side row.
4. Unravel the waste yarn.
5. Hand-knit the trim.

Crocheted trim at the start of the fabric

1. Crochet the trim using the desired number of stitches and courses. After the final course, cut a 15–20cm (6–8in) tail and pull it through the last stitch. Since there are no live stitches, the beginning or ending course can be picked up (depending on the trim orientation).
2. Hold the trim so that it lines up with the edge of the machine bed. If it has a right and wrong side, make sure it is positioned correctly.
3. Use a one-prong transfer tool to pick up the course of crochet stitches and rehang them on the machine needles as evenly as possible.
4. To make sure the first machine-knit course is smooth, place all needles in holding position (with the carriage set to knit them back) before passing the carriage across.

Crocheted trim at the end of the fabric

1. Machine-knit to the course where you want the crochet trim to begin, then knit one course of ravel cord and several courses of waste yarn.
2. Remove the knitting from the machine.
3. Fold the waste yarn out of the way and crochet into each live stitch. This can be with the right or the wrong side of the fabric facing, depending on whether the trim begins with a right- or wrong-side row.
4. Remove the waste yarn after completing the first crochet row.
5. Crochet the remaining rows of the trim.

Edgings

Two-needle hand-knit (top) and crochet (bottom) hems at the start and end of the fabric.

Bands of shaped crochet stitches combined to create a mixed media collar with feathers and beads.

Edgings are trims along the selvedges. They may be integrated into the fabric itself, in which case they are formed as you knit, or they can be applied to the fabric after it has been knitted. Applied edgings can be created by picking up stitches along the selvedge of the fabric, rehanging them and knitting the trim. Or they can be knitted separately and joined to the fabric afterwards.

Chain-stitch edging

This is the machine-knitted version of a popular integrated edging used in hand-knitting, also known as a slip-stitch edging. The result is a series of neat enlarged chains that travel the edge of the fabric, one chain for every two knitted courses. The line of chains can make seaming by hand easier, because the elongated stitches can be matched up more readily. Chain stitch is not recommended on edgings that will be picked up and rehung on the machine later. This is because each chain edge stitch represents two courses, whereas a plain edge stitch represents one. The difference can result in an uneven ratio.

To knit a chain-stitch edging on both sides:

1. Cast on and knit two courses. End with the needles in working position.
2. Manually undo the edge stitch closest to the carriage by gently tugging the working yarn coming from this stitch. As the stitch tightens, lift the working yarn up and back slightly towards the needle hook so that the stitch lifts off the needle. The stitch from the row below is now in the needle hook, and the working yarn is coming from the second needle on the edge.
3. Knit one course.
4. Repeat Steps 2 and 3.

TIP: *To create slightly larger chains, knit with the adjacent needle (the second needle from the edge) in nonworking position.*

I-cord edging

Knitting an I-cord on one or both selvedges is a simple way to finish a fabric so that the edges appear neat and lie flat. For I-cord edgings both sides:

1. After knitting with waste yarn and ravel cord, cast on again with the main yarn over the ravel-cord stitches. Knit two rows.
2. Set the carriage to the hold function. Place three or four edge needles opposite the carriage side in holding position. Knit across.
3. Place the held needles on the carriage side in upper working position, and three or four edge needles opposite the carriage side in holding position. Knit across.
4. Repeat Step 3.

Ribbed edging

Ribbing can be formed with a latch tool over a few edge stitches to give structure to the sides of the fabric and prevent them from rolling. It is easiest to drop and reconstruct columns of purl stitches into knit stitches in manageable amounts as the fabric progresses, rather than all at once at the end.

To create a single-rib edging, reconstruct the column of stitches from the second needle from the edge, then reconstruct one or more alternate columns of stitches depending on the desired width of the trim.

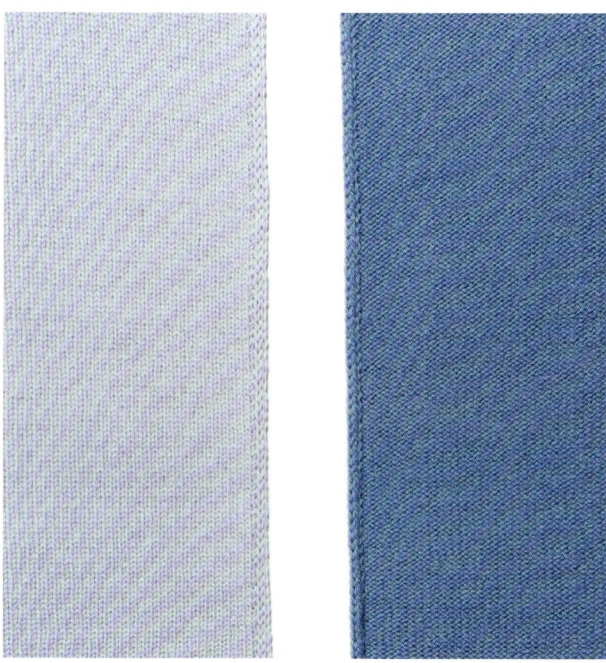

I-cord edging from the knit (left) and purl (right) side of the fabric.

Single-rib edging from the knit (left) and purl (right) side of the fabric.

Bias edging

A bias edging is formed by transferring a group of stitches one stitch over towards the edge of the fabric to create diagonal lines in the selvedge. It is most effective when worked over three or more stitches; the more stitches that are moved, the wider the bias edging appears. This edging adds a welcome detail and frames the fabric well.

This example is worked over three stitches at both edges of the fabric.

1. Cast on and knit two courses.
2. Use a three-prong transfer tool to move the second, third and fourth stitches from the right edge over by one place, away from the centre of the fabric. The first edge needle now has two stitches, the second and third needles have one stitch and the fourth needle is empty.
3. Fill the empty needle by picking up the purl bump from the adjacent stitch on the fifth needle.
4. Use a three-prong transfer tool to move the second, third and fourth stitches from the left edge in the same way. Fill the empty needle with the purl bump from the adjacent stitch.
5. Knit two courses.
6. Repeat Steps 2–5.

Decorative shaped edging

Some knitting methods cause the edges of the fabric to take on the shape of the stitch pattern, which may be curved or undulating. If the design outcome allows it, it is often better to celebrate the direction the fabric naturally wants to take, than to try to control it or turn it into something else. Lace, cables and ruched fabrics can all produce unique edges, with stitches that follow the movement and motion of the knitting technique. Methods such as these can also be used to form decorative borders to add a new texture, shape, stitch or pattern to the fabric. Stitches may also be transferred to create increases and decreases, forming zigzag or unusually shaped sides.

TIP: *Integrating a stitch pattern into the very edge of the fabric may involve trial and error. Stitches for cables, for example, can be crossed only on the fabric edge opposite the carriage. If crossed on the same side, the working thread gets caught as the stitches twist around one another to form the braid. Cables must therefore be crossed on alternate courses if they are to appear on both edges of the fabric.*

Bias edging worked over three stitches (left) and five stitches (right).

Six-stitch cable edging (left) and decorative points created through increasing and decreasing stitches (right).

Rolled edging

This is essentially a single-jersey trim that uses the natural roll of the fabric as a design detail. It can be created by picking up stitches along the selvedge and knitting additional courses. The trim courses roll towards the right side of the fabric. The simple appearance makes a good finish for a wide range of garments and accessories.

1. With the wrong side of the fabric facing you, pick up the stitches along the selvedge and rehang them on the required number of needles. To help the needles knit the first course, they may be brought to holding position (with the carriage set to knit them back).
2. Thread the carriage with the trim yarn and knit approximately ten courses (it may be more for a fine yarn, or fewer for a thick yarn).
3. Cast off all stitches.
4. The trim naturally rolls to display its purl side. It can be left as it is, or secured with a few invisible hand-sewn stitches.

Rolled edging from the knit (left) and purl (right) side of the fabric.

Folded edging

Folded edgings follow the same principle as folded hems (see page 162). The instructions assume the trim is to be knitted in a smaller stitch size than the main fabric, but this can be adjusted according to your preferences. To knit a basic folded edging trim:

1. With the wrong side of the fabric facing you, pick up the stitches along the selvedge and rehang them on the required number of needles. To help the needles knit the first course, they may be brought out to holding position (with the carriage set to knit them back).
2. Thread the carriage with the trim yarn and tighten the stitch size by two numbers (main tension -2). Knit one course.
3. Knit the required number of courses for the outside facing of the edging.
4. For the middle course, loosen the stitch size by four numbers (main tension +2).
5. Tighten the stitch size by four numbers (main tension -2). Knit the required number of courses for the inside facing of the edging.
6. To fold the trim, use a one-prong transfer tool to pick up the first course of the trim, placing it on the needles directly above.
7. Cast off.

To knit a 1 × 1 mock-rib folded edge trim (worked over an odd number of picked-up stitches), make the following changes:

- After Step 2, use a one-prong transfer tool to transfer the second stitch from the edge to the adjacent needle to the right or left. Repeat across the course, transferring every other stitch to its neighbouring needle. Place all empty needles to nonworking position.
- When folding the trim in Step 6, bring the nonworking needles to working position. Place the trim stitches onto the empty needles directly above.

This method can be altered to suit other mock-rib arrangements.

Hand-knitted and crocheted edging

Stitches along the selvedge of the fabric can easily be picked up with a knitting needle or crochet hook to form a hand-finished edge. Hand-knitted stitches that naturally create a flat and crisply structured trim are a good choice here. In addition, a few courses of slip stitch or single crochet can work as a quick and subtle addition to the textile. This is also a great opportunity to create decorative edges with lace, textured or dimensional stitches, or beaded trims.

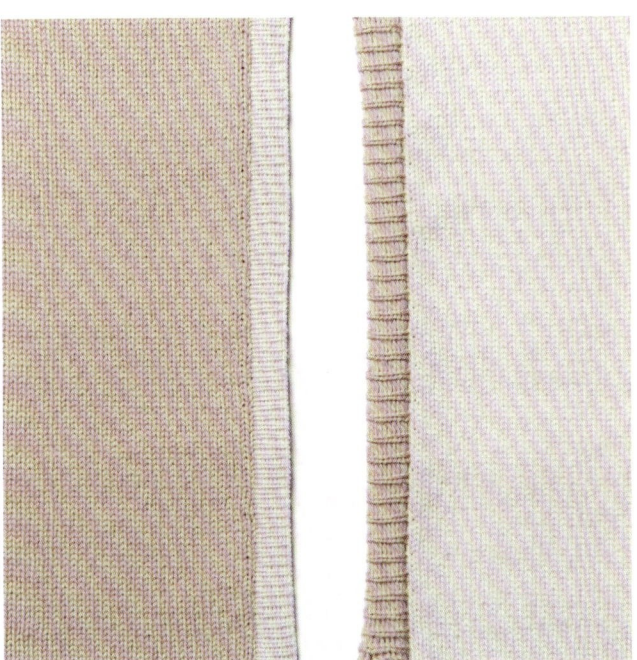

Basic (left) and 1 × 1 mock-rib (right) folded edging.

Dimensional hand-knitted (left) and beaded crocheted (right) edging.

Buttonholes

Separately knitted edging

In some cases, such as for detailed edgings, it can be easier to join the trim to the main fabric once it has been knitted.

1. Knit the edging trim using the required number of stitches and courses.
2. With the right side of the trim facing you, pick up the stitches from the edge and rehang them on the required number of machine needles.
3. With the wrong side of the main fabric facing you, pick up the stitches from the edge and rehang them on the same number of machine needles.
4. Bring the needles into holding position, with the carriage set to knit them back. Pass the carriage across to knit the stitches from the trim and main fabric together.
5. Cast off.

TIP: *Non-knitted trims can also be joined to the main fabric in this way. Keep in mind the transfer tool needs to be able to pick up the edge of the alternative material and so those with loose weaves, lace, cut-out openings or similar structures work best.*

Buttons are a popular addition to knitted trims, whether as a closure or a decorative detail. Simple buttonholes are formed horizontally within the fabric, and their size is dictated by the number of needles. Vertical buttonholes are knitted vertically, and their size is dictated by the rows knitted.

Simple buttonhole

A simple buttonhole can be made over one or two stitches in the same way that a single- or double-stitch eyelet is created (see page 116). If you wish, simple buttonholes may be finished with blanket stitch, sewn using a tapestry needle and the same yarn.

Lace-trim edgings.

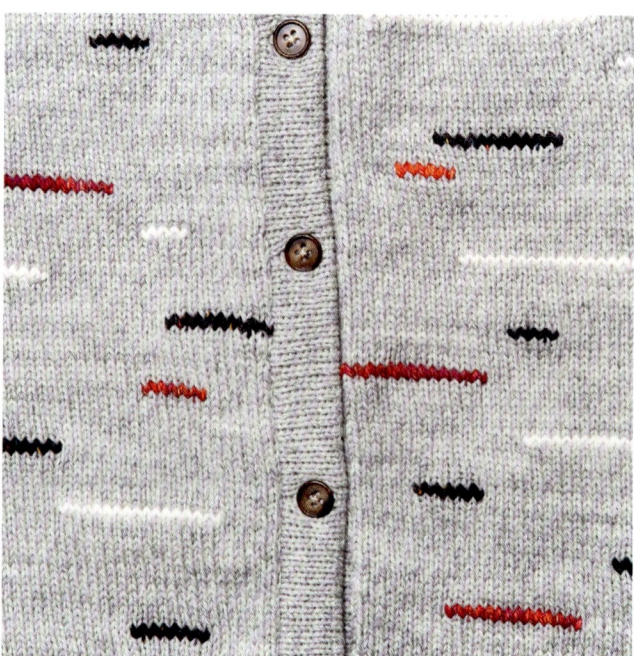

Simple buttonholes in a folded trim.

Simple buttonhole in a folded trim

Simple buttonholes can easily be integrated into folded trims. This method is worked by picking up and rehanging the edge stitches from the main knitted fabric, then making the following amendments to the basic folded edging trim (see page 170):

- Knit half the required number of courses for the outside facing of the trim.
- Transfer the buttonhole stitches.
- Knit the remaining number of courses for the outside facing of the trim.
- Knit half the required number of courses for the inside facing of the trim.
- Transfer the same buttonhole stitches.
- Knit the remaining number of courses for the inside facing of the trim.

Because the buttonholes must align exactly once the trim is folded, the inside and outside facing should consist of the same number of knitted rows.

TIP: *To create larger horizontal buttonholes, try creating openings in the fabric with cast-off surface holes (see pages 127–28). They can be reinforced with hand-stitching once they have been knitted.*

Vertical buttonhole

Vertical buttonholes are essentially slits in the fabric, knitted using holding position. To choose the position of the buttonhole, select two needles; the opening is formed between them. If you wish, vertical buttonholes may be finished with blanket stitch, sewn using a tapestry needle and the same yarn.

These instructions involve the carriage starting at the right side of the knitting, but they can be easily adapted if the carriage needs to start at the left side of the work.

1. Knit to the course where you want to create the buttonhole, ending with the carriage at the right side of the knitting.
2. Place all needles to the left of the buttonhole opening in holding position. Set the carriage to the hold function.
3. Knit the length of the buttonhole and break the yarn.
4. Place the held needles in upper working position and all the needles to the right of the buttonhole opening in holding position.
5. Rethread the carriage and knit the same number of courses as in Step 3.
6. Break and rethread the yarn if necessary, set the carriage for normal knitting, and continue to knit.

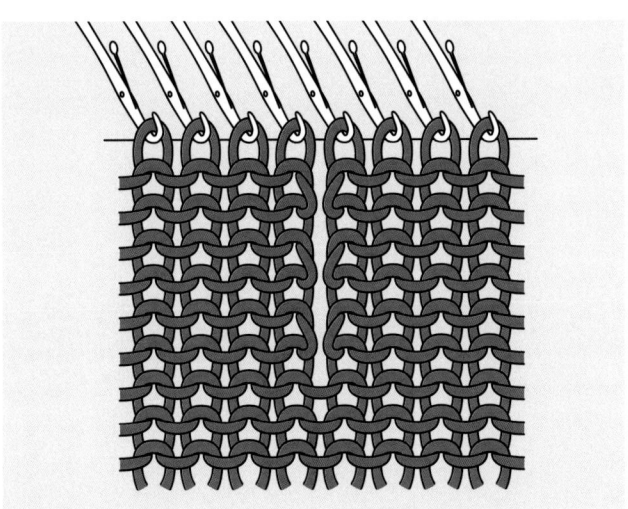

Vertical buttonhole. The stitches to the left and right of the buttonhole are knitted separately to create the opening.

Chapter 9

Finishing

Regardless of whether you are designing a textile collection, accessory, garment or other outcome, some type of finishing is generally required once the knitting is complete. The process of finishing can be summarized in these steps, and it is usually recommended to work them in this order:

1. **Weave in ends** Secure and hide all ends left after changing yarns, carefully trimming any excess. If the knitted piece requires a lot of blocking, wait until it is finished and dry to trim the leftover threads.

2. **Blocking** This evens out and enhances the knitted fabric, adding to the drape, hand feel and usability. It sets the knitted piece to the schematic measurements, fixes subtle inconsistencies in size and prepares the edges for seaming.

3. **Surface treatments** Work any effects such as embroidery or embellishment and sew on smaller details such as appliqués. It is much easier to do so now, while the knitting is still in flat pieces.

4. **Seaming and joining** Edges are seamed together on the machine or by hand. The knitted outcome will dictate the order of assembly.

5. **Additional blocking** If necessary, seams and edges can be blocked lightly to help them lie flat and to shape.

6. **Add fastenings** Closures such as buttons can be sewn on at this stage.

7. **Weave in remaining ends** Hide, secure and trim any additional yarn ends left from the finishing.

TIP: *Always consider the finishing methods at the start of the design process, and practise them to check that they complement the knitted piece. Work with large swatches to assess how the fabrication responds to blocking, seaming and other relevant processes. This will help you handle the end product with confidence while finishing it.*

Blocking

When a fabric comes off the knitting machine, it usually needs to be blocked to even out the stitches and reach the desired size and shape. Blocking involves pinning a completed piece of knitting into the exact proposed measurements, so that it can be wetted, steamed or pressed and left to dry. This finishing process enhances the appearance, hand feel and structure of a knitted textile or garment in several ways:

- The surface of the fabric will appear smoother, with more uniform stitches.
- Stitch patterns will open up and become more visible.
- Plain edges will become straighter and flatter, as the tendency to curl is greatly reduced or eliminated.
- The length and width of the knitting can be adjusted slightly for additional accuracy.

Blocking takes place before garment pieces are seamed and assembled. This order ensures the pattern pieces are set to the correct dimensions, eliminating any variations in size that may have occurred during knitting. Blocked edges are much easier to seam; they lie flat so that you can see and line up stitches more readily. Joining blocked pieces lends a more accurate fit and a professional finish to a knitted garment.

Blocking can also contribute to the tactility of some fabrics, by making them softer or fluffier. It can have an 'airbrushed' effect on a knitted piece, blurring out small inconsistencies in the stitches or yarn. Once pinned out to size, the full detail of the fabric can unfold and stitch patterns may appear clearer and crisper. Textiles formed from all-over transferred lace, for example, are often completely transformed by this treatment.

The full impact of knitted lace designs can be magically revealed after blocking. 'Kenchiku Wrap' by Julie Hoover for Brooklyn Tweed.

Tools

Blocking board A flat surface large enough for the knitted piece (or pieces) to be pinned out on, often made of sturdy foam and customizable in size. You can also make your own, using a material that can withstand pins, moisture and heat, such as corkboard, or even a folded blanket or a couple of towels covered with a cotton sheet. An ironing or steaming board can be used for swatches or smaller pieces of knitting.

TIP: *It is very useful to have a grid on the surface of the blocking board, to use as a guide during pinning and measuring. You could always customize a non-gridded board by covering it with a lightweight checked cotton such as gingham. Make sure the grid lines of the checked fabric run absolutely straight both horizontally and vertically.*

Pins For gently reshaping the knitting to fit the desired measurements. Longer pins, such as T-pins, are recommended over shorter ones. Make sure they are rust-proof and can withstand heat (avoid plastic-headed pins, for example).

Blocking wires Fine rust-resistant metal rods, useful for achieving an even, consistent long edge. They are usually sold in sets and may be configured to different lengths. Differing thicknesses of wire are also available, as well as flexible rods that can be inserted into curved edges.

Setting tools Depending on how you choose to block the knitting, different items may be required:

- Clean sink or washing-up bowl and clean towel, for wet blocking by soaking
- Clean spray bottle, for wet blocking by misting
- Steam iron or handheld steamer, for dry blocking by steaming
- Steam iron and clean cotton or linen cloth or thin towel (known as a pressing cloth), for dry blocking by pressing

Tape measure To check the measurements of the knitted fabric on the blocking board.

TIP: *It is very difficult to achieve a precise result without taking the time to measure, since the fabric is easily distorted once it is malleable after contact with moisture and heat.*

Blocking different fabrics

The blocking process must be customized according to the knitted fabric. Take into account the fibre and yarn type, as well as the stitch pattern. Blocking processes are categorized as wet (submerging in or spraying with water) and dry (steaming or pressing) (see pages 180–81). The correct method can transform a textile into a beautifully finished fabrication, but an unsuitable method might ruin it. Too much water may make a knitted piece stretch; over-pressing can result in a flat, dull surface; and too much heat can burn the fibres.

The various fibres and yarns respond to blocking in different ways, and it is always a good idea to check the manufacturer's care instructions on the label or ball band if you can. When working with blended yarns or a fabric constructed from a stitch pattern that uses several fibres, consider how each fibre will react to blocking. Always give priority to the fibre that is most delicate.

The way the fabric has been constructed is also an important consideration when deciding on the blocking approach. Openwork stitches and lace patterns benefit greatly from blocking, and such textiles can look significantly better once blocked. The weight of the fabric should also be taken into account; fine knits tend to call for more concentrated blocking than heavier-gauge ones.

It is very helpful to think about how the fabric's composition and stitch pattern can be handled together during finishing. For example, a fabric knitted using a stitch pattern that requires a lot of steam to open up, from a yarn that cannot be exposed to much heat, might need to be reconsidered during the design process.

TIP: *Blocking is not always essential, some fibres and stitch patterns may not require it at all. Certain novelty and metallic yarns made solely from synthetic fibres, as well as intensely textured or dimensional pieces, or those that are inherently very stable may be best left unblocked.*

Swatches of different fibres in their unblocked states (clockwise from top left): baby yak, silk, linen, and viscose/polyester.

The same swatches once blocked.

Wool and similar protein fibres

Wool can be wet- and dry-blocked, and it becomes loftier, softer and sometimes fuzzier. The temperature of the water or steam must not be too high, or the fibres can felt together (see page 137). While various other animal fibres (such as alpaca, cashmere and yak, but not silk – see below) can be treated in a similar way to wool, some are more delicate. For these, wetting the fabric by misting is advisable over completely submerging it, and dry blocking should also be done with caution. To avoid the risk of a matted and flattened surface, do not press long-haired fibres, such as mohair and angora, or other textured animal-fibre yarns.

Cellulose fibres and silk

Fibres such as cotton, linen, silk and hemp may be wet- or dry-blocked. They can withstand higher temperatures than wool and animal-hair fibres, but you should still be gentle.

Synthetic fibres

Yarns made from synthetic fibres require the most attention during blocking. Because synthetics such as acrylic, nylon and polyester contain plastic, they can melt, burn, flatten or become shiny when they come into contact with heat. Because of this, wet blocking poses significantly less risk than dry. Dry blocking should be carried out only using a very cool iron or with a pressing cloth to act as a barrier.

TIP: *Be cautious when blocking a fabric that is a mix of synthetic and natural fibres. If treated incorrectly, the fabric could be damaged – even if the synthetic is a very small fraction of its composition.*

Lace and openwork

When a fabric of this type comes off the machine, the stitch pattern may seem less clear than it was when it was stretched across the needles and tensioned with weights. To help the fabric open up and reveal the stitch pattern, it can be wet- and dry-blocked. Avoid pressing stitch patterns that are also textured, such as fully fashioned transferred lace.

Textured stitches

Stitches that impart tactility, such as cables, knit and purl patterns and tuck, miss and knit-weave should be blocked very carefully. Gentle wet blocking or very controlled steaming are the best ways to emphasize the surface relief without damaging the knit. During blocking, use your hands to tweak the fabric, making sure the raised areas remain dominant. Pressing is not advisable, since it is likely to flatten the raised details (unless that is an aesthetic choice).

Colour patterns

Multicoloured patterns such as Fair Isle, intarsia, tuck and miss stitches all generally benefit from the smoother finish that blocking can provide. They can usually be wet- or dry-blocked.

Ribbing and trims

Rib stitches and trims should be blocked according to how they are being used. Trims that must remain elastic or pull the fabric in, such as cuffs and neckbands, are generally not blocked, or are blocked very gently. Ribbing in particular will lose its stretch and appear flat if it is pinned out and set to dry. Leaving ribs unpinned to dry in their natural, relaxed position will ensure they remain stretchy. If you do choose to block a rib, avoid pressing it, since that can compress the structure too much.

In some cases, a rib or trim is not required to bring the fabric in. This might be an aesthetic choice or for certain applications, such as a cardigan placket, in which the trim is required to remain at a set size. A rib or rib effect might also be used for an all-over stitch pattern. These situations call for the ribbing or trim to be pinned out exactly to the desired measurements, and then wet- or dry-blocked.

TIP: *Test your selected approach with small swatches before moving on to a larger piece. Proceeding with caution allows you to remain in control; if you are unsure how the fabric might react, start gently and work up to adding more water, heat or pressure.*

Different stitch types call for varying amounts of blocking. The same swatches in their unblocked (above) and blocked (below) states.

A fabric swatch pinned on a board ready for blocking.

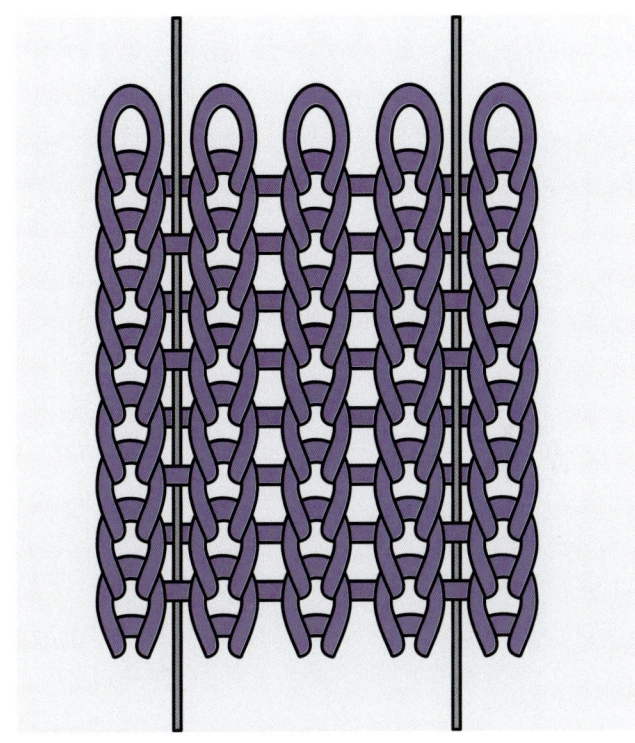

Blocking wires inserted into the fabric between the two edge wales of stitches. On the left, the wire is inserted under and over every other row, and on the right it is inserted under and over every two rows.

The blocking process
Pinning the knitting

Whether the knitting is pinned with the right or the wrong side up depends on the type of textile and your preferred way of working. Right side up may be favoured because it allows you to assess the fabric easily as you progress. This might be helpful if there is a stitch pattern or surface decoration that is not so clearly seen on the reverse. On the other hand, blocking with the wrong side up can prevent the right side from being damaged by excess heat.

- Lay the knitted piece flat on the board, arranging it into its general shape and size. Always use your hands to smooth the fabric evenly, working from the centre out. If necessary, secure the corners with pins.
- Pin the key areas of the fabric first. Identify the widest and longest parts of the fabric, and pin in place. Once they are correct, work around the edges, pinning to the desired shape and size. Place pins into the edge of the fabric at a slight angle, roughly 1.5cm (½in) apart, or closer if the edge starts to look scalloped.

- If using blocking wires, thread them through the space between the selvedge stitch and its neighbouring stitch at an even rate. As with pins, this must be frequent enough that the edge does not look tugged. Once the wire is inserted, it can be further secured with pins.
- For a garment piece, first pin important areas such as the shoulders, neckline, armholes, and side and bottom edges. Then secure the rest of the outline, avoiding ribbing or trims if they are meant to remain elastic and pull the fabric in.
- As each section is pinned, measure it and check it against the schematic.
- Symmetrical pieces should be measured from the centre point out, to confirm that the sides will be identical. If something is not correct, readjust the fabric, pin and check again. Avoid pulling at the edges of the knitting to achieve the correct size, since this can produce irregular or wavy edges. Instead, coax the fabric carefully from the inner area outwards.

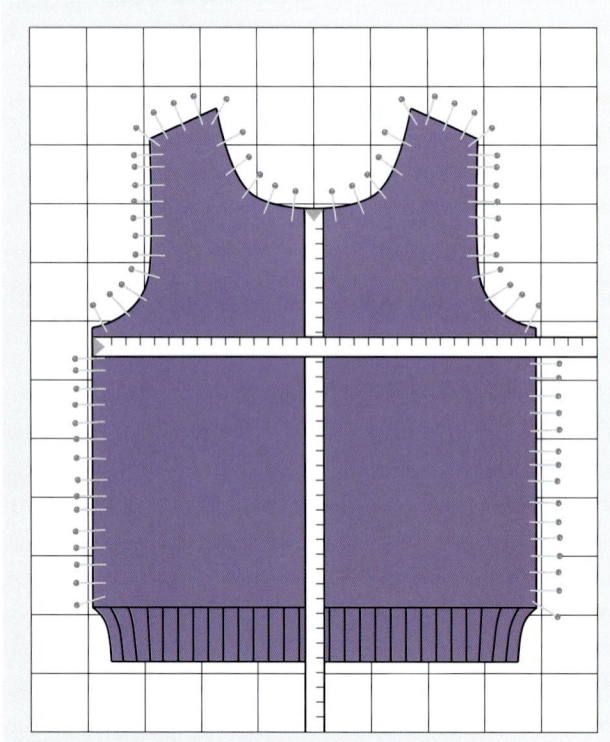

Garment panel pinned out onto a gridded blocking board with its key points measured to ensure accuracy and symmetry. The rib trim is left unpinned so that it does not lose its desired elasticity.

- If space allows, lay pieces that are the same size together on the blocking board. It is easier to match them up and mirror their measurements when they are side by side.

TIP: *Unless calculated before, the exact size of smaller pieces of fabric or swatches is usually unknown. Rather than pinning to a precise measurement, follow the general shape of the swatch, allowing the behaviour of the fabric to guide you.*

TIP: *Decorative shaped edges such as scallops or points can be accentuated if they are carefully laid out and pinned into shape. Place one pin in the top or peak of the shape to pull it out from the rest of the edging.*

Reshaping

One of the merits of blocking is that it allows you to make subtle adjustments to the shape and size of the knitting, if necessary. To enlarge the piece, ease the fabric from the centre outwards. To diminish it, work in the opposite way. Bear in mind that it is much easier to increase than to decrease.

Certain fabrics may be manipulated better than others during blocking, and retain their altered shape for longer afterwards. This is dictated by the fibre type, the flexibility of the material and the blocking method. Wool and wool blends, for example, may be controlled quite successfully and hold their modified form well, while fabrics knitted from synthetic yarns are much harder to change. Open, loose-gauge knits respond better to reshaping than those that are closely knit and compact. In addition, fibres are usually more malleable if they are wet-blocked by being immersed in water, instead of being misted or dry-blocked.

Reshaping is not technically a permanent fix; as soon as a knitted fabric becomes wet again, it will return to its pre-blocked measurements and require finishing once more. It is best not to rely on reshaping if a knitted outcome is significantly different from the design intention. Instead, address the root of the problem: check the tension, identify any issues and knit it again with alterations.

Wet blocking
Immersing

This method of blocking differs from the others in that the knitted pieces are wetted first, and then pinned to size. It calls for extra care when handling the fabric, particularly if the fibre is prone to felting.

TIP: *Never use hot water, place the knitting directly under running water, dip the fabric into and out of the water or agitate it while it soaks.*

1. Fill a clean sink or washing-up bowl with cool or tepid water (check the yarn label or ball band for the manufacturer's instructions).
2. If you wish, add a small amount of rinse-less laundry soap. This can soften some fabrics.
3. Place the knitting in the water and hold it down until it is completely immersed and all air bubbles are removed. Make sure all of the fabric remains underwater and leave it to soak for 15–30 minutes.
4. Use both hands to gather the knitting into a ball (so that

its weight is always supported) and lift it out of the water. Some fibres – especially wool – become very heavy from absorbing water and can stretch out of shape if lifted only by a small area or edge.

5. Carefully squeeze out as much water as you can. Keep supporting the fabric evenly, and never wring or twist it.

6. Place a clean towel on the floor or a table and lay the knitting on top, folding the fabric over if it is larger than the towel. Roll up the towel as if it were a burrito, and press it lightly so that it soaks up more water. By this time the pieces should be damp, rather than dripping.

7. Unroll the knitting from the towel and pin it to the desired shape and size. Leave it undisturbed to rest and dry completely before removing the pins or blocking wires.

Misting

Fabrics that are to be blocked in this way are pinned to the desired shape and size first, and wetted afterwards. This more controlled approach is particularly suitable for delicate fibres or heavier knitted fabrics that may be at risk of overstretching if they are immersed fully. Knitted pieces can also be easier to pin and measure when they are dry than when saturated. Misted fabric will dry considerably more quickly than soaked fabric, and that may be preferable if the fabric is thick or if you are working to a tight deadline.

1. Pin the knitting to the desired shape and size.
2. Fill a clean spray bottle with cold water and mist the fabric until it is thoroughly wet.
3. Leave the knitting to rest and dry completely before removing the pins or blocking wires.

Dry blocking
Steaming

This approach calls for the textile to be pinned to the desired shape and size, then exposed to moisture and heat through steaming. Adjust the heat of the steam according to the fibre type or the manufacturer's care instructions. If in doubt, use a low temperature and gradually increase it while keeping a close eye on how the fabric is responding. Always remember that there should be some distance between the source of heat and the fabric, since touching the knitting with the iron can damage it. As the heat of the steam comes into contact with the fabric, it sculpts and moulds the fibres.

1. Pin the knitting to the desired shape and size.
2. Hold a steam iron or handheld steamer at least 2.5cm (1in) above the fabric, moving it slowly over the knitting.
3. Keep applying steam over the entire surface area of the knitting in vertical and horizontal strokes, so that every part of the fabric comes into contact with moisture. As you do so, use your other hand to pat the fabric (being mindful of the steam heat), smoothing out any areas that appear uneven, or emphasizing those that need defining.
4. Leave the knitting to rest and dry completely before removing the pins or blocking wires.

Pressing

The knitted fabric should be pinned to the desired shape and size before it is pressed. A clean cotton or linen pressing cloth placed over the knitting acts as a barrier between fabric and iron. A dry pressing cloth combined with a steam iron may subject the fabric to enough moisture, but if more is required the pressing cloth can be wetted (and wrung out, so that it is not dripping). Adjust the temperature of the iron according to the fibre type or the yarn manufacturer's recommendations.

1. Pin the knitting to the desired shape and size.
2. Working in sections, place a wet or dry pressing cloth on the fabric and touch the cloth extremely lightly with the iron, moving from section to section and re-wetting the pressing cloth if necessary. As you proceed, pat the fabric with your other hand (being mindful of the steam heat), to adjust or open out any areas that need it.
3. Lift off the pressing cloth. Leave the knitting to rest and dry completely before removing the pins or blocking wires.

Final steps

For the fabric to remain in its blocked dimensions, it must be bone dry before the pins and wires are removed. Depending on the fibre type, the density of the fabric, the method of blocking and the air temperature, this may take a couple of hours or a couple of days. Keep the blocking board flat as the knitting dries or cools, and let the fabric do so naturally, at its own pace. Once the knitting is completely dry or cooled, carefully unpin it from the board. If it is to be seamed, store it flat until you are ready to do so.

TIP: *A warm room with good air flow will speed up the drying process.*

Seaming

Garments or knitted fabrics that have been seamed together might benefit from having small details set again through gentle steaming or pressing. This is particularly helpful for bulky or rigid seams that are not lying flush to the fabric. Turn the piece inside out so that the seams are facing up. Work on each join, using your fingers to pat and flatten the seam neatly, before very lightly steaming or pressing.

TIP: *A cotton or linen hand towel can help to set seams along curved edges. Roll the towel and place it under the seam to provide padding while lightly steaming or pressing the contour of the curve. As you progress up a longer edge, move the towel to follow.*

Seams can be used to assemble flat pieces into a garment, to attach trim to a textile, and to build modular compositions. There are many seaming techniques, and the one you choose will vary according to the structure of the fabric, the position of the edge to be seamed and the desired appearance. Some seams are nearly invisible, whereas others add a new layer of design interest.

It is advisable to use the same yarn for seaming as for the fabric, so that the seam is camouflaged. If a very thick or novelty yarn was used, however, it is usually easier to work with a finer yarn in the same colour. Choose one that is smooth and strong, and preferably the same fibre composition as the main one. Embroidery threads are often a good choice, since they come in a vast range of colours and in several fibre types.

Subtly textured knitted panels are creatively joined in selective areas. The deconstructed yet pieced together approach is further emphasized by colour blocking. By Ottolinger, Autumn/Winter 2020.

Usually, the knitted outcome dictates the order of seaming or assembly. Considering the position of each seam and where the eye will be drawn to first can help you determine this. It can be a good idea to begin with a prominent seam, since that will set the tone for the rest of the piece. Not only will this join be the most visible, but also, if it is executed well, it will help the others slot together precisely. When assembling flat pieces for a knitted sweater, there is an order that is generally followed for a neat outcome:

1. Join first shoulder seam.
2. Attach neck trim.
3. Join second shoulder seam.
4. Set in and seam sleeves to the armholes.
5. Join sides of sleeves.
6. Seam sides of garment.

TIP: *Always consider the important points of the garment, as it can be helpful to begin the seams there for extra control over the finishing. For example, even slightly mismatched hem and cuff joins can be very noticeable.*

Preparing fabrics for seaming

If blocking is required, always do it before seaming so that you are working with flat-lying edges set to the correct measurements. Inserting yarn markers into the fabric while it is knitting on the machine can be very useful. Marking an edge stitch on both pieces at regular intervals allows you to match the seaming edge clearly during finishing, and key central points can also be highlighted to make tasks such as setting in a sleeve much simpler.

To add a yarn marker, take a small piece of yarn in a contrasting colour, make a slip knot in the middle of it and place it on the selected needle's hook, tightening it gently. Alternatively, the cut yarn may simply be folded in half and laid over the needle's hook. Make sure to hold on to the ends of the marker strand to secure it as the carriage passes. The markers can be removed from the fabric easily once seaming is complete.

Although it takes a little more planning in terms of counting stitches and courses, markers can also be added once the pieces are off the machine. Pins and safety pins can also help you to create accurately matched seams.

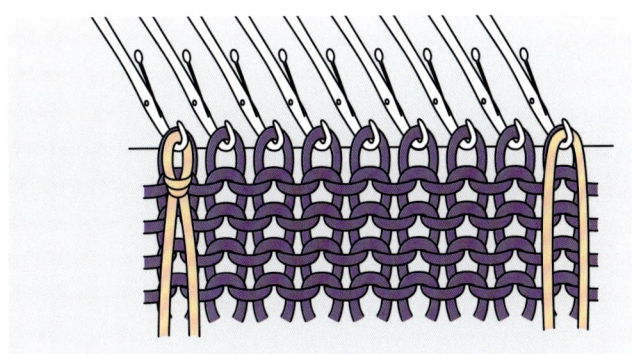

Adding markers to the fabric to help with seaming: slip-knot yarn marker (left) and folded strand of yarn (right).

Seaming on the machine

Joining two edges of fabric on the machine is an efficient way of seaming. It involves picking up and rehanging open or closed stitches along the edges, and joining them with one or sometimes two courses of knitting. It can create a very even finish, as long as you take care to be consistent when picking up and rehanging stitches. Most machine-seaming methods are limited as to the length of edge that can be joined. Picking up stitches along an edge is suitable only for pieces that are narrower than the machine's needle bed.

Test on a swatch before beginning to seam the final knitted outcome. It is necessary to evaluate:

• The stitch size that will be used to knit the joining course – this should be loose enough that the seam remains elastic.
• The size of the seam – if there is excess bulk, try knitting the joining course using a finer yarn than the main yarn, or picking up only half an edge stitch, rather than the full V.
• The finish of the seam – if the join does not lie flat enough, try a different casting-off method.

TIP: *It can sometimes be useful to begin the first centimetre (or inch) or so of seaming by hand, before picking up and rehanging the rest of the stitches from both pieces on the machine. This gives you more control when joining important areas that must match perfectly.*

Open stitches to open stitches

This method of seaming can be used to connect two sets of live stitches that have been removed from the machine

Two fabrics joined with the 'open stitches to open stitches' method.

with waste yarn and ravel cord. The edges are rehung so that the first piece of the fabric's stitches are behind the latches, and the second piece of fabric's stitches are in front of the open latches. The stitches from the second piece of fabric are then pulled through those from the first piece, leaving one stitch on each needle. The fabrics are seamed with their right sides together.

1. With the right side of Piece 1 facing you, use a one-prong transfer tool to pick up the open stitches from the main yarn course and rehang them on the machine's needles. Check that every live stitch is accounted for.
2. Place the needles in holding position and push the stitches so they are held against the sinker posts. (These stitches are now behind the needle latches.)
3. With the wrong side of Piece 2 facing you, use a one-prong transfer tool to pick up the open stitches from the main yarn course and rehang them so they are in the open hooks of the needles. Check that every live stitch is accounted for.

4. Close all the needle latches and use the flat end of a needle pusher or a long ruler to bring all the needles back to working position in a single motion. As the needles move to working position, the open stitches from Piece 2 in the needle hooks are pulled through the open stitches from Piece 1, which are against the sinker posts. There is now one stitch on each needle.
5. Place the needles in holding position and set the carriage to knit needles in hold.
6. Thread the carriage with the main yarn and set the

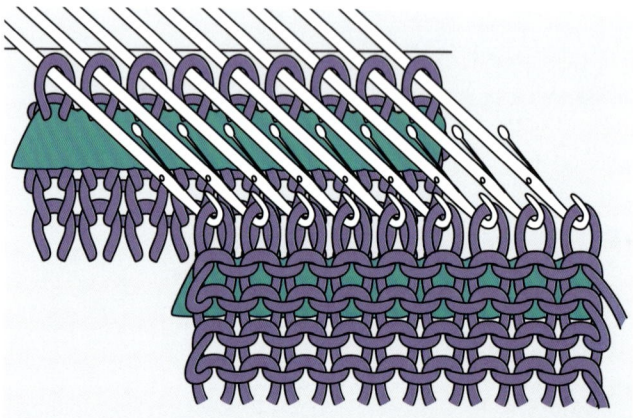

Open stitches to open stitches seam. Steps 1–3: Rehang the fabrics with their right sides facing. Place the stitches of Piece 1 behind the latches, against the sinker posts. Place the stitches of Piece 2 in front of the latches, in the needle hooks.

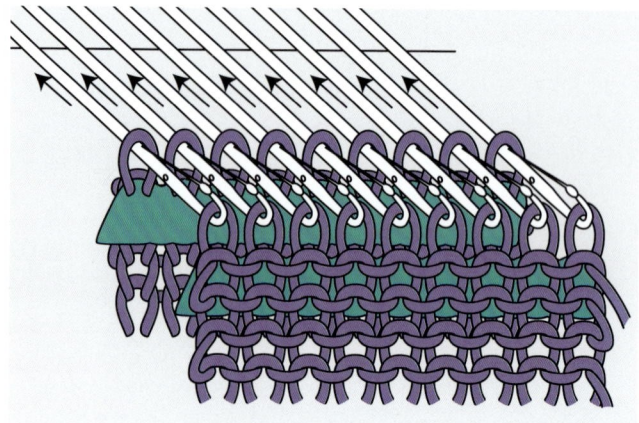

Step 4: With the latches closed, bring the needles back to working position so that the open stitches from Piece 2 pull through the open stitches from Piece 1.

stitch size to three or four numbers looser than the main tension. Knit one course. (If the main yarn tension is already at the loosest stitch size, knit the course by forming the stitches by hand on the machine.)

7. Cast off all stitches.
8. Remove the waste yarn and ravel cord.

Open stitches to closed stitches

This join is suitable for connecting an edge of open stitches, which has been removed from the machine with waste yarn and ravel cord, to an edge of closed stitches (those on the selvedge or cast-on or cast-off edges). The method is similar to the 'open stitches to open stitches' seam previously described, where one set of stitches is pulled through another. Always pick up and rehang the edge with the closed stitches first, for a more successful finish. The fabrics are joined with right sides together.

1. With the right side of Piece 1 facing you, use a one-prong transfer tool to pick up the closed stitches and rehang them on the machine needles. If picking up along a selvedge, remember to do so at the correct ratio to avoid gathering or stretching.
2. Place the needles in holding position and push the stitches so they are held against the sinker posts. (These stitches are now behind the needle latches.)
3. With the wrong side of Piece 2 facing you, use a one-prong transfer tool to pick up the open stitches from the main yarn course and rehang them so they are in the open hooks of the needles. Check that every stitch is accounted for.
4. Close all the needle latches, then use the flat end of a needle pusher or a long ruler to bring all the needles back to working position in a single motion. As the needles move to working position, the open stitches from Piece 2 (in the needle hooks) are pulled through the closed stitches from Piece 1 (against the sinker posts). There is now one stitch on each needle.
5. Place the needles in holding position and set the carriage to knit needles in hold.
6. Thread the carriage with the main yarn and set the stitch size to three or four numbers looser than the main tension. Knit one course. (If the main yarn tension is already at the loosest stitch size, knit the course by forming the stitches by hand on the machine.)
7. Cast off all stitches.
8. Remove the waste yarn and ravel cord.

Two fabrics joined with the 'open stitches to closed stitches' method.

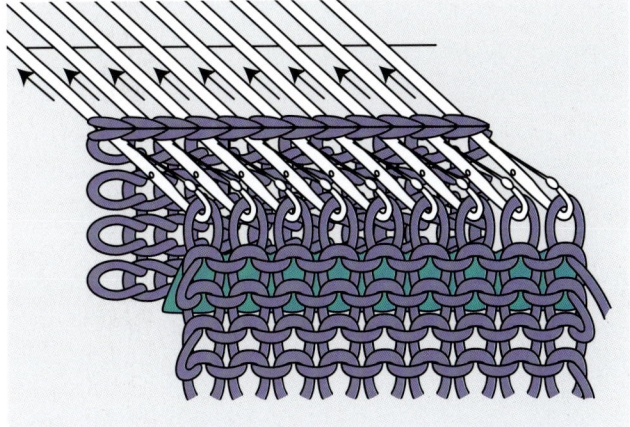

Open stitches to closed stitches seam. *Step 4: With the latches closed, bring the needles back to working position so that the open stitches from Piece 2 pull through the closed stitches from Piece 1.*

Closed stitches to closed stitches

Two closed stitch edges, such as the selvedge, cast-on or cast-off edges, can have their stitches seamed together using this method. If working with a selvedge, make sure you calculate in advance the number of stitches to be picked up and rehung according to the tension and schematic measurements. Extra care must also be taken when rehanging selvedge edges to ensure that any pattern or stitch layout is matched and mirrored in both pieces. The fabrics are joined with right sides together.

1. With the right side of Piece 1 facing you, use a one-prong transfer tool to pick up the closed stitches and rehang them on the machine's needles.
2. With the wrong side of Piece 2 facing you, use a one-prong transfer tool to pick up the closed stitches and rehang them on the machine's needles.
3. There are now two stitches on each needle. Place the needles in holding position with the carriage set to knit needles in hold.
4. Close all the needle latches, then set the stitch size so that it is one number tighter than the main tension.
5. Thread the carriage with the main yarn and knit one course.
6. Adjust the stitch size so it is three or four numbers looser than the main tension. Knit one course. (If the main yarn tension is already at the loosest stitch size, knit the course by forming the stitches by hand on the machine.)
7. Cast off all stitches.

Two fabrics joined with the 'closed stitches to closed stitches' method.

Seam as you knit

Also known as 'join as you knit', this method is used to seam two selvedges together. The seam of the two edges is formed at the same time as the second piece of fabric, or edge, is knitted. Because of this, it is a quick and simple way to create a vertical seam that lies flat with little bulk.

This method can be particularly useful when you are working with long or wide pieces of knitting. Seaming long pieces can be problematic if the number of stitches to be rehung exceeds the number of needles in the bed. Wide designs generally need to be split into two or more panels and seamed together to form the required size. As well as facilitating larger knits or modular constructions, seaming as you knit can help you make sure that very exact stitch patterns fit together flawlessly. This join blends in particularly well with textured stitch patterns.

To create a flat, even seam, the row tension of the two knitted pieces to be joined should be the same. If the row tensions differ, the number of courses knitted between the rehung stitch joins must be adjusted.

TIP: *A voluminous or gathered seam can be created by joining two very different length fabrics with the join as you knit method.*

1. Knit the first piece of fabric and note down the number of courses knitted.
2. If the seam is to be made on the right-hand side of the second piece of fabric (as you look at it on the machine), begin with the carriage at the left of the machine. If the seam is to be made on the left-hand side of the second piece of fabric (as you look at it on the machine), begin with the carriage at the right of the machine.
3. Cast on for the second piece of fabric.
4. With the wrong side of Piece 1 facing you, use a one-prong transfer tool to pick up the stitch from the cast-on row at the seaming edge of the fabric. Rehang this stitch on the seaming edge needle of the second piece of knitting. Place this edge needle in holding position (with the carriage set to knit it back).
5. Knit two courses.
6. Use a one-prong tool to pick up every other selvedge stitch from Piece 1, rehanging it on the seaming edge needle of the second piece of knitting. Knit two courses in between each pick up and repeat until the second piece has been knitted to the same length as the first piece.

7. Before casting off the stitches from the second piece, use a one-prong tool to pick up the selvedge cast-off stitch from the first piece of fabric, and rehang it on the edge needle on the machine.

Seam as you knit. *Step 6: Insert transfer tool into the selvedge stitch of the first piece of fabric, placing it onto the seaming edge needle of the second piece.*

Two fabrics joined with the 'seam as you knit' method.

Seaming by hand

Seaming using hand-stitching can give added control. It can sometimes be easier to see the fabric when connecting the knitting in this way, and it allows you to work very precisely when matching up stripes or heavily repeated patterns.

Pay attention to the tension: the seaming thread should be pulled firm enough that it blends well into the knitting, but not so tight that the seam ends up distorted or puckered. Work with lengths of yarn that seem comfortable and sensible, since anything too long can become tangled or weakened and frayed with the repeated friction of being passed in and out of the fabric. If you run out of yarn before ending a seam, join a new end and weave the tail in neatly.

There are several hand-worked seams that can be used to connect a variety of edges. Most methods used in two-needle hand-knitting are appropriate for machine-knitted fabrications, and directions for these can easily be found in hand-knitwear books. Popular methods for machine-knitting include:

Mattress stitch This woven-looking stitch is a very versatile way of connecting two selvedges using a tapestry needle and yarn. The resulting join is often undetectable, giving a professional finish. Mattress stitch allows a lot of control during seaming, and this can be particularly helpful when piecing together curves or shaped edges, or working with outcomes that require added elasticity. The way the fabrics are orientated during this join – laid side by side with right sides facing up – helps you be precise in matching up continuous stitch patterns and details.

Grafting Also known as Kitchener stitch, this method is used to join two sets of live stitches that have been removed from the machine with waste yarn and ravel cord. A grafted seam is constructed by inserting a tapestry needle threaded with the main yarn into the live stitches in the exact path that the knitted structure is formed. This means that the join appears as a knitted course, rendering it indistinguishable from the rest of the fabric. For this reason, grafting is an ideal seam in circumstances when the fabric must lie completely smooth, with no ridge or bulk. The two pieces of knitting are joined end to end, with right sides up. It is particularly important to watch the tension of the grafted seam; try to match the stitch size of the live edge courses as accurately as possible.

TIP: *Simple structures such as single jersey are much easier to work with during grafting, and so, for pattern stitch fabrics or shaped edges, it is recommended to end with one or two courses of plain knitting.*

Chained seam A crochet hook or latch tool can be used to create a simple chained seam that is suitable for joining two selvedges. If using a latch tool, make sure the loop is always behind the latch, and the strand of yarn is placed in the hook. The fabrics are joined with right sides together, and, depending on the fabric type, the hook or tool can be inserted into every other edge stitch rather than each one.

Seaming by hand: mattress stitch in progress using a contrasting colour yarn to highlight the sewn pathway.

Linking

Linkers are seaming machines used within the knitwear industry. While industrial models are reserved for commercial production, simpler versions are also available to suit the domestic machine knitter.

This round machine contains linker points distributed around the circumference, onto which the fabric's knitted stitches are placed. Seams are joined right side together wth a chain stitch made automatically by the linker. Because of the circular configuration, edges of any length can be joined easily. The markings on the machine allow fabrics to be matched up precisely, creating a finish that is neat and professional.

Decorative and Combined Methods

Not every outcome requires the finish to be invisible, and decorative or unusual seams can also be functional. There are numerous design options and approaches to working that can be explored thoroughly during design development. Eye-catching joins can serve as the primary ornamental feature of a minimal fabrication, or highlight an unconventional approach to construction. Pieces can also be connected in a way that reflects the visual mood of the knitted stitch pattern and the characteristics of the textile.

These seams can be worked on the machine, by hand, or using a mixture of the two. They can also involve less traditional materials and methods that are not typically associated with knitwear. Connecting two edges through eyelets or ladders can be a decorative and practical solution. These openings provide spaces for a transfer tool, crochet hook, latch tool or tapestry needle to be inserted so that the fabric can be joined on or off the machine.

Here are some starting points to provide you with ideas for designing personalized joins between knitted fabrics. You may also find unique ideas can come from researching linkages in spheres beyond knitwear.

'Seam as you knit' eyelet joins

Some popular approaches to machine-joined eyelet seams are worked in a similar way to the 'seam as you knit' method (see page 186), with the following amendments:

- Knit the first piece of fabric with lace holes created on the second stitch from the seaming edge every two or four courses.
- Cast on the second piece of fabric and knit two or four courses (the same number of courses before the first lace hole in the first piece of fabric).
- Instead of placing the one-prong transfer tool into a selvedge stitch from the first piece of fabric, place it through the eyelet hole and rehang the edge of the fabric on the seaming edge needle of the second piece of knitting. Place this needle in holding position (with the carriage set to knit it back) to secure the fabric.
- Knit the same number of courses between joins as there are between lace holes on the first piece.

TIP: *Because the joins occur only where there are lace holes, the very bottom and top of the fabrics will have some rows that are not joined. If you wish, they can be seamed in the same way as the standard 'seam as you go' method or by hand afterwards.*

Jo Bee's decorative approach to joining fabrics mixes machine and hand techniques. Openwork crochet stitches are used to link machine knitted cable panels, resulting in an extremely intricate outcome.

Seam as you knit eyelet join. *Insert the transfer tool into the lace hole at the edge of the first piece of fabric, placing it onto the seaming edge needle of the second piece.*

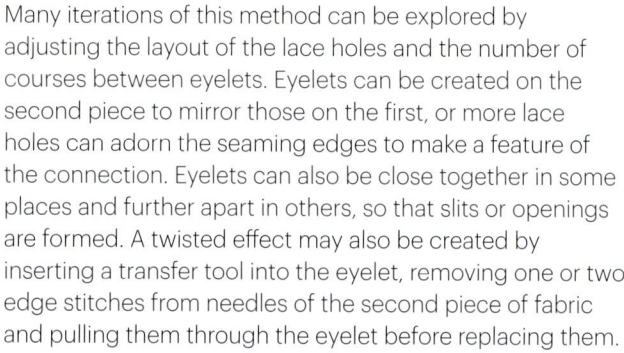

'Seam as you knit' eyelet joined fabrics.

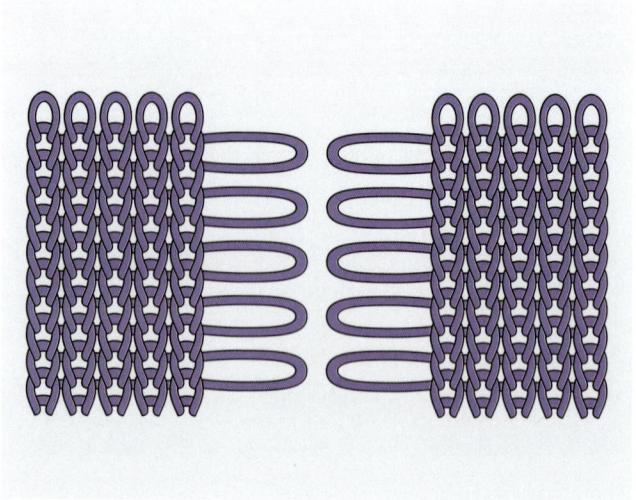

Dropped stitches at the very edges of fabrics create wide horizontal loops that can be manipulated to create unique lace-effect joins.

Many iterations of this method can be explored by adjusting the layout of the lace holes and the number of courses between eyelets. Eyelets can be created on the second piece to mirror those on the first, or more lace holes can adorn the seaming edges to make a feature of the connection. Eyelets can also be close together in some places and further apart in others, so that slits or openings are formed. A twisted effect may also be created by inserting a transfer tool into the eyelet, removing one or two edge stitches from needles of the second piece of fabric and pulling them through the eyelet before replacing them.

Eyelets on seaming edges can also act as markers for looping, weaving, sewing or threading in alternative materials to form the basis of an unusual join. They are ideal places to insert a crochet hook or tapestry needle to form a handcrafted join.

Laced joins

Ladders are another excellent foundation for decorative joins. The resulting laced-effect seams look intricate, and echo handcrafted needle- and threadwork. Ladders near the edge of the fabric (those formed over the second stitch from the edge) can be added during knitting, providing a vertical column that can be manipulated and explored during seaming. Alternatively, if the edge stitches of the fabric are dropped, the result is elongated horizontal loops that are perfect for creative joining. To create elongated horizontal loops in this way on the selvedge:

1. Knit the first piece of fabric as required, ending with the carriage on the side of the fabric that will not be seamed. At the cast-off course, remove one or more edge stitches from their needles (on the seaming side) by placing a stitch holder or spare piece of yarn into them to secure. The more edge stitches that are secured, the wider the dropped edge loops will be.
2. Cast off the remaining stitches.
3. Repeat Steps 1 and 2 for the second piece of fabric.
4. Remove the stitch holder or spare piece of yarn from the live edge stitches on both pieces of fabric and let them unravel to the cast-on edge. Use a tapestry needle or transfer tool to gently help the stitches release if necessary.

These edge loops invite a huge amount of exploration. They can be pulled through one another using a latch tool, forming a lacy connection between the two textiles, or several dropped loops may be crocheted together in patterns or linked using a tapestry needle and yarn. You might find inspiration in traditional needlework lacing stitches for connecting fabrics.

TIP: *For added control with delicate seaming techniques, it can be helpful to place the two pieces to be joined on a blocking board. Insert a few pins so that they remain in place while you are working the connection.*

Joining by inserting a trim

Another way of adding detail is to insert a trim or strip of fabric between the two knitted selvedges. This may take any form, knitted or otherwise, as long as a transfer tool or crochet hook can be placed through it.

The edge of the first piece of knitting is connected to the edge of the insertion using the 'closed stitches to closed stitches method' method (see page 186). The second piece is then connected to the other side of the insertion in the same way. To reduce bulk, or if you are working with thick yarn, it is advisable to pick up only half of each selvedge stitch when rehanging.

Pieces may also be joined with a crochet hook, allowing a freer approach. This is also particularly useful when integrating a more unconventional material or trim, such as metal chain, that could not be joined using the knitting machine.

To create this lace-effect join, elongated loops were formed on the seaming edges of the fabrics by dropping stitches. Loops from each edge were gathered into groups and crocheted together to form a connection.

To follow the openwork aesthetic of the two ladder knit fabrics, a band of lace crochet is used as a joining.

Troubleshooting

Encountering mistakes is an important part of the machine knitting learning experience. While they may happen frequently at first, practice lends expertise in identifying and rectifying potential errors. Machines are engineered to operate in a certain way, which when followed leads to trouble-free knitting. Most frequently, problems happen when these 'guidelines' are not adhered too. Incorrect threading through the auto tension unit, using too few weights, and a yarn that is too fine or thick are common examples of this, but are all simple to fix.

Detailed here are some common issues with possible solutions. In some instances, there may be two or more factors that are contributing to the problem. Keep in mind that even when following the correct procedures, more experimental techniques that push the machine can require an individualized approach to troubleshooting.

General tips
- Treat the machine with care and do not force the carriage if you think it is stuck. While some methods and yarns can make the carriage more difficult to slide across the bed, you should rethink your approach if it requires too much force.
- Before beginning knitting, and particularly when working on a machine that has been used by others, complete a set of checks. Needles should not be bent and the latches should open and close easily, the machine should be set for plain knitting, and the carriage should be aligned correctly on the bed.
- Stitches are most secure when needles are placed in holding position. When working with difficult yarns and techniques and if the method allows, place needles to this position (with the carriage set to knit them back) before knitting across.
- Always make sure the yarn is threaded properly through the auto tension unit before and during knitting.

Stitches/fabric drops off needles
- Make sure the yarn is correctly secured in the yarn feeder, particularly when making frequent yarn changes.
- Check if the yarn broke. Fragile yarns are more prone to this and even strong ones can snap if they catch on something.
- Assess if the fabric is weighted well enough. Use extra claw weights or your hand to carefully add tension to

the work if needed, particularly with partial knitting and tuck methods.
- Ensure the carriage passes all working needles before knitting back, especially when knitting very wide pieces.

Stitches not forming properly
- The stitch size may be too tight or the yarn too thick. In both instances, horizontal floats can span the width of one or more stitches.
- Check for broken needles, particularly if there is a build up of floats.
- Make sure the fabric has enough weight to provide tension to help stitches form.
- If loose stitches occur or slack yarn forms loops at the edges of the work, the carriage is travelling too far past the fabric edge before knitting back.

Carriage is difficult to move
- The stitch size may be too tight or the yarn too thick.
- Check that the yarn is flowing freely from the cone or ball and through the auto tension unit.
- Ensure there is no yarn wrapped around the wheels or brushes underneath the carriage.
- Clean and maintain the needle bed and carriage by removing dust and dirt and oiling. Only use a designated knitting machine oil and never put oil directly onto the machine without a cloth.

Videos
1. Closed cast-on methods (pages 54–57)
2. Cast-off methods (pages 58–61)
3. Troubleshooting (current page)
4. Punchcard knitting (pages 76–79)
5. Shaping the fabric (pages 146–51)
6. Picking up stitches (pages 158–59)

Credits
Featuring:
Florence Spurling

Videographer:
Marcie Revens

The extremely delicate knitted ground of Schiaparelli's Spring/Summer Couture 2020 creation lends the illusion of floating beads.

Glossary

Appliqué Decorative addition sewn or attached to a backing fabric. It can be of any material and is usually made up of ornamental shapes and patterns.

Aran Textured and dimensional style of knitting used in pullovers of the same name that feature intricate compositions of cables, bobbles and other relief stitch patterns.

Blocking Finishing process for knitted fabrics which uses water or heat to set pieces to the desired measurements and even out the stitches.

Broomstick lace A distinctive openwork crochet stitch that uses a large knitting needle or rod to create very large loops.

Cable Dimensional technique that forms rope-like twists in the fabric. Created when two groups of stitches swap places by crossing over each other.

Carriage Comprised of two parts, the main body and sinker plate, which houses cams, brushes, wheels and magnets. The carriage slides across the needle bed, carrying yarn and laying it into the needle hooks to form stitches.

Casting off Removing fabric from the machine by securing stitches to create a finished edge that does not unravel.

Casting on Introducing stitches onto the machine's needles to begin knitting.

Course A horizontal row of stitches in knitted fabric structure. Each time the carriage passes to the other side of the needle bed, it knits a course.

Crochet Constructed textile technique that uses a hook to form an interlocking chain structure. When crocheting, you have only one live stitch on your hook compared to a whole row of live stitches on your needle when knitting. Because of this, multidirectional, freeform and very lacy crochet fabrics are simple to execute.

Devoré Fabric composed of two or more fibre types with a semi-sheer appearance achieved by applying a chemical paste. The chemical burns though one of the fibres and leaves the other intact.

Eyelet Opening or hole formed when a stitch is transferred and its empty needle is left in working position. After the carriage knits a row, the empty needle receives a new stitch.

Face Surface of the fabric chosen as the right side.

Fair Isle Multicoloured technique used for small-scale patterns which uses two yarns to knit selected needles in the same course of knitting. As one yarn knits, the other is carried along the purl-side of the fabric forming floats. Needles can be selected manually or automatically with a punchcard.

Fibre The raw material used to produce yarn that may derive from natural or manufactured sources.

Float Yarn strand that is carried from one needle to another without knitting the stitch or stitches in between. Occurs in laddered, miss-stitch and Fair Isle knitted structures.

Gradient Colour effect where tones transition or fade into one another, usually achieved by combining two or more ends in the same yarn feeder when knitting.

Holding position Position where needles are as far forward as possible in the needle bed.

I-cord Narrow tab of fabric created by knitting stitches in one direction and missing them in the other direction. The resultant floats from each miss-stitch row pull the tab in widthwise to form a cord.

Intarsia Colour technique used to knit patterns of any scale that can be created with numerous yarns per row. No floats appear on the purl side as each block of pattern is knit separately with its own yarn.

Knit stitch The simplest stitch produced by the machine. Has a smooth V-shape appearance.

Knit-weave Textured surface effect in which a secondary yarn is interlaced under and over the needles as the main yarn knits. The woven yarn appears as floats of varying length on the fabric's purl side.

Ladder Vertical opening in the fabric displayed as a column of floats, formed when the carriage passes one or more nonworking needles positioned between two working needles.

Lanolin Grease or wax present in sheep's wool.

Lifeline Fine, contrasting colour yarn used to highlight stitches within a selected course.

Live stitches Open or unfinished stitches that are usually removed from the machine and held secure with ravel cord and waste knitting.

Machine gauge Defined by the spacing of needles in the machine bed. The gauge dictates the weight of yarn that can be used.

Main yarn The primary yarn used for main knitting differentiated from those used for waste knitting, contrasting colours or effects.

Manually knitting Manoeuvring needles to form stitches by hand rather than with the carriage.

Marling Combining two or more different ends in the same yarn feeder so that they knit together as if they are one.

Miss stitch Created when the carriage purposely skips a selected needle for one or more rows. Displays an elongated stitch on the face and a horizontal float on the reverse.

Mosaic knitting Maze-like effect that combines two-colour stripes with a specially designed tuck- or miss-stitch pattern arrangement.

Nonworking position Position where needles are as far back as possible in the needle bed.

Plating Double-sided effect using two different yarns that appear on alternate sides of the fabric. The main yarn lies on the knit side and the plating yarn on the purl side.

Ply A yarn constructed from two or more single yarns twisted together. Also refers to yarn weight in UK hand-knitting terms.

Punchcard Pattern cards that are used with designated machines to automatically select needles for Fair Isle, tuck, miss and knit-weave stitch arrangements.

Purl stitch The reverse of a knit stitch. Has a ridged arch-shaped appearance.

Ravel cord Smooth, slippery yarn that is used for casting on and knitting one row between the main and waste yarn.

Reconstructing a stitch Using a latch tool to turn a dropped stitch into a knit or purl before placing it back onto its needle.

Reverse Surface of the fabric chosen as the wrong side.

Ribbing Elastic structure commonly used for trims where columns of knit stitches alternate with those of purl stitches.

Schematic Visual rendering of a garment or other outcome illustrating the size, scale and measurements of each pattern piece.

Seaming Finishing process in which two edges of a fabric are joined together.

Shaping Adding or subtracting stitches to the fabric to create a wider or narrower piece.

Short-row knitting Also called 'partial knitting', used to shape fabrics within garment construction and create three-dimensional surface effects. Uses the holding position function which prevents certain needles from knitting while others continue to form stitches.

Single jersey Fabric formed from knit stitches on the face and purl stitches on the reverse.

Sinker posts Prongs at the edge of the needle bed that separate each needle from the next.

Space-dye Yarn dyeing method in which multiple colours are applied at intervals along the length of the strands. Once knitted, it creates a blurred effect.

Stitch transfer Moving a stitch from one needle to another needle.

Stripes Bands of pattern that usually runs horizontally in the fabric, formed from yarn or stitch changes.

Swiss darning Also called 'duplicate stitch', an embroidery method that resembles that of a knitted stitch.

Tension Describes the number of stitches and rows per centimeter or inch in a knitted fabric.

Trim Include hems, edgings, bands and borders and are used on the edges of knitted fabric for aesthetic and construction purposes.

Tuck stitch Created when a stitch is held on a needle without being knitted over one or more rows. Displays an elongated stitch on the face and raised floats on the reverse.

Upper working position Position where needles are slightly forwards so that their open latches line up with the edge of the needle bed.

Wale A vertical column of stitches in knitted fabric structure. Each cast-on needle represents a wale in the fabric.

Waste knitting Fabric knitted in a contrasting colour yarn to the main one.

Working position Position where needle hooks line up with the edge of the needle bed.

Wrapping a needle Prevents a hole from occurring in the fabric in short-row knitting.

Yarn A continuous strand created from fibre that has been spun or twisted together.

Yarn count Numerical system used to detail the fineness or thickness of yarn and indicates the relationship between length and weight.

Index